T0248347

SHATTERED

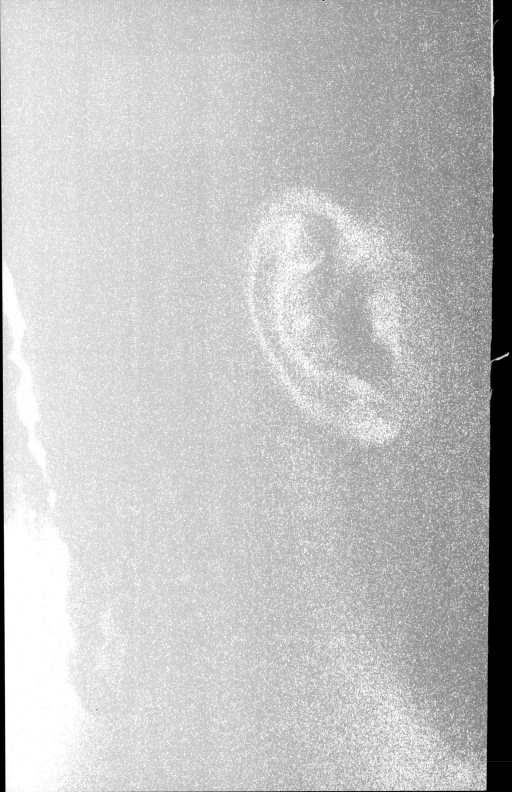

SHATTERED

FRAGMENTS OF A BLACK LIFE

WEST VIRGINIA UNIVERSITY
PRESS • MORGANTOWN

matthieu
chapman

ISBN 978-1-952271-92-2 (paperback) / 978-1-952271-93-9 (ebook)

Library of Congress Cataloging-in-Publication Data
Names: Chapman, Matthieu, 1984– author.
Title: Shattered : fragments of a black life / Matthieu Chapman.
Other titles: Fragments of a black life
Description: First edition. | Morgantown : West Virginia University Press,
    2023. | Includes bibliographical references.
Identifiers: LCCN 2023010643 | ISBN 9781952271922 (paperback) | ISBN
    9781952271939 (ebook)
Subjects: LCSH: Chapman, Matthieu, 1984– | African Americans—
    California—Biography. | African Americans—Psychology. | African
    Americans—Social conditions. | United States—Race relations. |
    California—Biography.
Classification: LCC E185.93.C2 C49 2023 | DDC 973/.04960730092
    [B]—dc23/eng/20230324
LC record available at https://lccn.loc.gov/2023010643

Book and cover design by Than Saffel / WVU Press
Cover image by LUMEZIA.com / Shutterstock.com

To my daughter, Roar Astrid Valkyrie

Author's Note

Afropessimism.

Many find the name off-putting, depressing, defeatist—all reactions I had initially. But once I began to interrogate my own aversion to the label and began to truly engage with the nuances and diversity of thought within the field, I found things I had never experienced before.

Radical hope.

Radical creativity.

Radical self-determination.

Afropessimism is a field of theory that distinguishes antiblack racism from other forms of racism. As such, the problem of race for black people is not white supremacy—in which all nonwhite races suffer equally compared to whiteness—but rather the problem is antiblackness—in which all nonblacks maintain a structural position of human from which blacks are excluded. In other words, black people are nonhuman, and everyone else is human. The distinction is that under white supremacy, all nonwhite beings are positioned as subhuman—less than the full white subject—and therefore the suffering of nonwhite beings can be analogized. For example, with white supremacy, we can compare the suffering of the colonized Indian to the suffering of the immigrant Mexican. In Afropessimism, blackness is incompatible with the construction of the human, therefore blacks do not exist on the scale that would allow us to compare black suffering to human suffering. Afropessimism is not a critique of black people. Rather it is a critique of a world that needs black suffering and black death to maintain its own mental health.

Throughout this book, I use "black" in the lowercase. And only in the lowercase—even when starting a sentence. I used to oscillate between various constructions of "black" and "Black" to distinguish between a color and a Concept. "black"—black as night, black tar, coal-black. "Black"—Black people, Black being, Black death. But "Black" is not proper in this context because the concept of black in this book is not proper. This book is not about blackness that is sanitized and proper and resilient and hopeful. This book is about the blackness that survives despite its death, despite a world that continually kills us. This book is about blackness that, as La Marr Jurelle Bruce says, is "a critique of the proper . . . a blackness that is neither capitalized nor *propertized* via the protocols of Western grammar; a blackness that centers those who are typically regarded as lesser and *lower cases.*"[1] It is a blackness that escapes what the world thinks of it and transcends any definitions I could give. I love the capital *B*, and I love those who use the capital *B*. But this book escapes designations of proper and improper. This book works beyond and between the anger and the rage and the joy and the love and the hope for a future and the hopelessness in the now. Nothing about this book is "proper," most of all its exploration and expression of blackness.

This is not a book about black life or about living life as a black man. This is neither a book about being black nor about black being. This book is about the resistance that occurs, the shattering, collapsing, and reconfiguring of being that happens in the collisions between competing conceptions of blackness. This book is about the struggle between a free, unbridled, uncontainable blackness and the cage that the antiblack world has built for it.

This book is about living in a world of the dying.

This book is about being dead in the land of the living.

This book is about the tension between wholes and pieces in a world whose whole is built on my pieces.

As such, the story is in the whole, but the story is also in the pieces: fragments, facets, shards, slivers, splinters, absences.

Fragments: Think of these as broader chapters that cover chunks of time.

Facets: Each fragment contains multiple facets—the large pieces of a primarily linear narrative of my trials and tribulations in navigating the world of difference between my blackness and how the world perceives, engages, and violates my blackness. Each facet is required to see the whole. The facets in the narrative, while numbered beginning with one in each fragment, do not necessarily come in chronological order— the pieces never fall organized or neatly.

Shards: Alongside the facets are various shards of story that have broken through time, space, and narrative to provide other experiences in my life that inform and enliven the facets.

Slivers: Adjacent to the facets and shards are the smaller slivers of being that provide light, brief bits of history, and contexts through which to view the other pieces.

Absences: But shattered objects are not defined solely by the pieces that scatter. The breaking produces negative spaces that define the separate parts of the former whole. These absences appear on the page as the unseeable that haunt and scandalize the whole.

Splinter: And just when I thought I had collected all the pieces, I found that splinters remain missing. Tiny, nearly imperceptible spears of emotion and imagery that cannot be put into tidy paragraphs.

This story is not about resistance and resilience in the face
of white supremacy.
This story is not about overcoming obstacles and
dismantling systemic racism.
The story is asking why black resistance and overcoming
always seem to fall short of creating lasting change.
This story is asking how, despite the many political and social
progresses of black people, we are still no closer
to the mountaintop.
This story is questioning if we've been having the wrong
conversations about how to change the world.
This story is about a world that needs antiblackness to function.
This story is about wandering the world of the living
as a dead man.
This story is about surviving in death.
This story isn't about changing that world.
This story is about destroying it.

FRAGMENT 1

FACET: 1

Age: 11
Place: Uniontown, PA
Status: Dying

I had never actually heard the word in person. Sure, I had heard the word's distant cousin, whose razor blade edges had been dulled by the softening of the hard *r* sound into "nigga," on albums from the Wu-Tang Clan and Dr. Dre. But even in those cases, the force of the word was always mediated through layers of hi-fi and audiotape.

But here, in the flesh, the word was too real. The word became tangible. The hard *r* re-sharpened the blade. The blade grew wings, eyes, a mouth—the razors becoming talons on a monster that cut through the room toward me with velocity and violence. It caught my chest and ripped through my flesh, leaving a wound in my soul that would never and could never heal. A taste overcame my mouth: a blend of sour rancidness and ferric metal—a mix of bile and blood that rose from deep in the pit of my stomach.

It was the taste of hate.

Up until that moment, I didn't know that hate had a taste.

"Nigger."

She said the word almost too matter-of-factly.

But she can't have said it.

Not her.

Not that.

Not my mother.

Her face. I'll never forget her face. That space of less than a blink. The distance between the tensing of her lips and flaring of her nostrils. That brief moment is forever seared into my memory—the slow baring of her teeth to form the *n* that would begin my destruction. I no longer recognized what I was seeing as my mother's face. Instead, it became a mask, a facade of love and nurturing that could no longer conceal the devil within. She had worn this mask with few cracks over the first decade of my life. Now, as her clenched teeth separated to form the short *i*, the veneer melted away, and the demon beneath the alabaster glamour showed through. As she shifted from the short *i* through the *g* and to the fateful hard *r*, she ceased to be a woman and became a beast, the final "ger" losing its vowel, becoming the low, sustained growl of a wounded animal: "Grrrrrrrrr." The twisted, demented anger had always lurked just beneath the surface, but for the first time, she revealed the creature within. That face will never leave my mind because it is the last memory of my life.

"That nigger was supposed to have you home by seven," she said.

My eleven-year-old self suddenly became acquainted with a concept that had always structured black people's existence and would soon come to structure so much of my own: casual hate. Until this moment, I had always thought that hate was irrational—an emotion that often arose disproportionately in response to a slight, either real or perceived. But she said it with such casualness, as though that word was nothing more than an item on a shopping list: a gallon of milk, a dozen eggs, a nigger, and a loaf of bread.

My sister cried, but my brother screamed. I had seen my sister in tears before. But I had never heard my brother scream. I'd heard my brother shout in anger when we'd fight. I'd heard him yell when being whupped for breaking too many rules. But now, he didn't shout or yell. He screamed—long and loud and incoherent. The sound waves left his mouth and traveled through the intervening space, colliding with me with a meteoric force that impacted my soul. I still feel the visceral echoes and reverberations of that sound—it is the gritting of teeth and the tension of sinew that exists for a brief second between the squeal of brakes and the crunch of metal.

We attempted to process what just occurred to the best of our young minds' abilities, but the sound of the word short-circuited our understandings of the world. It was the hard *r*. The hard *r* can only be the sound of malice. The hard *r* rips apart the white liberal myth of mixed-race and multicultural. The hard *r* reached into my being and ripped out the parts of myself that came from my mother. The white parts. The hard *r* that exists in the middle of the one-drop rule now formed a barrier between my mother's whiteness and her children's blackness. With this hard *r* in our home and my father living a hundred miles away, our single-parent household became a zero-parent household.

My sister cried, but my brother screamed. In that instant, everything became real. I now know what that scream was. That was the scream of someone being obliterated: the being of a being rupturing and being replaced with a being whose being could never be. It was the death of a human and the birth of something else, something monstrous, unknown, and unknowable. It was the scream of Aunt Hester, originating on a plantation in the childhood of Frederick Douglass, warping through time and inhabiting the bodies of Emmett Till, Malcolm X, and Fred Byrd before possessing my brother, rendering his being torn, incoherent, and incommunicable. At that moment, my mother was Captain Anthony, and I was young Frederick, engulfed in the sound of disintegration, the sound of someone not knowing who or what they were anymore. Of someone being ripped from the womb all over again—a birth into death. A crossing over in time, space, and place.

My sister cried. My brother screamed.

My reaction, however, was quite the opposite. It was silence. It was clarity. It was knowing, for the first time in my life, precisely what I was. The word reached my ears with cold determination, as though both she and her words knew of the coming unmaking. The word didn't arrive in letters, syllables, and sentences but in a flash, a crash, a clatter. The razor-sharp claws of the disyllabic harpy crashed into my developing psyche, and scattering spider cracks converged into absolute destruction. And at that moment, my self, all I ever was, came crashing down within me, shattered into a million tiny pieces.

My white mother had just called my black father "nigger."

May 27, 2020

"i started reading . . . he writes well . . . but this is an angry book not a good strategy . . . he has a story to tell for sure . . . but too close to home . . . he should wait a few years i think . . .

i will read more but from the beginning i thought that rage and resentment were more important than figuring out what he wanted to do with this book . . ."

Yes, this email is real.

So is the date.

The irony lies in the date.

Maybe if this anger more frequently got published,

distributed, read, and listened to,

the world wouldn't think these things came out of nowhere.

SHARD: 1
Status: Ancient History

My parents never had the best relationship.

They met when my mother was eighteen years old. She is of German, Irish, and English descent, with features that remove any doubt of her pure white heritage. She is a small woman, no more than five feet, three inches tall, with reddish-auburn hair and green eyes that lived behind tortoiseshell glasses. Although her maiden name was Epling, that name derives from her father's German heritage. On her mother's side, she is of the Canterbury line, a name that hearkens back to Chaucer tales and massive cathedrals. My father was almost four years her senior. He is a black man whose heritage reaches only as far as South Carolina before the line dies in the hold of the slave ship. He has kind, brown eyes—eyes that live on in me. Based on the few old photographs I have seen, he also had a sense of style that would have been right at home in any Motown band or James Brown audience. He was a slick cat: a bad mother—*shut yo' mouth*.

They could not have been more opposite. I don't know how or why they met, and I'll never understand how or why they got together. At this point, I'll never ask. I do not speak to my mother and have not since I was twenty-five years old. Likewise, I will not ask my father. He is now retired, and his courtship with my mother was a lifetime ago for him. I don't have the heart to drag him to his cemetery of past mistakes and have him dig up the corpses. He doesn't have the strength for such a journey. Or maybe I don't have the strength.

They met in Charleston, West Virginia. He was my mother's

second husband. As soon as she reached West Virginia's age of consent, which was sixteen, she hitched herself to the first man who could take her away from her redneck upbringing and left for Oklahoma. She was one of nine children born to a working-class, coal-mining family, part of the silent majority whose current population made America great (?) again. Something must have gone wrong with her marriage because, within a year, she returned from Oklahoma. She went back to her family and the ragged collection of wood and blood that constituted her home. Here, she met my father. They met, had sex, got pregnant, and got married—a revolutionary act for a white woman and a black man in 1979 in West Virginia. Both were old enough to have conscious memories of *Loving v. Virginia*. But their two bodies collided, a sperm found an egg, and neither of them recoiled from the responsibility that entailed. Lust plus irresponsibility equals child. Maybe love was part of the equation, and maybe it wasn't. Regardless, love is a variable whose insertion into the equation doesn't alter its outcome.

Although they were married and had three children, I don't remember them showing each other any physical or emotional affection. Grand gestures like standing in the rain with a boom box or rushing through a crowded airport to stop a flight, which movies and TV shows had taught me equaled romantic love, were utterly absent from our lives.

Our lives were empty of any evidence of their love, except for a small anniversary clock that always hung on the living room wall of our house in Dunbar, West Virginia. The timepiece was a cheap flat panel printed with blue and purple flowers and some vain, generic poem about the virtues of love. It was the type of drivel that underpaid, contract copywriters hated to produce but needed to write for Hallmark and Things Remembered so they could secure the fifty dollar remunerations in order to survive until their novel took off.

It couldn't have cost more than twenty dollars when my father purchased it for their first anniversary in December 1980. Still, at the time, the purchase must have been both financially and emotionally significant to a couple of my parents' means.

The date is why I question the role of love in the equation. My parents celebrated their anniversary in December of 1980; my brother was born that June. The timeline positions his development as a fetus, the progression of the pregnancy to the point where miscarriage is much less likely—the point where the birth of my brother became not just a chance but a likelihood—alongside their decision to wed. I can't say whether or not he was the sole cause of their holy union, but knowing the parties involved, he was undoubtedly a factor.

I can't imagine the problems they must have faced before he was born: 1979. West Virginia. Mixed-race couple. I won't write out the equation this time, but I invite you to use your imagination to arrange those variables in a way that has a peaceful, productive outcome. While I can't say there was no love between my mother and father, I can say there was no love lost between their families. Although both of my grandfathers passed before I was born, I never saw both of my grandmothers in the same room in my seventeen years before my maternal grandmother died. Growing up, we would visit my dad's family or my mom's family, never both. We'd have my dad's family or my mom's family over for holidays, never both. My parents' union was solely their union.

Maybe they engaged in the stilted, disgusting TV trope perpetuated by the most banal sitcoms that a baby would fix their problems. If they showed up at their parents' homes with a baby, their parents would somehow come to love, or at least accept, each other. Maybe they were in love and used my brother as an excuse to show their love to the world.

If that was the plan, it was an utter failure. While the segregated nature of our family's dynamic went unspoken, it never went unnoticed. Even as a child, I realized that my mother's family was more likely to come to our house: my cousins Jeremy, Justin, and Jason each lived with us for brief stints during my childhood. On the other hand, we were more likely to go visit my father's family, often without our mother accompanying us.

As a child, I noticed these things, but thoughts about them didn't linger. I was acutely aware of my uncle Brent—my mother's drunk, redneck brother—stopping by with his kids. He would drink beer while my cousins, brother, and I explored the woods around our house. But my dad's brother, Bobby, equally derelict in his livelihood, never came to our home. Perhaps there were more significant family dynamics at play between my parents and their siblings and their families. In hindsight, my dad's family possibly didn't want to be around my mother. Maybe they were ashamed that he would step outside of his race. Or maybe my father didn't want his family around his white wife, unaware of what some of the more outspoken aunties, such as Kay or Bee, might say when he stepped out to the bathroom or to turn the food on the grill. Maybe my mother's brother just stopped by unannounced and uninvited. But as a child, I just noticed who came to see us and who we had to go see.

What finally unified the two sides of my family in my life was their absence. Many of those cousins who we'd visit or who visited us—Jeremy, Justin, Tanika, Kimiyatta—had children in their teens and early twenties. While parenthood took over their lives, I was going to college and moving states. My mother disavowed most of her family, and I lost contact with all of them except for my cousin Jason.

Shortly after enrolling in graduate school in Virginia, however, I went with my father back to West Virginia to visit my grandmother.

I hadn't been to the state in eight years. During this trip, we made stops to see my cousin Tanika in Orchard Manor, my uncle Allen at the community center, my cousin Kimiyatta at her home, and others. Each of these conversations went one of two ways. One: a vague pronouncement of pride followed by reminiscing on memories they had of me that I could not remember. Two: a condescending remark about how I thought I was too good for them followed by an inquiry into how much money I was making. When we tried to discuss the present, we had nothing to say. There was no path to understanding, no touchstone of comprehension. We had taken different paths, which led us so far apart that we had nothing in common anymore. They took the road that society and history repeatedly shoved in their faces, one of survival and welfare and teen pregnancy and drug use. I took a course to something else and, unfortunately, in their eyes— or maybe in my eyes reflected in theirs—it was a path that made me lesser.

To them, I had forgotten where I came from.

To them, I was trying to forget I was black.

It's true what they say: you can't go home again.

Maybe my parents' pregnancy wasn't about unifying the family. Maybe they made a mistake, and my father's Baptist upbringing weighed heavily on his conscience, guilting him by the threat of shame and coercing him by the threat of hell into making an honest woman of my mother. But unfortunately, the true reason for their marriage has been lost to time, buried under decades of rationalizing and cognitive dissonance. Nowhere and no time was happily ever after. If they ever loved one another, they had long lost that love by the time I was able to form memories.

FACET: 2

Age: 11
Place: Uniontown, PA
Status: Just before Dying

It was a brutally cold November day in Uniontown, Pennsylvania—
the kind of day where the air hurts your lungs and no number of
layers can remove the chill from your spine. It was a Sunday. My dad
had visitation rights every other weekend, and he always came to get
us on Sunday. Sometimes we'd do Saturday and Sunday, but always
Sunday. This Sunday followed the first snowfall of the year, and the
landscape glittered with a light dusting of snow illuminated by the
streetlights of Lawn Avenue. Suppose one had an appropriate privilege in their upbringing and an inappropriate amount of naïveté. In
that case, this pristine image could easily be mistaken for the idyl-
lic worlds presented in Thomas Kinkade paintings and Bing Crosby
songs. But zoom in on the peaceful panorama, and you'll find our
home was far from perfect. I grew up in a household where single-
parent was a positive descriptor as it rescued us from the fighting and
violence of an unloving marriage. I spent the morning checking the
grocery store circulars for sales on Thanksgiving essentials that were
good enough for us to afford a traditional dinner. We weren't poor,
at least not in any meaningful way. We usually had food and, with
enough diligence and foresight, we could even fund holiday meals.
They were, however, never quite as robust as those in Norman Rock-
well paintings and holiday films led us to believe.

As a child, I saw my father as larger and more intimidating than his size and demeanor should warrant. He isn't a large man; he was more than a shade under six feet tall, and the scale certainly couldn't have touched 200 pounds, even fully dressed with a pocketful of change. However, as the years piled on, so did the pounds, and he has thickened some with age. Now, same as then, he keeps his head shaved. Although now, when his hair grows between trimmings, there is more gray than black. He sometimes wore a goatee, and I never saw him without at least a mustache in my entire life. He has kind eyes. His mouth is stoic and straight, afraid to venture too far south for fear of being mistaken for an expression of anger and guarded against smiling except when warranted. His demeanor usually alternated between a fun, engaged father and the quiet fatigue that afflicts most black men of a certain age—one that seems to be getting younger and younger as black death floods our media. He was always willing to try whatever activities his children were engaged in, whether video games or drawing. We would even have dunk contests, not that any of us could reach a regulation rim. Instead, we'd have them in the bedroom with the small Nerf hoop that hung over our bedroom door.

"Off the bed, between the legs, and with the left hand," he said.

And through the door. The rim—a small, plastic loop attached to a cardboard backboard—could neither support my father's weight nor stop his momentum. And while he completed his dunk, he also hit the door with such force that it cracked and splintered in two.

My mom put an end to the dunk contests after that.

Like all good fathers, he tried to raise us as best he could, even some of his teaching methods were a bit unorthodox. He didn't teach us the value of a dollar by underpaying us for the labor of mowing the lawn or washing the car. Instead, he engaged in small skirtings of the rules that keep stores and businesses from taking his money excessively. For example, our local movie theater offered free refills on large popcorns and drinks. Instead of purchasing refreshments when we'd go to the theater, he'd simply ask someone heading toward a trash can after their film if he could have their cup and popcorn tub. He would then take them into the restroom, wash them with the hand soap from the dispenser, and let the theater refill them for free. "This theater makes a million dollars a year. Why should I pay them eight dollars for a nickel worth of popcorn?"

Sometimes, when his less direct lessons didn't hit the mark, he would take a more direct route to keep us in line. He wasn't necessarily quick to get the belt, but he certainly wasn't afraid to use it. I only got the belt once as a child because I learned from my brother's behavior and its consequences. My brother got whupped more times than I can remember. My father, however, took no joy in it; it was a necessary measure to keep us from going too far over the line. In his mind, keeping us in line with the belt was better than the police keeping us in line with bullets.

My mother and father soon separated, and when he left the house both the basketball and the beatings went with him. But on this day, my dad was on his way to pick us up. Waiting for my father on these days was always interminable. Not because I dreaded spending time with my father, but mainly because the time spent always felt like a waste of time. Everything about the visits was liminal: our house would suddenly have the feel and tenor of a bus stop—we'd wait at home for a ride that we would spend counting the minutes until it was over. Even the relationship was liminal: he would be my dad for four to six hours and then return for the next thirteen days to being the disembodied voice on the other end of the phone line.

Once he was no longer with us all the time, the days spent with our father were bland and repetitive. Most of the time, we'd go to the mall, and his few short hours with us functioned more as a commercial exchange than familial bonding. As soon as we'd arrive at whatever monument to capitalism served as that visit's outing, he'd hand us twenty dollars or so. We'd then go our separate ways only to meet up when we were out of cash or energy. At the time, I never stopped to think how much it must have hurt him to spend his few short hours with us that way, but I also recognize that perhaps we didn't know how to spend them any other way. For the entirety of our lives before his split from my mother, he was the primary breadwinner, which meant our mother governed our lives day-to-day while he worked. He was at the time, and every time until his retirement, a compression station operator and project manager for Consolidated Natural Gas and remained so through the company's merger and buyout by Dominion Resources. During his forty-plus years with the company, he had multiple opportunities for promotion into management. However, he always turned them down for fear of losing the protection of the United Gas Workers of America Union. As a black man, he knew that he needed that union more than his white colleagues because the boss would not afford him the same second chances.

This time, the worn-out capitalism that structured our relationship would lead us to end our visit with a trip to the grocery store to get the essentials for a Thanksgiving dinner. Even though he couldn't be with us on the holiday, he wanted the four of us—my mother, my brother, my sister, and me—to be as much of a family as we could.

Usually, when we would leave to go with my father, my mother would ask what time we would be home. But this time was different. As we stood in the small foyer of our nineteenth-century house that was never quite a home, putting on the coats and gloves that would be our armor against the bracing wind, my mother stood directly in front of my brother and issued a decree:

"I need you home by seven," she said.

"Why?" my brother asked.

"Because you have school tomorrow," she responded, kissing him on the forehead.

Both the words and the kiss were out of the ordinary for our send-off, although unremarkable at the time. My mother had never before made a demand on our time with our father. More often than not, she approached our days with our father as a relief—a small respite from the tedious struggles of single motherhood.

She then knelt to help me put on my right-hand glove. Putting on gloves was always an ordeal for me as a child. Being right-handed, I could easily pull the thick, polyester ski glove onto my left hand. Once the extra padding dulled my dexterity, however, I struggled to pull on the right one. If I were at home, my mother would usually help. If at school, some teacher or resource officer would come to my aid. God forbid the glove ever came off while playing. In these unfortunate instances, my brother and cousins would take the glove and play a harmless game of keep-away that we called the less benign name of "monkey in the middle." They would toss the glove back and forth in time with mocking chants, "Fat Matt, the water rat, couldn't get through 'cause he was too fat." Their laughter increased in direct relation to my anger as I fruitlessly tried to reclaim my property. I huffed and puffed to regain possession before my hand went numb— my eleven-year-old, already 180-pound body struggling too much under its girth to ever win the game.

I always hated when they did that.

"We always have school," my brother said, recognizing the weird-ness of her request. He was four years my senior and always more perceptive of the context of our surroundings. So while I focused on making sure I had my stubby fingers correctly inserted into the fleece-lined gloves, my brother was busy trying to determine what threat level, if any, to attach to my mother's demand.

"Just tell your father to have you home by seven." She turned, kissed my brother on the cheek, and handed him the list of groceries we'd need to purchase for Thanksgiving. At that moment, a car horn blared. And as my mother went to open the door and send us off with our father, I saw the confusion on my brother's face.

My dad greeted us with the typical questions, trying to engage with the lives of the children he saw only 7 percent of the time. "How are you?" "How's school?" And in this case, "What do y'all want for Christmas?"

We answered his queries with answers that had become rote: Good. Fine. And, I don't know.

This day with our father was a little more special than our usual shopping excursions. Since this was the last time he'd see us before the Thanksgiving holiday, he took us to see a movie. Going to movies with my father and siblings was always an adventure—less because of the fantastical worlds on the big screen than because none of us ever wanted to see the same movie. Being old enough to be concerned with what his friends would think even if they weren't present, my brother typically wanted to see the more violent action films—anything with Jean-Claude Van Damme or Sylvester Stallone. My sister, two years my elder, had just become a teenager. Her taste in movies was a strange polarity of Disney princesses and art films—both Disney's *Beauty and the Beast* and Godfrey Reggio's *Koyaanisqatsi* equally enthralled her. My dad didn't care what we watched, as long as we watched it together.

I just wanted to watch cartoons.

"I want to see *To Wong Foo*," my sister said.

"You don't even know what that's about," my brother retorted in a way that only older brothers can, where an empirical truth becomes a condescending insult.

"It's better than anything else playing," she responded, her tenor shifting toward the nagging that always ensured she got her way.

"How do you know? You haven't seen anything playing," my brother tried to continue, but my dad cut him off.

"If y'all start fightin', we aren't gonna see anything," he said.

My dad had a way about him. He was the strong, silent type whose constant need for strength often left him tired and battered. He was a black man, and he needed that strength to survive every day in a society that would love nothing more than for him to fail. But he wouldn't let that happen. He wouldn't let the world revel in his misery and use his life to perpetuate myths of racial inferiority. Not to himself and not for us. So, he persisted. He protected me from that society as best he could. But sometimes, that society was at work in our home, and his absence from that homelife left me unguarded.

"Fine," my brother said.

"Don't give me that lip," replied my father.

The argument was over before it began. We were all familiar with that particular tone of my father's. While most parents only threaten to turn the car around, my dad would actually do it. With the argument over, we compromised on a movie that none of us wanted to watch, but none of us refused to watch. We settled into the theater with our recycled popcorn bag and soda cup filled to the brim with complimentary refreshments—thanks to my dad exploiting a loophole in capitalism.

After the movie, we made our way to Foodland: a grungy, off-white grocery store in the small ten-block area that constituted downtown Uniontown. While we watched the movie, the snowfall increased to blizzardy accumulation. With road closures and power outages on the horizon, the store was a madhouse of activity and energy. People jostled and bumped impatiently up and down the aisles, leaving the shelves bereft of essentials such as milk and bread.

As we fought through the crowds, my brother's mannerisms shifted toward agitation. I assumed it was the cacophony of the holiday shoppers and their blatant disregard for civility and personal space, but it was something else. He was anxious about a more immediate threat. As I watched him nervously look up and down, debating whether I should ask if he was okay, I noticed something peculiar: he kept trying to steal a glance at my father's watch. I suddenly realized what he was doing, and I began to tense too. He was checking the time.

6:53.

We hadn't told our father that our mother wanted us home by seven. When she said it, I didn't think this was a big deal. Now, however, my brother's stilted and tense breathing changed my mind. My breathing began to match his, but it was too late to tell our father. With our pulses racing, we finished maneuvering the aisles and made our way to the checkout line. Although the line was only three or four people deep, this was still in the days before Visa checkout and Apple pay, when each patron would count out their cash and await change. Or worse, write a check. As we slowly inched forward in the line, I looked at the big clock that hung over the plate glass windows at the front of the store and began to do calculations in my head . . .

6:58.

If we left right at this second, hit no red lights, and drove ten miles over the speed limit, we could make it home by seven. I looked at my brother, and he was doing the same calculations. It was too late to tell my dad we were supposed to be home by seven. I stood in the line, hoping my mother had forgotten her decree.

7:07.

Checkout took nine minutes. We had missed our curfew. The mingled hopelessness and anxiety of being late made the car ride last forever. I tried to convince myself that it was nothing, that she wouldn't mind. But I knew better. She would not have issued the ultimatum unless she had planned to enforce it.

We pulled up to the curb in front of our house and loaded the groceries onto our arms. I didn't know the time, but I know it was well past seven. My dad, unaware of our torment, ended the visit the way he always did. He gave each of us a hug, said, "I love you," and, "Call if you need anything." He then got in his car and disappeared around the corner to make the ninety-minute drive to his small townhome in Chambersburg.

We made the same return from this visit every week. We'd walk in the door with whatever toys and trinkets we had purchased, perhaps with a few groceries or leftovers from one of the "good" restaurants: Ponderosa, Shoney's, or maybe even Bob's Big Boy. We'd immediately seek out our mother to let her know we were home. She'd ask how it was, although she never really cared about the answer. We'd answer, "It was fine"—because we had learned that speaking of our father in her presence often led to disastrous results.

This return home, however, was different. We trudged through the newly fallen snow to the porch and slowly opened the door. Part of me hoped that we could all sneak into the house and our beds without our mother noticing, although I knew the grocery bags and wet soles of our shoes would certainly alert her to our arrival.

We walked in the door carrying our family's Thanksgiving traditions: a couple of Jiffy corn muffin mix boxes, a frozen Sara Lee pumpkin pie, sage breakfast sausage for the dressing, the disgusting can of red jelly that stores try to pass off as cranberry sauce, and a turkey that none of us seemed to like but ate anyway. We slunk with our hands full across the cheap frayed rug that covered the scratched hardwood. But we didn't have to go and find our mother. Instead, she waited on the curved staircase in the foyer. (The notion of a curved staircase and foyer may create the impression that we were something we weren't—I can assure you that despite these features, we were living the same middle-class fantasy as whoever put these features into the poorly built and even more poorly maintained home we occupied.) Her elbows were on her knees with her hands folded tight enough to see the skin bunching around her knuckles. She was silent and still—the type of complete silence that makes an audience hold its breath in the theater. The kind of silence where you hear your heartbeat in the back of your ears and your blood rushing through your head. The type of stillness whose breaking can only be interpreted as violence.

The door closing caused the grocery bags to flutter in the cold winter wind. Then, the scene settled to match her silence. The stillness was so intense that I could feel my brother inhale and exhale. He took a step forward from the door, sensing that in the peace of my mother lay danger. He put himself in the line of fire, overcome by a primordial instinct to protect the younger members of the pack.

"Mom?" The word escaped his mouth, his confidence and bravado betrayed by the slight raising of pitch that made his greeting sound like a question.

"What time is it?" my mother asked in a low, steady voice, barely louder than a whisper.

Her earlier demand flashed into my head: "I need you home by seven."

"Six something?" my brother responded with hope, but we all knew the answer.

"No," she said, with so much venom that the word dripped from her mouth onto the floor. It slithered its way across the faded floorboards of the foyer and made its way up my spine, triggering my fight or flight response. Unfortunately, I had nowhere to fly and had no weapons with which to win the fight. My stomach knotted, sending bile and acid up into the base of my throat. I suddenly recognized the danger that my brother had responded to mere seconds earlier. As my esophagus burned, my vision shifted into soft focus and my eyes threatened to well. I wanted nothing more than to burst back out through the door and run off into the cold, snowy November night.

"It's almost 7:20."

7:18.

The sounds emanated from her mouth in a mix of grizzled air and seething rage that made the walls close in. My chest became tight—I couldn't even draw enough air to hyperventilate. I thought I knew what was coming. My mother was prone to mood swings. Her storm of emotions would swell into a maelstrom that rocked our ship, but we knew clear skies would come soon enough if we could just weather the waves.

"We're sorry," my brother tried. "The lines at the store were crazy."

I didn't know how meaningful the almost twenty minutes between 7 p.m. and 7:18 p.m. would come to be for my life. I didn't know that eighteen minutes late was a capital crime.

But my mother's response assured me that eighteen minutes was more than enough cause to die.

"That nigger was supposed to have you home by seven," she said.

SHARD: 2
Status: Fractured

My earliest memory of my parents would be them going down to the basement. I couldn't have been older than three or four. Our small red house at 424 Westmoreland Drive in Dunbar, West Virginia, stood near the top of a hill. The facade of the ground floor sat at street level, and on the left side of the house was a gravel driveway that followed the sloping land directly to the dual-purpose garage/basement. Every other Friday, payday for my dad and his working-class friends, my parents would put us to bed and head downstairs. Every other Friday, my brother and I would stay up late and watch the cars pull up to the curb. Every other Friday, we watched my working-class parents' friends stroll down to the basement with twelve-packs of Bud Light and other products designed to wash away the workaday drudgery.

These friends, mostly my father's friends, were very different from his family. There was Joe, a long-haired white man with a mustache and goatee who I never saw in a shirt with sleeves. Carl, a rotund man with dark black hair and a toothpick hanging out of his mouth. Jimmy, a man who my father affectionately called "San-CHEZ." There were countless others whose names and features I don't remember, save this: these friends who would come to drink in our basement were white.

As a child who was still largely unaware of his blackness, their whiteness did not strike me as unusual. Why would it? My mother was white. The presence of both whiteness and blackness were constants in my life. The world had yet to confront me with how all-consuming the distinction was.

When these friends would come over, my brother and I would sit over the furnace vent and listen to the sounds echo from the basement through the ducts into our room. I don't know why we did it; it wasn't particularly entertaining or enlightening most of the time. Most of the time, we'd just hear them listening to music and talking. Maybe it was the risk? The voyeuristic pleasure of hearing something you weren't supposed to and the tension of potentially being caught. I would ride this wave of secrecy to fantasies of my brother and me as spies hiding in the air duct of the supervillain's lair, waiting for them to reveal the secret that would allow us to stop their nefarious plans.

Every so often, I'd hear something I didn't understand, and I'd cock my head to the side like a confused puppy and look at my brother. Every time, my brother would shush me before I could break the silence and get us caught. And as we huddled over the furnace vent, my parents and their friends would sit in the basement and talk about their day-to-day lives, never looking further back than the previous week at work and never looking further forward than the next beer. Sometimes, along with the voices, were the sounds of Led Zeppelin, The Temptations, and Pink Floyd. Sometimes, along with the voices, was the odor of bad pizza and fresh-cut grass that I would later learn was the smell of marijuana.

Sometimes, the other voices were gone, and it was just my parents. Sometimes, when it was just my parents, we didn't need the vent to hear them. Most of the Fridays when their friends weren't over, my parents would put us to bed and go to the basement to fight. Occasionally, they would argue in front of us, but those arguments would always stop short of yelling or physical violence when we were present. They tried to stay together for us, and they wanted to protect us from the fact that they were falling apart. But my brother and I would hear the truth rattle up the pipe from the basement.

"How could you do this to me?" my mother would wail at my father.

"Now look here . . ." my father would start but never finish.

"How could you do this to me?" My mother would shout with a volume and anger that dwarfed her petite frame.

The question was so common and their fighting so frequent that both lost all meaning before I enrolled in kindergarten. More than the words, I remember my mother's tenor. It was an anguished keening: sharp, shrill, funerary—a wail that could only be the product of a divergent mind forced to adapt to a life and a living for which it had no manual for navigating. The percussive orchestra of property damage often accompanied her cries: a hammer pounding on my dad's grill or a crowbar slamming into his car. This banging would shock me away from the vent and into bed, where the pillow could absorb my tears, the weight of the moments sopping into my ThunderCats pillowcase. To calm myself, I would make up fantasies of what was happening in the basement. I often imagined that my parents were knights, defending our home from monsters and Muppets. These figures escaped from my favorite fantasy films and invaded our home through the mysterious drain in the center of the basement floor. I imagined the Fire Gang and Skeksis and all the other terrifying creatures from my childhood emerging through that empty hole, only to be beaten back by my mother and father. Or sometimes, I'd pretend they were forming a rock 'n' roll band. I'd heard enough of John Bonham, Ozzy Osbourne, and Jimmy Page through that vent to convince myself that they weren't fighting but were inspired. I imagined that the irregular thrashing of metal on metal and glass on concrete were just odd time signatures that my preadolescent mind couldn't calculate. I dreamed that perhaps they were trying to influence us into creating art that our strained finances couldn't afford to incubate and nurture.

But imagination can only go so far. In the moments that I was honest with myself, I knew what was happening. My fantasies shattered every time the police arrived.

On more than one occasion, I saw my father in handcuffs. But never my mother—my introduction to the societal assumption of black criminality coming courtesy of my own family. Holding the accusations of children to a higher evidentiary standard than those of adults, my voice and tears served as the evidence necessary to confirm whatever assumptions the officer had when he asked his question.

"Hey there, son," the officer said.

The first time the man in the black uniform with yellow embroideries and gold badges made this introduction, I was five years old. Alongside learning the ABCs and 123s in kindergarten, I also learned how to deal with the police. I couldn't respond. I was not his son, and this man was not my father. Although he tried his best to be comforting, I knew what his job was even at that young age. His job was to arrest criminals. Was I a criminal?

"Have you ever seen your father hurt your mother?" he asked. Always that question. In all the times the police came to our house, it was always that question. Never if my mother had hurt my father. Not even if he was bruised or if his clothing was torn when the cops arrived would they ask if she was the one who had hurt him. Never if either had hurt my siblings or me. Always if my father had hurt my mother. Always if the man had hurt the woman. Always if black had hurt white.

"No. He's never hurt her," I replied.

Unfortunately, my answer didn't match his assumption. He disregarded my testimony, and he turned and walked the twenty or so feet across the living room to my father. I couldn't hear the exchange, but I heard how it ended.

"Not in front of them," my dad half-asked, half-commanded.

With that, my father walked out the front door with the officer close behind at his left shoulder. Once out the door, my mother quickly herded us to our room. Unfortunately, her attempt to shield us from further trauma was destroyed as I looked out of the bedroom window I shared with my brother. Here, we saw the officer leading my father off in handcuffs and shoving him into the back of the cruiser.

I saw this sight far too often as a child. Whenever the police would come, my dad would go away. Sometimes, just for the night. On most occasions, both my parents slept off whatever poisons they'd put into their systems and allowed the light of a new day to burn away the sins of the past evening. But sometimes, he'd be gone for a few days. Whenever he'd go away, I never knew if he was in jail, crashing on a friend's couch, or out of town for work. I was just a child, and when I asked, "Where's daddy?" my mom wouldn't answer with where he was, but always when he'd be home. Not in any absolute manner. With vague, obfuscating phrases such as "soon," "in a bit," or "once he's done with work."

Whenever he came back, he'd always bring a gift whose value was proportional to the time he was away. If it was overnight, he might sneak a Little Debbie cake out of the Coleman cooler he used as a lunchbox and hand it to me. I still to this day love Oatmeal Creme Pies and Star Crunch—small remembrances of what could colloquially and delusively be called "good times." If it was a weekend, he might return with an action figure. If it was longer, a LEGO set. I now know that those gifts were to distract me from asking where he'd been. It was an effective tactic: the sight of a G. I. Joe or a LEGO space set immediately overwhelmed and drove whatever frightful thoughts were haunting my mind.

This pattern of vocals, percussion, flashing red and blue lights, questions, and spending the night with only my mother home continued for what—to me—was forever. It is among my first memories and, at the time, bookended the entire span of my memories. Until the day the pattern broke.

SHARD: 3
Status: Lost

One day, my dad went away and took his belongings with him. My parents were separating. My dad was moving into his own apartment, and we'd only see him on weekends. I didn't truly comprehend what this meant since we were used to really only seeing him on weekends because of his work schedule. During the week, our encounters were primarily between a man exhausted from the day and his son exhausted for the night. I have stronger memories of his stereo being gone from the house than of his presence. He had this colossal console stereo with a turntable, an equalizer, two cassette decks, and speakers as tall as I was. The mixer, equalizer, and console unit stood in a solid wood cabinet made from spalted oak. A glass door adorned the front of the case, shielding the delicate electronics from atmospheric threats. It occupied a wall in our living room opposite the TV, creating dueling tennis court configurations between our entertainment appliances and both couches. I never knew which served to organize the other, but I valued the distractions of the electronic devices far higher than the interactions of the face-to-face seating. Our living room served as a symbolic monument to the macro systemic paradigm of our existence: the day-to-day of our lives led to nothing but pain, so we prioritized a series of visual and aural distractions. I focused on losing the stereo because there was already too much pain to cope with losing my father.

My father's exile turned our single-family home into a half-family home, with the other half sentenced to living in a shitty one-bedroom apartment across the street from his favorite bar, The Smokehouse. The every other Friday night basement parties became me and my siblings pilings into his white Plymouth Breeze every other Friday evening and heading to the outskirts of downtown Charleston. We would spend the weekend camping out on cheap foam mattresses my father had procured from a nearby military surplus store. We'd unroll these mats each night to lay them on the dirty grayish-brown carpet in the living room that never got clean no matter how much we vacuumed. Then, each morning, we'd roll them back up and place them in the closet, an act that reinforced each day the temporary and transient nature of our relationship with our father.

My father worked hard to make these weekends fun and productive. We'd mostly play board games or cards and watch TV. Some days, we'd go to the mall or one of the many nearby parks, usually Shawnee or Wine Cellar, and hike or swim or play on the playgrounds. More often, though, we'd go to the Smokehouse, where we'd play pool or watch TV while he drank with his friends. Sometimes, I felt blessed that I had a father who, despite the animosity between him and my mother, tried his best to be a part of his children's lives. Sometimes, I felt like an imposition; here was a man trying to live his best life, and best became far from so by the burden of his fuck trophies. I wonder, however, if perhaps our frequent trips to the Smokehouse and his regular drinking were his way of coping with our presence. Not because he didn't want us in his life. But because when we were around, we were painful reminders that we weren't in his life more.

SHARD: 4
Status: Foreshadowing

My mother filled her newly single life with religion. She flirted with many belief systems during my childhood: the Church of the Nazarene, the Salvation Army, Scientology. But she only ever brought me into one. Less than a month after my father's departure, we received a knock on the door. I answered to see two clean-cut, gentle souls, asking if there was anything they could do for us. The man on the right was tall and thickly built, with short hair and a tie just a bit too short. By his side was a thinly built man with longer but still orderly dark hair. Both of them wore the same white button-up shirt and black slacks. I went to get my mother. When she met them at the door, they began talking. After a few minutes, she invited them in.

If I were perhaps a bit older, I would have interpreted these two well-dressed white men as a governmental threat, but since I was only six, I returned to my video games. After what couldn't have been more than ten minutes, my mother called all of us to the living room. My brother and I reluctantly paused our game, and we met our sister in the hallway on our way to our mother.

"Hi," said the thickly built man, "I'm Elder Watt."

"And I'm Elder Peck," said the other. "What's your name?"

"Gabe," said my brother, interrupting my attempt to respond.

My brother is four years older than me, and even at ten years old, he seemed wise. Maybe wise isn't the right word, but he was certainly more experienced with the troubles of our lives and thus more discerning of impending threats.

"And you are?" asked Elder Watt, turning to me.

He again cut me off. "This is my brother Matt and my sister Staci."

"Hello, Gabe, Matt, and Staci," said Elder Watt. "We're members of the Church of Jesus Christ of Latter-day Saints. Your mother asked us to share a lesson from the Book of Mormon with her. Would you like to join us?"

"Not really," said my brother. I don't know if he was uninterested, skeptical, or afraid, but he was definitely cautious and defensive.

"Is that any way to treat guests?" said my mother, asking us as much as telling.

"That's okay," said Elder Watt. "We will only share if you ask us."

My mother shot us a look that said we should reconsider our response, or else.

"Okay," said my brother.

My family sat together on the couch with the two Mormon elders seated across on the loveseat. I didn't understand anything they were saying; instead, I spent the time counting the grains on the wood flooring in our living room. With my video game on pause in the other room, their reading felt like lifetimes. Then, just when I thought I was about to lose it, they broke the monotony with a question.

"Would it be okay if we prayed for you?" asked Elder Peck.

Before any of us could speak, my mom answered for all of us, "Of course it would."

We all stood, joined hands, and bowed our heads. Then, Elder Peck began his prayer, "Our Father in heaven . . ."

As he spoke, I shifted uncomfortably. Even though my head was bowed and my eyes were closed, I could feel my siblings' nervous energy reverberating through the floor. I cracked my eyes and slowly rose my head a millimeter at a time to try to catch a glimpse of my brother or sister. I was surprised when I reached my brother to find that he was already looking back at me with a secretive glance. I could see just enough of his eyebrows furrowing to know we were thinking the same thought: *this is weird.*

"In Jesus's name, we pray, Amen," said Elder Peck.

"Amen," repeated Elder Watt.

They left immediately after. My brother and I exchanged awkward glances with my sister as we returned to our rooms. We didn't speak about what had just happened, but I saw reflected in their eyes the same relief I felt: *I'm glad that's over.*

But it had just begun. Our mother had invited the elders back the following weekend for dinner. And the next. And the next. And the *next* week, my mom woke us up early, dressed us up, and we attended temple. And we attended the week after that. And after that. And slowly, methodically, week by week, more Mormon books found their way into our house, and we spent more of our time at temple and other social gatherings. As time went by, the awkwardness wore away, and I actually came to enjoy the fellowship.

But I was still only a child, and I had little knowledge of the actual teachings and history of the church. We would go to temple every Sunday and sing hymns and hear a sermon. But the most I ever got out of them were the typical, vague Christian messages of love and forgiveness. The church has endless media to aid in engaging children with the doctrine of Joseph Smith and the angel Moroni, ranging from comic book versions of scripture to animated videos and video games. Still, in each case, I was more interested in the images than the actual message. So I continued to sit through temple each Sunday, oblivious to what was being said—these two hours spent every Sunday were the toll we had to pay to enjoy the cookouts, baseball games, and camping trips.

So, when I reached eight years old, I was baptized into the

Mormon religion. Mormons will only baptize someone if they choose to do so of their own free will. The person must look into their heart and find that the truth is in a personal relationship with Jesus Christ, our Savior. Mormons decided that people are accountable enough to consent to this at age eight. I had no idea what I was agreeing to. I looked into my heart, and I found that I wanted to be like my brother. And since he decided, so did I.

When I agreed to baptism, I had no idea that I was joining a religion with a long history of hating black people. According to the *Book of Mormon*, the congregation aspired to be "a white and delightsome people."[1] And church lore is full of stories and biographies of black members who longed to change the color of their skin or pronounced themselves white despite reality—misguided efforts to become closer to God's purity and light. The earliest configuration of the church under Joseph Smith allowed black men to participate fully. However, the church under his successor Brigham Young decreed that black men could not hold the priesthood. In subsequent years, Young's church barred both black men and women from attending temple.[2] For over a century, from 1852 to the 1970s, the church preached explicitly antiblack doctrine and operated on antiblack rules. Their interpretation of heaven consisted of multiple levels, with the higher levels closer to God and inaccessible to blacks. The church preached the policing and control of black bodies even in the afterlife. The church did not formally renounce these racist teachings until 2013.

I was an active member of the church from 1990 to 1993.

I am less concerned, however, with the history of Mormonism and race than I am with what this history meant for my family and me. It means that my mother, my white mother, decided to indoctrinate her three children—at the time, ages six, eight, and ten—into a religion that has a foundational canon that viewed her relationship and our existence as a sin. A faith that preached that the antiblack violence of mortal life extended into antiblack violence of the metaphysical, spiritual afterlife. And she did it while her children's black father was out of the home. In hindsight, I cannot help but view our foray into a religion that hated half of what I was as my mother's attempt to purge my father and my father's blackness from her children, and in doing so, purge the black sin of his flesh and ours from her history.

Being in this environment as a child was an interesting phenomenon. Despite being consciously unaware of this history and these teachings, I could feel them in the eyes and hear them in the voices of the elders and parishioners at our temple. What my childish mind took for kindness, my adult mind now interprets through years of encounters with antiblackness as pity. Elder Peck didn't bring us small gifts every time he came to the house, usually some form of scriptural paraphernalia, because we were his favorite family. He brought these extra materials because our souls needed extra help to overcome our skin. Ms. Judy wasn't giving me additional cookies at the picnic because she liked me, but because she wanted to provide me with earthly pleasures to make up for the fact that I would be denied eternal paradise.

SLIVER

A Simple Question

"Is an extra cookie violence?"

We are inundated so often through the nightly news and Hollywood blockbusters with images of spectacular violence against black bodies that we often overlook its more insidious forms. While it's easy to lash out against police lynching a black man, it's less easy to lash out at what George W. Bush, of all people, called "the soft bigotry of low expectations." Bush was speaking of the corporeal and conscious expectations that primarily manifest through lessened opportunities—we expect black people to make worse grades, go to worse colleges, and work in lower-paying fields. However, these lowered expectations also manifest in the remnants of decades- to centuries-old beliefs that black people are metaphysically incapable of redemption and salvation.

These beliefs are so much a part of the world that even kindness toward blackness—giving an extra cookie in my experience, or the current trend to hashtag every unjust black death across social media—is not kindness, but rather the pity and violence of lowered expectations. The truly living expect black death and black eternity to matter just as little to them as black lives.

SHARD: 5
Status: Hopeful

A couple of years after he moved out, my father and my mother reconciled. I don't know what exactly led to their reconciliation, but their reunion was joined by a hardened determination to make life better for all of us. My parents decided to give up the drugs and alcohol and enter an in-patient rehab program. They were committed to having my mother be a stay-at-home mom so that we kids would always have a parent engaged in our lives. They were committed to getting us help in processing the effects of their destructive behaviors and moving forward to happy, productive lives.

They were so committed, in fact, that they had to separate themselves from the friends and family who contributed to their reckless and toxic behavior. My dad had asked for and received a transfer at his job to take us away from bad influences and give us a fresh start. So, in the middle of the summer after my third grade year, we left our friends and families and moved 180 plus miles north. Less than a month after his request for a transfer, my family arrived at our new house in Uniontown, Pennsylvania.

With my dad again a part of the household, we stopped going to temple. Perhaps with my father back in her life, my mother no longer needed religion. Or maybe, she recognized the violent hypocrisy of remaining involved in a faith that reviled and condemned her chosen lover as unworthy of the highest levels of heaven. One of the most sacred rituals in the Mormon church is "the sealing." Mormons believe that civil marriages do not extend to eternity but end with earthly life. Until 2013, official church literature advised against interracial sealing, as the covenant of the sealing was at odds with the church's beliefs regarding blacks: while a civil marriage dissolved at death, a sealing connected the couple for all eternity. Sealing a black person to a white person, however, would create a conflict in the afterlife: the two would theoretically be sealed in eternity, but some levels of heaven are inaccessible to blacks. Hence, interracial sealing creates a paradox either by granting access to the inaccessible or by denying access to the otherwise deserving.[3] In the end, whether through conscious objection or a product of circumstance and convenience, my mother chose her civil marriage over eternal salvation.

Our new house in Uniontown was built in the nineteenth century. The builders must have been a middle-class family who wanted to feel much wealthier and more important than they were—an early version of keeping up with the Joneses. There was an oddly situated foyer with a library off to the side before walking directly into a bathroom with a stained glass window that looked into the formal dining room. I never could grasp precisely why someone would build a window between where they shit and where they ate. There were two staircases: the first rose off the foyer with a small landing where it turned 180 degrees after four steps in an attempt to emulate the grand sweeping curved staircases of pre-bellum plantation mansions. The second staircase was at the back of the house, leading directly from the kitchen to the fourth bedroom, which the landlord politely called "the servant's quarters" in the presence of this mixed-race family. The home was built for features, not function, as though reconstructed from a fading memory of grandiose largesse, full of what would have been upscale if constructed and configured more thoughtfully.

For a short time, everything worked out great. My parents went to rehab and got clean. Over twenty-five years later, my father remains sober. My mother, sadly, fell off the wagon so often that it was hard to tell if she was ever indeed on it. I began attending Benjamin Franklin Middle School, where I excelled academically. I had friends. I had a family.

It is the last time I can remember being truly happy.

I was nine years old.

Of course, it wouldn't be long before my parents began fighting again. Without the drugs and the alcohol clouding their judgment, they began to recalculate the equation that led to their marriage. In this iteration, the damage *to* their children by staying together outweighed the responsibility to stay together *for* their children. They separated again. Our new house suddenly felt as old and empty and cold as it looked. And this time, my dad didn't move to a shitty apartment in the next town over but instead took a transfer to a compression station two hours away in Chambersburg. This way, there would be no chance encounters between Mom and Dad, no unannounced arrivals, and no salvation from my mother.

FACET: 3

Age: 11
Location: Uniontown, PA
Status: Dying/Reverberation

"I told that nigger to have you home by seven."

I felt what it meant to be a nigger at that moment. Being a nigger meant I had no family. Being a nigger meant I had no honor. Being a nigger meant that my life was a concept that was undergirded by white myths of blissful racial integration that ignored my lived experience. That my "life" is forever and always contingent on the desires of a world that needs my death. Blood is thicker than water. But at that moment, her words were a centrifuge separating my blood into the pure, milky plasma of my whiteness and the sticky, viscous serum of my blackness. That serum was thicker than any experience or filiation assumed by the consequence of my birth.

SLIVER
Nigger is . . .

"Nigger."

One of the greatest philosophers and social commentators of our time, Richard Pryor, called it a "devastating fucking word."

The English language contains dozens of racial epithets intended to demean black people: ape, colored, coon, crow, golliwog, jigaboo, Sambo, tar baby, jungle bunny, monkey, porch monkey, spade, thug—the list is as long as our nation's history. Each of these terms has faded in and out of fashion along with the times, but not nigger. Nigger is unique. Only nigger has maintained its power across time and space. The word is so devastating that its presence is banned from discussions of racist terms, replaced by the semantically identical "N-word."

What is the power of nigger? If we are to believe white, liberal integrationist narratives of progress and a post-race society, nigger should be as archaic as gator bait or bluegum. The word should spark confusion, not anger.

Every race has been subject to various slurs. I will not recount them here because they are not mine to say. But none of these slurs carries such a burdensome history that it squashes every letter but the first. There are no a-, b-, or c-words for any nonblack race.

But there is an N-word for us.

If it was just a word, it should have faded from fashion alongside biting one's thumb. But nigger is not just a word. No. Nigger is a machine. Nigger, Negro—black object, inhuman. Nigger is an idea. A concept. Nigger is gravity. Nigger holds all of whiteness together against blackness. Nigger brings Germans, Irish, Polish, English, French, and even the Spanish and Italians together, marking them each ontologically as human.

Nigger is the ether, the glue, the ontological sutures fastening those between white and black

to humanity. All nonblack races
can deploy nigger to obliterate
black being—and many have,
in their own histories and their
own ways. For example, when the
Chinese sailed across the ocean to
the eastern shore of Africa in the
tenth century, they created new
words, new labels, new ontologies
to contain blackness. Although
already practicing slavery in their
homeland, the Chinese decided
that black Africans were not
worthy of the current slave status.
Instead, they occupied a special
place as "devil-slaves": Inhumans
that could neither digest human
food nor speak human languages.
Their very own private form of
nigger.

From the Manicheans in the
fourth century, through the
Moroccans of the seventh and
the Chinese of the tenth, to the
Portuguese, Spanish, and English
Renaissances into Point Comfort,
peoples and cultures worldwide
have long linked blackness
with inhumanity. They did it
with absence. They did it with
castration. They did it with devil

and imp and anthropophagi and Negro.

And now, they all can do it with nigger.

Nigger has crossed boundaries to become a term of endearment in many communities. White fraternity boys confidently call one another the word after a careful look over each shoulder. Asian teens greet one another as such when giving dap. Even young white girls become emboldened with the word when they find a black boyfriend. Within communities, the word has been adopted, appropriated as a term of intraracial community and belonging.

But when the word crosses the boundaries of race, it becomes recharged with the violence of antiblack presents and histories. Nigger is what remained of the Africans who exited the hold onto the shores of Jamestown. Nigger is the paradox of being owned as human chattel, which Saidiya Hartman eloquently calls the "captive's bifurcated existence as both object of property and a person."[4] Nigger is being bred like cattle on

plantations in Virginia. Nigger is
having your children be not your
children, but the master's farm
equipment. Nigger is a history.
In American history, nigger is the
offspring and memory of forced
labor and bondage and slavery. For
them, nigger is ironic belonging.
When they use it against us, the
word is unfettered violence.

   With the history of niggers not
contained to whiteness, I can't help
but wonder about the role of white
supremacy in black life. White
supremacy certainly exists—all
nonwhite races suffer under white
supremacy. But how do we reconcile the suffering of Asians under
white supremacy with the suffering
of blacks in Asia? How do we analo-
gize the suffering of Latinx people
with the suffering of blacks when
Afro-Latin people are subject to
violence in Latin cultures? Why
does no other race have to argue
that their lives matter?

   While the people between the
limits of white and black—the
brown, the yellow, and the
red—are each subject to white
supremacy, they are also capable

of antiblackness. As such, we must question Charles Mills's statement that "all white people may not be signatories of the racial contract, but all white people are beneficiaries of the racial contract." Who in this equation is white? Politically, he is correct: all nonwhite beings suffer under white supremacy.

But what contract have all nonwhites signed that allows them to perpetuate antiblack violence? The human contract must read, "All humans may not be signatories of the contract of antiblackness, but all humans are beneficiaries of the contract of antiblackness. Your humanity depends on it."

White supremacy is *A* problem for blacks.

Antiblackness is *THE* problem for blacks.

A sick, antiblack world that cannot extract nigger from black being.

"That word has nothing to do with us," Pryor continues.

And he's right. Nigger has nothing to do with black people. Nigger has always been and will always be about the world—its history and present of colonization, genocide, slavery, violence, and oppression. Nigger is a concept. Nigger is a position. Nigger is an absolute negation of being in relation to the human subject. It has nothing to do with black people.

Except that black people have to live in a world in which the concept of nigger exists. And that world has decided that blackness and nigger are one and the same. A force, an idea, an abject—a being that is in the world but not of the world. A being through which all nonblack people can confirm their humanity, one dead nigger at a time.

ABSENCE
Status: Biracial?

I used to struggle with my parentage.

My inheritance

of domination from my mother's blood

and obliteration from my father's.

Growing up

I longed to belong.

But my biracial body was always too much and never enough:

Too black for the white kids.

Too white for the black kids.

Not black enough for the black world.

Not white enough for the white world.

I slowly slid along the in-between and

I acutely felt a longing to step off the tightrope

and fall into place either here or there.

It wasn't until I was much older that I came to realize

that the problem this time wasn't the world.

It was me.

I was desperately clinging to something I could never be,

and in doing so, kept myself from ever being the other.

I am not biracial.

Not in this world.

Not in this nation that made slavery an inheritable trait,
leaving children born either to or from slaves
nothing more than nothing:
black and white mixing into biracialism is a white myth.
A liberal fantasy of reconciliation and absolution
for terror and violence and history
that cannot be redressed, undone, unmade.
So I released the presence that would never be present
and I embraced the absence.
I am not biracial.
I am black.
And in admitting so,
declaring so,
loving so,
I was welcomed so,
into a world of unspeakable joy,
unbridled hope,
unbreakable spirit,
and uncontainable love.
I love black people.
I love the black community.
And I find it loves me back.

FACET: 4

Age: 11
Location: Uniontown, PA
Status: Dying

That cold day in November was dusted with the first snowfall of the year. The glittering light from the streetlamps reflected off the falling snowflakes, painting the world with peace and stillness. Inside, however, a word shattered the stillness and continues to reverberate in my marrow.

"That nigger was supposed to have you home by seven."

She knew what she was doing. She had to have known. On many occasions, my mother said demeaning things to us about our father. She attempted to turn us against our father. She would blame him for their separation. She would say he didn't love us because if he did, he would be there. She would often invent ways in which he had damaged her. Sometimes, it was as simple as expressing a different opinion than her on an issue and her claiming my father poisoned us against her. Other times, it was her saying he sabotaged her car—sugar in the gas tank or some other nefarious act—when the over-a-decade old, $600 piece of shit Honda Accord she owned would break down.

But these psychological attacks failed. I was a child who still loved our father. Partially because I loved him. Partially because, as a child, I knew no alternative. I met her repeated attempts to turn us against him with something between apathy and disgust. I couldn't help but wonder if she talked herself into believing her attacks backfired. No, of course not. She was never one to take responsibility for her actions. She must have just assumed whatever tactics he was using to poison us, of which there were none, were more effective. In her mind, she had no choice but the last resort. If we did not choose her over him, she would destroy him. She knew that nothing she could think or say or do would have the same life-altering impact as that word. She would unleash all the history of black abjection and violence onto his being, rendering him not the less preferable choice but not a choice at all.

"Nigger. . . ."

Before this moment, my mother had never been overtly racist. She didn't hate black people. She didn't wear a white hood. She had black friends. She *married* a black man. Hell, she had black children! But when things didn't go her way, antiblackness was a bullet she always had in her chamber. She didn't have to be antiblack; society allowed her a trump card in any interaction with my father or her children. She could at any moment pull the trigger and unleash a salvo of antiblackness against which my father had no recourse.

The white liberal likes to think that they can cure racism with love. With time. That, if we just spent more time with each other, that if different races just hung out, we'd realize we aren't so different, and racism will just—*poof*—fly off into the breeze like dandelion fuzz, disappearing over the horizon, never to return to earth.

And maybe for some races, that is true. Perhaps time and love will build bridges between their differences.

But twenty years of marriage and three children did nothing to cross the chasm of antiblackness. Perhaps the chasm between blacks and nonblacks is too large for any bridge this broken world can build.

"Nigger . . ." The rest of the sentence faded into the dark recesses, and that word echoed through every cell of my body.

I don't know what transgression my father could have committed in her grotesque imagination to convince her that only his utter destruction would suffice as justice. Still, whatever it was, it certainly could not have been accomplished in the eighteen minutes between her curfew and our arrival. No. This hatred had to be simmering for years, if not decades—from the first moment she surrendered herself and her whiteness to his black dick. Whatever this transgression was, it was enough to make her disregard the potential for any collateral damage. She sat on those stairs and waited—waited for us to return home so she could destroy our father.

"Nigger . . ." her voice echoed.

And at that moment, she destroyed her youngest son. Her purpose was so myopic that she failed to see that by destroying my father, she was destroying a piece of me. The fact that such a word existed in her epistemology meant I could never be more than nothing in her eyes. If he was a nigger, then the nigger blood that ran through his veins now coursed through mine. How could I ever be more?

"Nigger." The one-drop rule of past decades echoed in the present.

"Nigger." Not mixed-race. A motherless child. Her whiteness could not overcome his blackness.

SHARD: 6
Status: Fratricide

With a single word, my mother destroyed our family. Her mother-hood and my sonhood became a void, a phantasmagoric absence that haunts my very being. My defining moment—the keystone of the arch of my life—was a word spoken across the color line that broke every barrier and every connection. I had become natally alienated; she could never be my mother, and I could never be her son.

Nigger.

I don't mean destroyed our family in a purely metaphysical manner. While her antiblackness affected our metaphysical capacity to continue to exist as white mother and black children, the moment produced an actual severing of our family. My brother moved out shortly after that word. He packed his things and went to live in San Diego with Aunt Rose and Uncle Jeff. It was a late summer evening as we stood on the sidewalk of Lawn Avenue. The lightning bugs flickered on and off in their silent ventures through the thick, humid air that was just breaking as the sun began its descent. After loading his bags into the trunk of the taxi that would shuttle him off to the airport, my brother hugged my sister and my mother with all the enthusiasm that accompanies the typical funeral.

When he approached me, he clasped my hand in the Rocky Balboa–Apollo Creed grip that has been the favorite of black men since civil rights days and brought me in close. Then, in the grasp of his hug, he whispered in my ear the last words he'd ever say to me as his brother.

"Take care. Good-bye," he said, with a weight that I would later come to interpret within the long history of blackness in America: if we were niggers, then we couldn't be brothers. Brother is a relationship between humans, and human is something we never were and could never be. Not again. Not anymore.

His good-bye was more prescient than I ever could have imagined. A few years later, he would leave California and return to the East Coast to live with my dad. I never lived with my brother again. And while we remained in touch over the phone and saw each other at significant life events, we never really got to know one another. We never talked beyond the surface-level distractions of sports and music and video games.

FACET: 5

Age: 11
Location: Uniontown, PA
Status: Dying

"Nigger."

The pain was excruciating—the type of intense pain that super-sedes all physiological responses. The pain stopped all that I was: my breath, my thought, my being. And then it passed. It passed just as quickly as it arrived, passing through my obese body and my young mind like a big game hunter's .50 caliber gunshot through the sun-dried flesh of an elephant and with much the same effect—in, through, and out. I did not experience the pain for more than a moment.

Although the bullet left my body, it did not do so cleanly. The bullet shredded the nonphysical parts of me. In the space between a blink and a tear, I ceased experiencing the pain and instead became the pain. I was no longer in pain. *I was pain.* The violence of her words ricocheted throughout the layers of my psyche, tearing through the rules and bounds of the superego and recomposing my very being around its wake. The bullet ripped through history, creating a wormhole from me to my father to his mother, Elnora Hill, to the plantations of South Carolina to the transatlantic slave ships. To Oroonoko and Othello. To Peter Negro. Time collapsed around the pain that composed us all. And in that black hole, we were all one, joined by a violence that has no limit—forced by a pull stronger than the gravity of a neutron star into a being we cannot resist.

And a feeling washed over me as I fell, collapsed, into time and into myself. And once all that I was finished ricocheting off the cold, hard, concrete of reality, I felt . . . relief. Overwhelming relief. I looked at my mother, and her visage faded into the faux wood grain lining the stairs. What remained was a woman devoid of all meaning and connection. I inhaled, slow, calm, and deep—my first true breath. My first breath of the void. The first breath of my new life.

My first breath of Social Death.

My being, although conferred physically at birth, *was*, for the first time confirmed metaphysically in relation to the world constructed by antiblackness. This shattering was my graduation, from searching for my place to finding it. From wondering and wandering to knowing and *no*-ing—*no* time, *no* place, *no* being. For the first time in my life, although not the last, I knew what I was.

I was an orphan. My mother had, at that moment, knowingly or not, disavowed two of the primary components of what I was. In the first instance, her words positioned my father and me within a history that relished the obliteration of our presence and the denial of our humanity. How could she not recognize that I was made of his material as much as hers? Once the embryo grows, there is no separating the egg from the sperm. Due to my proximity to her, I felt the violence more acutely than he ever could, and I recognized that her actions were a disavowal of our already tenuous filial ties.

In the second instance, she disavowed my flesh—not just the parts derived from my father, but the whole of it, stained in her eyes by the same stain that afflicted Aaron the Moor, Kunta Kinte, Bigger Thomas, and so many others throughout time, space, and imagination. At that moment, I ceased to exist as a physical body. Instead, I existed on level ground with the myths and stories and rumors that preceded my physical presence in any space I entered.

I was an orphan. With one word, she decreed that I was neither family nor flesh, neither kin nor skin. Yet, without my family and without my flesh, what was I?

I was nothing.

Imagine learning as an eleven-year-old that you are nothing. What could possibly cause such total and complete destruction of all that you are?

Whatever led to the uttering of that slur, that most despicable, destructive of phrases, so imbued with a history and a here and now and always of violence and violence and violence, it must always have been there. Through the fights in the basement and the separation, through the reconciliation and the relocation. Through the Christmases and birthdays and Easters. Through the school concerts and T-ball games and parent-teacher conferences, it was always there. Always there, just below the surface, infusing each and every moment with the potential for earthshaking destruction.

My brother's scream echoed.

It echoed through the space of our small foyer and the seconds between utterance and comprehension.

It echoed through time immemorial.

It caught the pitch of Aunt Esther. Of Emmett Till. Of J. B. Stradford. Of Malcolm X and MLK. Of Trayvon Martin and Rodney King. Of Askia Ishaq II being conquered by Ahmad al-Mansur. Of Sengbe Pieh leading a revolt on *La Amistad*. His scream matched their pitch, and together they ventured off into the timeless ether of black death.

His scream was their scream.

And as this scream reverberated through all of time and space, it also reverberated through me. Through skin and flesh and bone and marrow. Through mind and thought and heart and soul. I felt it all crack, splinter, shatter, and clatter into a pile of what used to be myself. And in the void that remained, the echoing stopped.

And at that moment, I was born again. My mother was no longer my mother. She could not be, nor could she ever be, nor was she ever. No one who can harbor that much hate for blackness, despite the conditions of birth, could ever indeed be my blood. I was born again for the first time, no longer a child of a mother—no longer flesh of her flesh and blood of her blood.

I was her bloodstain.

FRAGMENT 2

FACET: 1

Age: 9
Location: Benjamin Franklin Middle School
Status: Why Can't We Be Friends?

Growing up in West Virginia and Pennsylvania, I was constantly the target of children's honesty and cruelty. In a child's eye, I was the motherlode of exclusionary criteria. I was always a heavy kid—one hundred eighty pounds in the third grade, and by the time I was a teenager, I was six feet tall and over three hundred pounds. I was poor. Not wholly impoverished, but we couldn't afford name-brand clothing and would shop at second-rate clothing stores such as Value City, Gabriel Brothers, and Burlington Coat Factory.

Also, I was not white.

Any child who decided to bully me could find a reason. There were Glenn and Carl, two athletic black students in my fourth grade class, who mocked me for my weight. Josh Hodges, a boy four years my senior who beat me up because he tried to steal my brother's jacket and I foolishly tried to stop him. There were Terrence and Terence, who mocked me for not being black enough, and there were Suzanne and Anne, who mocked me for being too black.

But of all the bullies, the one I remember most is Steven Knight.

SHARD: 1

Status: Framework

I've had a lot of bullies in my life.

People say children can be cruel. I am not so sure. Children are not cruel, not in the basest sense of the term. Sure, some children suffer from one of a dozen divergent psychologies that can affect their capacity for empathy or lead them into cruel acts as a manner of seeking attention. Still, for the most part, I believe that your average child's actions lack the intention of damage and pain that we associate with cruelty.

From where, then, does a child's cruelty derive? It derives primarily from their lack of complete indoctrination into the manners and expectations of "polite" society. Children aren't necessarily cruel, but honest. Children speak the truth without a verbal filter and with a poor understanding of empathy. They often respond to stimuli with pure emotion and raw thought unobstructed by the threat of consequences, immediately remarking upon and structuring their communities through the same physical and economic differences as adults. Yet, adults hide their cruelty behind economic policy, politics, and exclusion while children openly declare the characteristics of others that cause their separation and exile.

According to the National Center for Education Statistics and Bureau of Justice, 19 percent of children ages nine to twelve and 20 percent of children ages twelve to eighteen experience bullying.[1] Based on my own experiences as a child, who witnessed nearly all of my peers experience some form of bullying, that number seems preposterously low. I can't think of a single child in my elementary school who wasn't subject to some form of bullying, either from fellow students, a teacher, or a parent. Some students experienced physical bullying—being jacked up against a wall between classes or shoved into a locker. Some were subject to verbal bullying—vicious taunts and jagged insults that hurt worse than sticks and stones. Others were victims of psychological bullying—points and snickers from more popular students or out-of-line comments from teachers on assignments.

My brother was bullied, but not at school. He wasn't fat; he wasn't short; he wasn't a nerd—the most noticeable differences on which grade school bullies focus their attention. Yes, he was black, a common target of bullies in West Virginia, but not as black as the black kids. My brother and I both have the brown skin and curly hair that are the signature marks of miscegenation. Our mix of black and white left children on both sides of the color line wondering on which side we stood. Sometimes, both sides included us—we were black enough to hang out with the black kids and white enough to hang out with the white kids. Other times, both exiled us—too black for the white kids and too white for the black kids.

Adults were more likely to bully my brother. My brother was, if I'm being polite, strong-headed and rebellious. If I'm being less kind, he was a bad kid. My brother often tested the limits of adult authority. He talked back to teachers and got into fights, which often resulted in detention. He also talked back to my dad, often resulting in the belt. While corporal punishment was a sign of the times and culture—everyone in my family believed in spanking—sometimes the punishment overshot the crime. Looking back on these spankings with twenty plus years of hindsight, I don't remember any of my brother's outbursts or misdeeds, but I do remember the crack of the belt and the wailing from his lungs.

My sister didn't face the same bullying at home. She was the favorite. Among the three of us, she is the most unique. First off, she is the only girl—always daddy's little girl. My father never spoke this sentiment, but I felt it in my father's tendency to give my sister her way in the insubstantial choices of our lives—should we buy cookies and cream or mint chocolate chip ice cream? While these choices were without dire consequence, the pattern where her side was left happier than mine affected me.

Second, my sister doesn't look much like my brother and me. While my brother and I have dense, tight curls that grow into an afro and brown skin, my sister's hair falls in long, dark waves that frame her pure white skin. She certainly got a more significant proportion of my mother's genes than my brother and I. Both of us also have our father's eyes. Sometimes I wonder if these seemingly insignificant physical differences governed more of our lives than my adolescent mind could decipher. Is this why she had more birthday parties growing up? Could this be why my mother allowed her friends to sleep over more often?

While my sister could easily pass as white in school, she has always been overweight, and fatness is one of the favorite targets of bullies. I couldn't have been more than six years old when I first became aware of her being bullied. We were still at Ford Elementary in Dunbar, West Virginia. One day, the principal, Mrs. Sanders, came and got me out of class. I had no idea why she was calling me into the principal's office. I was a good kid, mostly—I got good grades, and, aside from the occasional outburst, I stayed out of trouble. However, Mrs. Sanders's unexpected summoning left me confused and scared. I dragged myself from my desk and into the hallway for my slow, tentative perp walk to her office, terrified of what awaited me.

When we arrived, I found my mother sitting in a chair across from Mrs. Sanders's desk. My sister was in another, crying. My mother was irate. She held in her hand a small piece of folded cardboard, which she shook violently as she began berating Mrs. Sanders.

"How could you let them get away with this?" my mother demanded.

"Now I know that this is insulting," said Mrs. Sanders, "but please calm down. I will take care of this."

"I want those boys kicked out of school," my mother said.

"Now, I can't do that," said Mrs. Sanders. "This doesn't rise to that level."

"Then I'm taking my kids out of this school," my mother threatened.

They went back and forth for a bit, so intensely that I joined my sister in tears. Finally my mother grabbed my hand and marched my sister and me from the office. I still had no idea what had happened, but I knew it had to do with that small, folded piece of cardboard.

When we got home, my mother went straight to the phone, and my sister went straight to her room. I followed my sister and hesitantly knocked on the door.

"What?" my sister shouted.

I took that as permission to enter. I slowly opened the door and popped my head in. "Are you okay?"

"No," she said through her tears.

"What happened?" I asked.

I looked at my sister, and around her were dozens of tiny shreds of cardboard. One had a bit of black skin; another, a red heart. Another contained the unmistakable bald head of Michael Jordan.

"What happened?" I repeated.

"Get out," she yelled.

I quickly turned and left the room.

I learned later that one of the students in her class, a boy named Brandon—who happened to be black—had decided to use the

Valentine's Day card exchange as an opportunity to insult my sister. She received the card from Brandon, sealed in a small, red envelope, and opened it immediately. Inside, was a Michael Jordan valentine, one of the cheap pieces of printed cardstock that come in packs of thirty for a couple bucks and are available at every grocery store and pharmacy for the months of January and February. This particular card had Jordan bent at the waist, hands on his knees, taking a rest in front of a red and white background of hearts. Appearing in a speech bubble of small printed text was "Time out for friends and fun!"

Brandon had taken the time to add to the speech bubble in red pen two simple words that crushed my sister and brought her to tears: "And food."

SLIVER

The Mason-Dixon Line

West Virginia has a fascinating history.

Once part of Virginia, the Virginia Succession Convention of 1861 revealed a deep split in the population between supporters of the Union and the Confederacy. Instead of engaging in a protracted legal battle over the fate of the entire state, delegates from the northwestern part of the state decided to hold a convention to discuss options for remaining in the Union. Almost as soon as Virginia declared it had seceded from the United States, the northwestern counties announced in a 96 percent landslide vote to secede from Virginia. Lincoln would admit this new state, West Virginia, into the Union on June 20, 1863.

The complete one-eighty in West Virginia's reputation from

that progressive vote in 1861 to today is astounding if you believe the whitewashed history surrounding this vote. Although purportedly founded on fighting against slavery and the Confederacy, the state, as all of America, has a more nuanced history than grade school textbooks include. Many of the delegation who voted on secession actually did so in hopes that the federal government would allow them to become a state without an emancipation clause—they wanted to remain in the Union while keeping their slaves. Becoming a state with the hopes of having their cake (being part of the Union) and eating it too (keeping their slaves) aligns strongly with the state's current status as a national symbol for regressive politics. With its shuttered coal mines, poor health care, and opioid crisis, the state exists in most Americans' minds either as a cautionary tale of failing to progress with the times or as a rallying cry for the plight of white America.

Pennsylvania has quite the opposite reputation.

Pennsylvania is a swing state known for its blue-collar history of steel, mining, and railroads. But unlike West Virginia, Pennsylvania evolved into white-collar industries of health care, finance, and publishing. William Penn, a man whose Quaker religion serves as a coat of pure-white lime concealing the state's slave-owning history, "founded" the state in 1787. Like every colony in America, Pennsylvania allowed slavery at its conception. The earliest documented slaves in Pennsylvania arrived in 1639. Their legislation on abolition served as a historical foreshadow of their present swing status; Pennsylvania was at the forefront of statewide abolitionist movements, outlawing slavery in 1780. But this legislation had a funky interpretation of abolition: it did not free existing slaves. Instead, the children of current slaves would be born "free," although how free can a child be when their parents are in bondage?

Moreover, the state placed conditions on the "freedom" of slave-born children. Slaveowners had to

register these births with the state,
and the children would have to
serve a twenty-eight-year inden-
ture to buy their freedom from the
master. That's right; these "free"
children were born indebted to the
people who enslaved them—the
loss of the slave commodity was
valued higher than the gain of
free black lives. This policy meant
the state was not documented as
slave-free until 1847, although
these records do not account for
any unregistered slave children.
And this was in Pennsylvania, a
state whose southern border is the
Mason-Dixon Line, the symbolic
divide between North and South,
nonracist and racist, free and slave.

FACET: 2

Age: 9
Location: Benjamin Franklin Middle School
Status: Why Can't We Be Friends?

I experienced far more racism in Pennsylvania than I did in West Virginia.

I am sure I experienced racism in West Virginia, but not overtly. Instead, I experienced the implicit meta racism that informs all of our experiences, regardless of our race. Although no one ever spat on me or called me the worst racial epithets, racism surrounded me like a fish immersed in water: all-consuming and inseparable from my very existence.

It was the implicit racism of all the Orchard Manner housing project residents where—being black—much of my father's family lived. Of the playground equipment there being a little less clean and a lot more worn out than the playground in my predominantly white neighborhood of Dunbar. But as a child, I never linked the black dirt embedded in the injection-molded plastic slide in Orchard Manor to the black melanin that imbued the residents' skin. Regardless, I was never the target of explicit racism in West Virginia, but this could be because I was young and didn't recognize it for what it was. Or maybe my parents were still able to shield me from it.

Within a week of starting school in Pennsylvania, a bully confronted me with my blackness. Steven Knight. I changed his name to protect the guilty, but his real name rings in my mind on occasion.

He was a short white boy with blond hair meticulously landscaped with military precision into a classic high, tight cut. He had piercing green eyes that glimmered with malicious intent that adults excused as mischievousness. On his cheek was a scar about one inch long just below his left eye. I never bothered to ask how he got it; I always just assumed that it was a well-earned reward for his behavior. He was loud and cocky and aggressive—he behaved with overbearing masculinity to conceal his insecurity. He also had a twin brother, Scott, who, although visibly indistinguishable from Steven, had his exact opposite personality: polite, quiet, and unassuming. I often wondered how two fetuses who shared a womb could grow into two such different children.

Steven was my bully. Or at least he tried to be. He was always aggressive and challenging toward me, often commenting on my weight or clothes to goad me into a physical confrontation. But his combination of minute stature and grandstanding posture led me to pity him more than fear him. Occasionally he would get me riled up. But like most bullies, he always had a friend ready to "hold him back" from any physical encounters.

Had it not been for my mother, Steven's attempts at bullying would have been wholly unremarkable. I would have written off his taunts as I had those of so many others: children are assholes and idiots. But, instead, one day, my mother met me at the edge of the schoolyard to walk me home, and our conversation deviated from the standard one-word answers I would volley back to her questions.

"How was school?" she asked.

"Steven called me fat," I said.

"Oh, honey. You're not fat," she lied, "just growing. You'll grow out of that baby fat."

"But today, he did it in front of everybody," I said. "They all laughed."

My mother then offered advice that was far too saccharin for the real world but was rather the stuff of Disney Channel movies and teen church pastor propaganda. "He just wants to be your friend and doesn't know how," she responded. "Why don't you break the ice and try to be his friend? I'll tell you what—let's invite him to a sleepover."

"Are you sure?" I asked. At the age of nine, I already recognized that her conclusions regarding Steven were unlikely.

"Positive."

Although initially reluctant, her advice progressed into a plan: I would invite him for a sleepover and show him that I was just a normal kid from a normal family. We'd eat the same foods and play the same video games with which he was familiar from his own home, and through these commonalities, we would forge a friendship. I was skeptical of the plan but decided that the worst-case scenario was he'd say no to the invitation.

Much to my surprise, he agreed to the sleepover. So, one Saturday night, his parents dropped him off at our house. My mother had cleaned and cooked to prepare for his arrival: we had fried chicken and mashed potatoes. Not knowing his preferences, we purchased close to a dozen bottles of various sodas and a half-dozen different chips and cookies for late-night snacks. We rented video games for our Sega Genesis and prepared my brother's bed in our shared room while my brother relocated to a makeshift bed in my mother's room.

Much to my surprise, the sleepover went off without a hitch. Steven was polite the entire night. He complimented my mother's cooking, and we played video games and traded basketball cards until well past my usual bedtime. I turned out the lights as the clock approached midnight, thinking that my mother was perhaps wiser than she often acted and that her plan, against all likelihood, had worked. In one night, I turned my bully into my friend.

"I'll see you at school tomorrow," Steven shouted the following day as he jogged to his parents' waiting car with a smile on his face.

"Bye," I shouted after him, smiling as well.

"That seemed to go well," my mother said as I returned to the small foyer inside our front door.

"Yeah. He's actually pretty cool," I responded.

"He just had to get to know you." She gave a gentle smile and bent down to kiss me on the forehead.

Monday morning at school revealed how wrong I was.

I arrived to find Steven holding court among a group of other white students: Richard, Cory, David, and a couple of others with whom I was at least familiar but not friends. Upon my entrance, their conversation turned to stifled laughter pointed in my direction. I paused in confusion—what was going on? Before I could figure it out on my own, Steven told me and everyone else.

"There's the half-breed!"

Half-breed. A term that I had never heard but whose meaning I automatically understood. Half-breed—a slur meaning mixed-race that compared not only me but also my entire family to animals. Half-breed—his pronouncement to the world that I was the product of two different species whose miscegenation was a crime.

Steven had duped us. Steven never intended to be my friend. Steven was smart in the way that makes one wish his powers could be used for good. Our sleepover was pleasant, even fun. But none of that mattered. Now, Steven regaled our white classmates with stories to strengthen his position within their community. He told them that he spit out my mother's food on the floor. He made up lies of a dilap-idated house with carpets stained by animal feces. They laughed at his story of jumping up and down on the bed and calling me a half-breed as I cried in the corner.

None of the children cared to question the probability of any of these statements. They didn't need to. Steven had infiltrated my home. He had infiltrated my life and used his exploratory journey to concoct fairy tales of his strange adventures and stranger encounters with the strangest people to take back with him to his homeland. And in Steven's stories, the class got what they needed: community. Steven's evidence confirmed their worst assumptions of me, of black people. Steven had reenacted centuries of colonization on my life and my being, and he used my race to play on his colleagues' worst fears and exile me from their community.

I was stunned. My brain shorted, unable to process this destruction. I knew it was wrong; I knew it was violent, but my nine-year-old self didn't understand all of the ways it was. But Steven's mocking was not the most painful part. The worst violence was how quickly the others—Richard, Cory, David—discarded every interaction we had in favor of Steven's racist mocking. Steven's lies hurt, but he was nobody, a bully who had no intention of ever being my friend. But the others, I thought they were my friends. And I discovered that the only thing keeping them from hating my blackness was that no one else told them it was okay to hate me for it. That was devastating. It left me wondering what I was in this world, and it made damn clear what I wasn't.

"Resistance—the refusal to accept or comply with something;
the attempt to prevent something by action or argument."
I am tired of stories of black resistance.
Refusal to accept. Refusal to comply.
In most cases, black resistance refuses white supremacy.
Tucked deep inside the narratives of resistance is
a capitulation that the world is
and must be
white supremacist.
And as blacks, we must resist.
We must refuse to comply.
We must refuse to accept our position
within the world.
What has resistance gotten us?
According to a 2020 study from Auburn University,
the stress of living within systemic racism rapidly ages the cells of
black bodies,
resulting in shortened life-spans.
Racism causes blacks to experience time differently—it pushes our
lives past us.
Our time is shorter than that of others

because we expend so much energy resisting.

How do we resist time?

How do we resist a death that speeds toward us

like an asteroid to the dinosaurs?

Resistance has yet to offer redress.

It's time to retire resistance.

Re-brand.

Re-focus.

Re-start.

And seek redress through a new re-:

Re-bellion?

Re-volution?

Re-structure?

Let's retire resistance.

Let's move past reform. Let's re-form.

Re-kindle.

Re-ignite.

Re-duce the world to ashes.

Let the world be re-born.

Let's re-create the world from scratch.

SLIVER
Reflection

While the event shattered my nine-year-old psyche, my thirty-five-year-old self sees this moment for what it was: a microcosm of the long continuum of antiblack violence creating and affirming white communities. The deployment of black violence to secure communities is not new. In the pre-bellum South, white folks made the physical pain of the whip and the psychological pain of the cakewalk community spectacles. They would drag black bodies into high-class parties and force them to perform for the landowners and debutantes, who then grew closer together over their mutual distaste for and denigration of blackness. Violence was their entertainment.

After the war, whites took antiblack violence as entertainment off the plantations and into the cities. Picture a lynching. What comes to

mind? A few rogue operatives—
the real racists, with hoods over
their heads, grabbing some poor
black soul under cover of darkness,
the whole town awakening to
the terrible sight of a black man
hanging from a tree. That is what
I was taught. But lynchings were
not always random acts of violence
perpetrated by a few hate-filled
outcasts. Often, lynchings were
well-attended community events.
Spectators took souvenirs to brag
to their friends—sometimes, a
photograph; other times, a piece of
Negro genitalia.

The spectacle of black violence
to confirm white life continues
today—why else do you think the
murder of black bodies by police
is national news while the death of
white bodies by police goes unre-
ported? Every time the police kill
a black person, the media blasts far
and wide the message that white
people are safe and protected from
blackness.

This is what Steven did to me.
He made me part of a continuum
with the whip, the noose, and the
bullet—he used violence against

my blackness to confirm his
community. Although he left my
body intact, he shattered my being.
He solidified his community on a
foundation built of my flesh.

FACET: 3

Age: 9
Location: Benjamin Franklin Middle School
Status: Why Can't We Be Friends?

While many students bullied me for various elements of my life and appearance, this was different. Steven saw that his words and actions as an individual had little effect on me, so he mobilized the whole class against me. Steven's bullying was the earliest encounter I had with white supremacy. He was the first person to make me understand that the world is built on black exile—that the world needs blackness to set the boundaries of human communities. He was the first person to subject me to the gratuitous violence that structures black life—the violence of exclusion that turns even innocent childhood interactions into potential devastation. How young is too young to teach children about race? Steven taught me at nine years old. He had been taught even earlier. Did someone sit him down and teach him that he could weaponize his whiteness to violently assault my blackness? Possibly. But more likely, no one ever taught him anything about race, leaving him to form his own conclusions based on who he was exposed to in life and through media—everything from the movie stars he saw on the big screen to the newscasters bringing him information about the world to the politicians who decided how that world was run reinforced that whiteness was important. Whiteness mattered. Whiteness was superior. And by not sitting him down and teaching him about race, the world taught him to be racist. So much so that at nine years old, Steven was able to deploy that racist violence against my blackness. While I was not physically injured, my suffering became the basis for his community, and those around him were eager to join.

I don't know if I should curse Steven or thank him.

FRAGMENT 3

FACET: 1

Age: 14
Location: Uniontown, PA
Status: Madness

My relationship with my mother continued to deteriorate after my brother left the house. She went back to work a few miles from home as a night manager at McDonald's. Although she had only a tenth-grade education, she always made the most of it. She was quite good at what she did, as far I could tell. She managed the restaurant's books, handled their scheduling, and made the orders every week. Most of the time, she was good with people, although she would occasionally have an episode with an employee or a customer that put her job in a precarious position.

She would come home from work and tell us about these incidents. "The owner passed me over for regional manager because I'm a woman, and they said they'd fire me if I sued," or "A customer was livid that we got his order wrong, and when I stood up for the staff, he called the owner trying to get me fired." She was always the victim or the martyr—things happened to her; she was never an agent in them. Her actions never played a role. When something went wrong, it was never her mistake, and it was never her fault. It was always an intentional attack with someone out to destroy her.

As a child, I wasn't able to put the pieces together. Still, the paranoia, the blaming others, the way she'd seem to turn on a moment-to-moment basis from a laughing, loving woman to a shrieking, crying demon should have been more troubling. While I found myself crying or hiding from her quite often, I assumed she was just like all of my other friends' mothers. I had no idea that being woken up in the dead of night and marched to the kitchen in my pajamas and berated for some minor infraction—perhaps not sweeping behind the stove or forgetting to feed the cat—was, at best, an odd occurrence. At worst, it was abusive. But when we faced actual spankings, losing a couple hours of sleep and being yelled at was the preferable alternative. Now, as an adult diagnosed with ADHD and depression, I recognize these behaviors for what they were—symptoms of mental illness.

She was aware of it, too. After she separated from my father, she began to see a professional. Every few weeks, she'd go out and return home with a few small, round, orange prescription bottles filled with multifarious drugs whose names I couldn't read then and don't remember now. But I felt their effects—she was more stable, which I measured by how often I got a full night's sleep. Sadly, despite the positive effects these visits had on her, they didn't last. One day, she left for her appointment and returned home empty-handed and angry. I had no idea why, and she tried her best to hide it, but I learned the truth later that evening.

While my mother was aware that my weight was a problem, she didn't do much to repair my health. Once our household became single-parent, home-cooked meals became scarcer and scarcer, and my siblings and I were often left to fend for ourselves. As such, our house was always well-stocked with junk food. With my mother working, we needed things that children could prepare on their own while their parents worked: frozen pizzas, fish sticks, cookies, chips— things that no one should eat but far too many of us do.

Being aware of the caloric treasures awaiting in our cupboards, I would sneak into the kitchen long after my bedtime to steal a snack.

As I slowly crept down the back stairs from the "servant's quarters" of the house on Lawn Avenue to its kitchen, I heard my mother's voice.

"He's trying to give me brain cancer," she said, matter-of-factly.

I have no idea to whom she was talking, but as I listened to her half of the conversation, the events that led her to return to the house so angry earlier that afternoon unfolded. Instead of asking the doctor for help, she had told him off, accusing him of malpractice. It was impossible to process this insanity: I furrowed my brows, narrowed my eyes—the left one slightly more than the right—and slowly parted my lips to shape my mouth into a confused 'what?' I couldn't believe what I was hearing. My mother claimed that the doctor had conspired with her sister, and they formulated the pills to give my mother brain cancer.

As I sat on the narrow back steps, I lost my grip on reality. Was what I heard real? It can't be real, my preteen brain thought, but why would she lie about that? I began chipping away at the brown paint that covered the wood stairs as the debate continued in my mind. It went on so long that by the time I snapped out of it, my mother had gone to bed, never seeing me eavesdropping at the base of the steps.

Her temperament made her nightly absences from my life a blessing. Her standard work shift was 4:00 p.m. to 1:00 a.m.—the closing shift—which left my sister and me largely unattended in my late adolescence. During this time, I learned how to run a household. Because my mother was quite impulsive with her finances, it fell on me at the age of twelve to balance her checkbook and make sure all of our bills were paid. Our relationship was now purely symbiotic—she provided the funds, and I provided the wherewithal to make sure we spent them appropriately. It was a functional, if not loving, relationship.

Although her physical presence had largely ceased to be a determining factor in my actions, her psychological issues continued to govern the direction of life. I could manage her day-to-day mood swings and unpredictability. For instance, when she'd spend our carefully budgeted money unexpectedly on frivolous things, I would always be able to find room in our budget to make up for it. I would either alter our food budget or delay a utility bill to a month with three paychecks. These things I could manage. But I was still a child, and sometimes her impulsiveness altered the course of our lives.

Like when she decided on relocating us to San Diego.

Which slights had occurred and which she concocted in her diseased mind, I'll never know. Still, she had let the thoughts and memories of what she interpreted as a coordinated conspiracy against her success and well-being fester and engorge themselves until they began to poison every environment in which she would interact. She had to escape. She had to flee the corporate office who passed her over for a promotion to regional manager because she wouldn't sleep with her boss. She had to escape my father, who, although he lived two hours away, was not far enough for his agents to interfere in her life. She had to escape our landlord, who would raise our rent unless she slept with him. In her mind, everyone was working against her, demanding her body and her dignity if she wanted to get ahead. At least some of these claims were not true. But she either couldn't see or refused to see that she was culpable in creating her damaged world. Rather than seek help, she sought to escape. She sought to find a place where she could move and no one would know who she was or from where she came. She needed a place where my father couldn't find her and where the sleazy men who tried to destroy her—her boss, her doctor, her landlord—wouldn't be able to pressure her into surrendering herself.

Of course, that place did not exist. So, my mother chose San Diego.

She framed her decision as though it was a decision made by all of us. But it wasn't. She tricked me into conceding to her desire out of guilt, coercion, and fear. When she first said we would be moving three thousand miles away—away from my school, away from my friends, away from my father—I couldn't comprehend her reasoning for such distance, so I did the only thing I could bear.

I cried.

I don't know if it was a product of her illness, her education, or her experience, but my mother was a master manipulator. To stop my tears, she moved into rationalization phase one: guilt.

"Don't you want what's best for us? Don't you want your mother to be happy?" she asked.

Despite her lack of education, she deployed the Socratic method with the deftness of a seasoned defense attorney. She phrased her questions to displace the moral and ethical burdens of the decision onto her youngest child, a fourteen-year-old who had no idea what was happening. I had no choice. My answer: "Yes."

Of course, I wanted what was best for us. Of course, I wanted her to be happy. But, at the moment, I was so overcome with emotion that I never even considered my own happiness.

"But I don't want to move," I said.

Once my emotions calmed and I verbalized resistance, my mother progressed to phase two: coercion.

"I have to do this, and I can't do this alone. I need you. I couldn't live without my children," she said. The words hit me so hard that I forgot our history. She did love me. She did. The stain of past trauma began to fade away, the emotion of the present bleaching away the incompatibility between our blood and our races.

She used her love, or at least her false performance of love, to coerce me into answers that served her purpose. At the time, I knew that I was always just one bad moment away from the same destruction she unleashed on my father. I knew that at any given moment, she could again shatter me to pieces. At the time, however, I had yet to learn how deeply her disdain for me dwelled. My still-developing brain rationalized away the trauma: my mother wasn't bad; she was just in pain. She didn't hate me; she just didn't know how to love me. She isn't a person who needs excommunication; she needs love. I fell for her words, and I felt her words, and, in the end, I succumbed to her coercion.

"But what about school? What about my friends?" I asked.

And this is where phase three began: fear. Her framing of a family decision turned to an ultimatum as quickly as her moods often did.

"I'm going, and if you don't want to go, you can move in with your dad," she said. Her threat penetrated the air like a dagger, piercing my heart and making me wince with an inhale as sharp as her tone.

I didn't know my father. My mother had made sure of that. He wasn't absent, but he was part-time. For most of my life, my father had been nothing more than every other weekend and two weeks during the summer. So, I had no idea what would transpire should I choose to live with my father. While my mother was less a parent than a joint tenant, at least I knew how to navigate those waters. But life with my father was a great unknown. She left me with two options: move three thousand miles west and continue the pseudo-business partnership I'd entered into with my mother, or venture two hundred miles east into the unknown that was living with my father. Both choices would place me in an unfamiliar location, but the latter would also put me in unfamiliar surroundings with unfamiliar people. Moving in with my father would be jumping into a sea, one polluted with years of my mother's toxic verbal refuse, with no life vest and no method of navigation.

I had no response. I was defeated. I had lost.

Within three months of this encounter, my mother, sister, and I were on an Amtrak train from Pittsburgh to San Diego.

SPLINTER
"Father"

He's always much older than I remember.
His lines a little deeper. His hair a little grayer.
His eyes a little dimmer.
Still he bears the marks of a life of labor.
Hard hands and strong back framed by shoulders once strong and
    high
but with time have eroded.
He bears the image of a once proud mountain
worn, carved, and caved into a man.
He still bears the marks of a life of hatred.
Hard soul and strong heart framed by resolve once impenetrable and
    untiring
but with pain has eroded.
He bears the image of a still proud man
worn, carved, caved from resisting.
He is at once stone and flesh.
Heart and ash,
fire and life.
He is kindling and kindles. The spark is not
gone, but it flickers with fatigue
and aches with age.
I know, like the pit that exists when the impossible becomes reality,
in the split second between hope and despair,

more of a feeling than a fact, I know
that he will be gone soon.
And I will miss him when he's gone.

FACET: 2

Age: 17
Location: San Diego, CA
Status: The Dangers of the Internet

My parents finalized their divorce in September of 2000.

Their marriage had hit the twenty-year milestone before it was legally ended. When the ink dried on the last of the papers, my mother got half of my father's assets, which didn't amount to much. They never owned property, and his savings were as liquid as coal. His only significant asset was a retirement plan through his job that approached six figures. Although he had been working for the same company for over twenty years, the constant withdraws and loans against the account left it far smaller than it could have been.

Nevertheless, my mother received just over $50,000, and she pledged to be responsible with the money. She even went so far as to hire a financial advisor. She planned to take the money and place it in mutual funds to begin saving for her retirement, minus what she needed to pay the credit cards and bills that had been piling up since the move. She also allowed us one luxury: we bought a home computer.

The stated purposes for purchasing the computer aligned with the generic, company-approved sales pitch given to us at Best Buy: homework, email, job searches, etc. But my inexperience with the emerging World Wide Web left me completely unaware of the potential dangers made possible by that box: the capacity to connect to others across distance and without accountability. The chatrooms of the early twenty-first century allowed for strangers to connect freely and openly through a stated shared interest; there were chatrooms based on hobbies, musical interests, and even location. In this computer-mediated reality, everyone in these chat rooms was free to be whoever they wanted. While the internet today is just as full of catfish and bots as ever, modern social networks allow users to choose with whom they want to connect, quickly limiting their online friends to however many degrees of separation they decide. Early chatrooms, however, were the Wild West. Anyone, anywhere, could pop up on your screen and indulge in whatever fantasy they chose.

The internet was the topic of frequent public service announcements in the early years of the twenty-first century aimed at parents to protect their kids from cyber threats. Most of these public service announcements piggybacked off the same dangers to our youth in the twentieth century, only rewritten to position the threat as existing in the electronic ether: don't talk to strangers, say no to drugs, and other issues the average eight-year-old was bludgeoned into believing they would encounter every day. So often in those days, the news had stories about older men who would use the anonymity of the internet and cheap, manipulative psychological tricks to prey on innocent children. In 2006, the *New York Times* published a warning to that effect titled "*On the Web, Pedophiles Extend Their Reach.*" The article details how pedophiles use the internet to share schemes for exploiting the daycare and foster systems, camps, and other events to groom and abduct victims. Meanwhile, a reality TV show based on that premise aired from 2004 to 2007—but when the pedophile would arrive for his rendezvous with a prepubescent girl, he would instead be met by Chris Hansen, the host, who would begin to interview the perp. The children that the pedophiles had chatted with were actually police officers; the pedophiles were more legally referred to as potential child abusers.

The announcements aimed to alert parents on ways to protect their children. The time and money that went into them, however, would probably have been better spent had they been directed toward advising kids how to protect their parents. My mother frequented chat rooms with the intention of reconnecting with a world she had recently claimed to be fleeing. She would spend all of her days off in front of the computer, typing feverishly in multiple windows. I can't say for sure she was only chatting with men, but based on the visitors I caught leaving our apartment as I returned home from school, my mother primarily used the computer as a means to fulfill her sexual urges.

My experience with internet hookups via my mother removed any lingering doubts about my relationship with her. One day in March of my senior year, I came home to find my mother sitting on the single half-step outside of our apartment door that served as a sad reminder that we had no porch. Something about her—perhaps her face or her posture—triggered an overwhelming sense of déjà vu. Ghostly images of the day she called my father *nigger* and the day she ripped us three thousand miles away from him assaulted my mind. The glimpses of the present appearing between these attacking memories told me that my life was about to change. I knew that she was about to drop a bomb. In the back of my head, I began to hear the high-pitched squeal that I had learned from so many Wile E. Coyote cartoons. The wail continued as I opened my mouth, inviting impact.

—*eeeeeeeeeeeeeeeeeeeee*—

"Hi, mom."

—*oooooooo*—

"We're moving to Oregon."

—bomb explodes—

"What?" I couldn't believe it. I was mere months from graduation. Leaving now would mean repeating my senior year.

"We're moving," she repeated, "to Oregon."

"Why?" I asked, but I already knew the reason.

"I've met someone," she said. "His name's Ahmet."

Ahmet Turkmenoglu was a Turkish immigrant who owned a nightclub in Medford, Oregon. He had proposed to my mother on the internet, and she decided to accept his marriage proposal despite never meeting him in person.

I was shaking with rage. How could she do this to me? She already moved me three thousand miles across the country because she hated my father. Now, her "love" for another man threatened to upend my life again. What about her love for me? Wasn't the bond between a mother and her child supposed to be the purest, strongest love imaginable, unbreakable by time or space or action? Shouldn't the psychological transmogrification of my father into a white man by my mother's love made the offspring a being composed just as much of whiteness as blackness?

Unfortunately, that mother-child bond manifests differently across the color line. When the white mother has a black son, the mother/son dynamic collapses under the black/nonblack antagonism. At that moment, perhaps my mother and I had more in common than at any point in our lives—we both longed for human contact and human connection. Our longings, however, derived from very different places: hers came from not being able to connect with her black son, and mine came from not being able to connect with her antiblack world. She could find the answer to her longing in another place with other people. My longing was for a place to simply be. When she called my father "nigger," she destroyed our family. Since that moment, I have longed for a connection to this world—to not just take up space, but to find my place. Not the places that this world prescribes for blacks, but a place of my own choosing with people who understood the struggles of black belonging in this world. But a resolution to that longing for belonging remains beyond possibility.

Even though I understood her longing, I could not understand her cavalier attitude. Not only did she approach the situation with little inhibition and even less foresight, but she was going to drag her son into the impending debacle. I could think of millions of reasons why this was a bad idea: when deciding to travel 1,200 miles to marry someone you've never seen and have no evidence even really exists as described, the potential for poor outcomes far outweighs the good. This particular scenario had a million possible results. Only one was that they would live happily ever after. The other 999,999 were scenarios that eventually led to unmitigated disaster—anything from catfishing to human trafficking. Worse yet, she intended to take her youngest son, the only one of her children who was still speaking with her, along on this quest.

I did what I wish I'd done the last time her impulses had overcome her sensibilities and threatened to displace my life: I refused.

"No," I said. "I'm not going." The anger had reached a point where every muscle in my body had tensed, the words escaping my lips like steam from a boiling kettle.

"Yes, you are," she replied; my agency and my life meant less than nothing to her.

I took a breath, and the slightly moist spring air filled my lungs. Anger, I knew, would get me nowhere. Screaming, I knew, would get me nowhere. Not with her. To her, my feelings were nothing more than a mild inconvenience. No, I couldn't attack her with my hurt. I had to use her hurt. I had to be tactical—what would she care about? Not me. And not being a good mother. Perhaps what she cared about was that others thought she was a good mother. More so than actually being a good mother, I thought, she cared about the shunning and exile from her kind that would come if they thought she was a bad mother. I tried to use this to my advantage. I went after her with the same Socratic deception and emotional manipulation that she had used on me all those years earlier. I played everything perfectly; every last variable accounted for, convinced that victory would be mine. I used her weapons against her—first: guilt.

"Don't you care about my happiness?" I asked.

"What about my happiness?" she responded.

Strike one.

Next up, coercion.

"I'm not going. I'll live on the streets if I have to," I threatened.

"That's your choice," she firmly stated, calling what she assumed was my bluff but was, in fact, a sincere promise.

Strike two.

How could I have miscalculated so poorly? Neither guilt nor coercion had worked. What variable was I forgetting? The one that I should have had more knowledge of than she did. While she cared what others thought, I now realized that she didn't care what others thought about her *as a mother*. At least not in the way we're all taught to believe mothers should care for their children. She cared about the story that she could create around her motherhood, and she cared about the questions she would be asked. As long as I was breathing, she could answer any question about me with "he's in San Diego." But if I died—well, admitting that only opens more questions, which would eventually lead to admitting her culpability in my death.

Final pitch: fear.

"What if I die because of your recklessness?"

This tactic, while not effective enough to dissuade her impulses, was enough to open negotiation. Over the next few weeks, our brief passings between school and work turned into our own mini Camp David. She first offered to wait until immediately after I graduated from high school. I met that with a hard pass, as the fact that I was going to college in San Diego in the fall meant that moving to Oregon and back made no sense. So I countered with staying until I started school; she responded with a red flag that she interpreted as passion—they had to get married this summer. A stranger from another country who had a deadline for marriage? I couldn't help but wonder if this was his way to get a green card.

After a few weeks of negotiation, we settled on a compromise: she would move to Oregon immediately while continuing to pay for our apartment until I finished school in May. After that, I was on my own; either I could move to Oregon and stay with her until classes started, or I could live on the streets for all she cared. So as I began my final semester of high school, I watched my mother pull off in a U-Haul truck loaded with her belongings. All I had left was my bed, my clothes, and my computer.

She took every memento of my childhood with her—every photo album, every report card, every baby book. The green Tyrannosaurus rex that was my favorite childhood stuffed animal. My yearbooks from grade school and middle school with the missives of "See you next fall!" and "Have a great summer!" from all the girls I had crushes on. The certificates confirming my grades had landed me on the principal's list. The letter I earned playing football as a junior. We couldn't afford the $180 for a letterman's jacket, so we had the blue-and-white felt "SD" logo framed. Every tangible remembrance of who I was up to that point was in the back of her rented truck.

I would never see any of those objects again. A stranger purchased them at auction when my mother stopped paying for the storage unit where she kept them. It makes me sick to think that some stranger picked through my childhood like a vulture, keeping any valuable morsels—slim pickings since most of it only had sentimental value—and throwing away the rest.

I believe my mother's side of the compromise was a subtle recognition from her that we had no meaningful filial bond—that our relationship as mother and son was nothing more than shelter and wishful thinking. She no longer had any children. Sure, she had given birth, but the blood that was supposed to connect us had coagulated and spoiled, dried into dust, and scattered into the ether, never to be recomposed. So, she left San Diego, looking to begin a new life with a new last name, unburdened by the stains of her past.

It turns out that my earlier suspicions of a green card were accurate, although unbeknown to my mother. Within a year of her moving to Oregon, she fell out with her husband. Unfortunately for him, their breakup also resulted in his deportation. She liquidated his assets and, as his legal wife, was the beneficiary of the sale of his home, his nightclub, and his vehicle. I have no idea how much she received from these sales, but I know that within a year, all that remained of this part of her life was his last name.

I had already been an orphan, but now I became a lost child. She became a former mother.

SLIVER
Man and Woman

In *Black Skins, White Masks,* Frantz Fanon's seminal 1952 work on the specificities of the black psyche, he discusses the "Man of Color and the White Woman." Fanon argues that the black man's desire for the white woman coexists alongside the black man's desire to be white. "By loving me, she proves to me that I am worthy of white love. I am loved like a white man. I am a white man."[1]

The desire to be white has nothing to do with a transmogrification of flesh and denial of black *being.* Instead, this desire for whiteness is a pathological manifestation of the unfulfillable desire to belong. Fanon recognized that the structural mechanism through which our world gains coherence is the absence of black relationality. To recognize blacks as not only "in" the world but also "of" the world is to unmake the paradigm of antiblackness—an unimaginable fantasy. With reimagining the world an impossibility, the black man imagines his belonging through changing his being and becoming one who can belong.

Fanon's work is on romantic love and desire, but what about when the white woman is the mother, and the black man is her child?

Shard: 1

Status: The Space between a Blink and a Tear

Growing up, I never really got to know my father. My father was present, although my parents' custody agreement would not allow him to be there as much as he and I desired. While our relationship was superficially pleasant, I never dared to dive below the surface for fear of finding anger and resentment lurking beneath. As a child, I could not analyze my parents' relationship. Emotions preempted any attempt; as much as I understood that my father wanted to be with us, I could not fully understand why he couldn't be with us. So I spent my childhood angry and resentful of him.

When I grew older, life gifted me the opportunity to get to know my father more as a man. What I learned was much different from what I felt as a child. I spent my childhood wondering why he wasn't there and how much he loved me. It shocked me to discover that he spent his whole life fighting as hard as possible with no goals in mind except to give his children a better life than he had. He didn't separate from my mother out of ill will; he did it because he thought it was best for us. He didn't uproot us from our home in West Virginia for his own good; he did it because it would allow him to get clean and get us further from the path of life that leads to alcohol, drugs, poverty, and an early grave.

I didn't learn any of this until his mother died. I was in grad school in Virginia. On his return to his home in Stafford, Virginia, from her funeral in Charleston, West Virginia, he stopped by where I was living in Staunton, and he took me out to breakfast. The moment we shared recast our relationship. As we sat in our booth at Shoney's, a chain of restaurants known for their artery-clogging southern cuisine and all-you-can-eat breakfast buffet, he began discussing the strife that had afflicted him and his siblings. I knew that drugs and abuse and jail stints ran rampant through his side of the family, but I was less familiar with the betrayal and lies and backstabbing. He had always kept it from us, again for our own good. But today, the cold, gray fog that often accompanied mornings in the Shenandoah Valley was brought both by the weather and by the death of his mother hanging in the atmosphere.

"All she ever wanted was for us to be a family," he said.

He paused for little more than a blink and exhaled heavily, purging his lungs of hope. "All she wanted was for us to love each other, and we couldn't even do that," he continued. "She had to die for us to be together again."

As he spoke, his voice never cracked, and his cadence never broke, but his eyes began to well. I didn't see him cry when he and my mother would fight. He didn't cry when he broke his finger in a company softball game, sliding headfirst into second base. I saw no tears as he loaded his belongings into the old white Plymouth and drove away from his wife and children. But sitting in a cracked vinyl booth, the eggs and bacon becoming cold and inedible on our plates, he calmly removed his glasses and dabbed at the tears that had slowly begun to flow down his cheeks. Then, after a brief pause, he said, "That's all I want for you guys. For you to love each other."

In the years between when my mother left and when I got to know my father, I had thought of him often. Unfortunately, while growing up, I had never had the courage to ask about his past: his childhood growing up black in West Virginia during the civil rights movement, his drug use, or even past generations of our family. I certainly hadn't dared to ask about his relationship with my mother.

Instead, in these years of my early adulthood, I would often try to articulate my feelings through imagined conversations with my father. I would record these conversations in whatever structure best fit the moment, often reflecting where I was in my life and career. Some came out as dialogues, some as songs, and some as essays. Most of them, however, came out as poems.

FACET: 3

Age: 26
Location: San Diego, CA
Status: Motherly Love

In the intervening years between abandoning me for her Oregonian soulmate and my graduate pursuits, my mother and I would speak semi-regularly. Although "speak" may be a word too strong for the half-sigh, half-grunts of vague confirmation that I elicited throughout our near-monthly conversations. More often than not, she'd call and ask how I was. Before I could even conclude my typical monosyllabic response, she'd launch into some long-winded, off-kilter diatribe about her most recent conflict. These conflicts were always meaningless and easily solvable if she would take half a second to admit that she, too, was culpable in their escalation. Unfortunately, her focus was not on resolution. It was on victory. In her mind, she was always in the right, and others were just too blind to see.

I had no idea why she continued to tell me these things, but I know why I kept listening. In my mind, I was still hoping for a redemption narrative. I was hoping for happily ever after. I was hoping for my mother to find herself so I, in turn, could find my mother. In the tradition of *Driving Miss Daisy* and *Crash*, I was hoping that our story had hit its obstacle and would come out the other side—that she would come to recognize the errors of her ways and love me as a son. I kept hoping that one day she would begin seeing a therapist and address her issues both with mental illness and with blackness so that we could have a future as a family. I kept praying for a day when she would meet my future wife and hold her future grandchild. Every syllable of our conversations carried on dreams of Thanksgiving meals and Christmas presents and laughter and love.

But with every conversation, those dreams moved closer and closer to nightmares. The few times I tried to guide her closer to accepting responsibility, closer to loving me, she only ripped our severed filial bonds further apart. She met every challenge to her viewpoint, every question of her actions, with the same phrase: "no son of mine would ever . . ."

No son of hers would ever, and I did. Was she trying to change my behavior or remind me of what I could never be? Soon, I stopped listening with any intent. My end of the conversation was nothing more than a noncommittal, subverbal "mm-hmm" that punctuated the pauses in her speech so vaguely that she was free to interpret them as she chose.

But I continued to hope, and in doing so, continued whoring myself out to my own mother. By the time I graduated from SDSU, my brother and sister had cut my mother out of their lives. I don't know the full details of the final straw for either's decision, but based on my own experiences with her, they have my support. With my brother and sister both having ceased communication with our mother, I exploited her lack of confidants for personal gain. Nothing substantial, but I was a broke college student, and the small pittance of twenty or fifty dollars she could muster every month or so offered considerable aid. Our conversations would allow her to feel like a mother. And in return, she'd send me a small check. If you strip away the sentimental bonds and semantics of holiness that society imposes on mother-child relationships, our interactions were no different from those of a businessman who hires a prostitute with no intentions of conjugal engagement but instead only the desire to pour out his soul.

This all changed, however, in December of 2010. Just a few weeks before Christmas of the inaugural year of my PhD, my mother went beyond the pale. I returned home from the LA Fitness across the street from the apartment I shared with my friend from undergrad, Scott, to find my voicemail overflowing with close to a dozen messages from my mother. Upon seeing the volume of missed calls, my first instinct was, as would be the first instinct of any decent human being, to panic. I picked up the phone and hit the buttons to retrieve my voicemails. As soon as I pressed send, my ears, my thoughts, and my very humanity were suddenly subjected to a violent assault of near-incoherent ramblings.

Beep. "It's your mother . . ." she vomited into the recording, "I need you to call me . . ." *Click.*

Mother. Not mom. *Mother.* She spoke the word as pure violence. The word long ago ceased being a term of endearment and became a taunt for what she would never be and for what I could never have. Hearing the word on my voicemail made me shudder. I knew that whatever was forthcoming would not be pleasant.

Beep. "I don't know what I did to you to deserve this, but how could you do this to me . . ." *Click.*

How could you do this to me? Those words transported me back to the bedroom, to the furnace vent, to the Friday nights spent huddled with my brother, separated from the violence by nothing more than the cold, metal tube whose end vents mirrored prison bars. I had heard that refrain so many times directed at my father, and I knew what followed: accusations, shouting, violence, and, ultimately, flashing blue and red lights, handcuffs, and creme pies.

Beep. "Dammit, Matthieu! Answer your phone! He came for me. He came for me, and you sent him . . ." *Click.*

I had no idea what was going on. Who came? What was going on?

Beep. "You know what? If you needed money, you could have asked. *You could have asked!* You didn't have to try to sell me!" *Click.*

Try to sell her? Not that I could imagine something so grotesque, but even if I had intended to do so, I had no idea how to go about it. Moreover, I had no idea where she was living at the time. The number was an Oregon area code. But I can't imagine she would have stayed there after the devastation she let loose on her poor, unsuspecting internet tryst.

I did what any son, any human being, would do—either out of concern or curiosity. I took a deep breath, gathering the air as my armor for the impending assault, and steeled myself as I dialed the number saved in my caller ID.

"How could you?" she answered, forgoing even a hello.

"How could I what?" I asked in all sincerity.

"How could you do that to me," she shrieked.

"I didn't do anything!" Another flashback to my childhood, all the times when my brother and I would deny whatever trouble our mother was accusing us of.

"He grabbed me in an alley and said, 'I paid your son, and now you owe me.'"

"What?" The word escaped my mouth not as a question but as a plea for sanity.

"He tried to rape me! I fought him off, but he said he paid my son, and now I owed him! I don't know what you promised him or how much it cost, but I hope it was worth it."

The accusation cut me deep—too deep. It bypassed my heart and my soul and wrapped back around the tonsils. Here, it pierced my emotional center and caused everything I ever felt toward the woman who birthed me but could not be my mother to seep out, evaporating into the stale air of my bedroom.

My own "mother" ambushed me with the oldest trope of blackness that exists in Western epistemology: the black buck, the rapist, the threat to white women everywhere. From Othello to Emmett Till to the Scottsboro Boys, many black men faced imprisonment, mutilation, lynching, and death for having the audacity to even look at a white woman. No judge. No jury. Only executioner. All from nothing more than the words, true or false, of a white woman. And what was I but a constant reminder of her place within this continuum? She had fucked a black man, but instead of him losing his life, she had his children. I was not her child—I wasn't even her bloodstain. The blood still ran fresh for her. I was her wound. I was her violence. I was a constant reminder that the three hundred fifty plus years that preceded her relationship with my father always made their encounters already into rape. While the laws may have changed in the last fifty years, the trope still exists in the collective unconscious—still part of the world's pathologizing of blackness. My mother pulled the trope from the subliminal and recontextualized it for the twenty-first century—with the internet, I didn't even need to be in the same state for her to accuse me of rape. The mere fact of my existence was always reperforming her rape.

Her accusation hit so hard it stopped my breath. As I regained the ability to breathe, each exhale expelled the shock bit by bit. Each inhale brought new feelings. Not anger or apologies. Instead, for the first time in a long time, I felt peace. For the first time, I stopped fighting for my mother. I stopped praying she'd find help. I stopped hoping she'd ever meet her grandchildren.

I let go.

And this time, letting go brought peace.

I let her continue to rant while I gathered my thoughts. As soon as she broke for air, I intercepted the flow of the conversation and calmly spoke my piece, "I don't know what I could have said or done in the past to make you think I am capable of such a thing, but the fact that you think I could do such a thing means we have nothing to say to each other. I know you have had issues with mental illness, and I empathize, but I can't deal with them or you anymore. What you just accused me of, no mother of mine, hell, no mother at all, could ever do such a thing. I don't think you mean it, and I forgive you. But until you get help, do not call me. Good-bye."

"Your father raped me when we conceived you! If it were up to me, you'd have never been born." The last words I ever exchanged with my mother.

My phone rang nonstop for close to an hour, only resting long enough for her to leave a voicemail. Once I realized she had no intention of relenting, I turned my phone off, poured myself a whiskey and Coke from the ample supply Scott and I kept in the kitchen, walked back to my room, and wept.

A couple of days later, when I finally mustered the strength to turn on my phone and leave my room, I discovered my voicemail was full. I deleted the messages without listening to them. To this day, she will call every so often. I never answer, but I at least attempt to listen to the voicemails, hoping that maybe this time, just maybe, she would be calm and tell me about her doctors and her medication. Every time, the voicemails are the same tired accusations against me and my father I had heard since I was a child. Every time I hear one of these voicemails, a little piece of me breaks again.

SPLINTER
"(R)(D)ecomposed"

Have you ever been broken?
Heard the crystalline snap of a thousand threads of existential
    coherence severing at once?
Seen the world of color fall from its frame in disjointed slivers
    revealing only black and white beneath?
Tasted the perspiration, grit, and despair that composes the
    atmosphere?
Felt the longing anguish of the simultaneous grasp for and fear of
    breath?
Smelled death and the decay of death, only to realize that the
    emanation is from yourself?
I have seen the void.
I gazed into it as the world crumbled.
A black hole filling a colorless nothing.
Sometimes, they say, the void gazes back.
Sometimes, however, the void is gripped in whiteness,
daring, challenging, determined to show me what I am—
what I am not.
What I cannot be.
Leaving only what I am:
recomposed of all that never was,
and never can truly be.

ABSENCE
Status: Fatherhood.

I have a daughter now.
Her name is Roar.
She is barely a year old.
Everywhere we go, people tell me how adorable she is.
She's tall for her age.

I wonder what age she'll be when
they stop approaching to tell me she's cute
and start crossing the street when they see us come near.

I wonder what age she'll be when
they stop seeing her curiosity as precociousness
and start seeing it as the mark of a troublemaker.

I wonder what age she'll be when
they stop seeing her as a child to be protected
and start seeing her as a woman to be neglected.

I wonder what age she'll be when
they stop seeing her potential death as a tragedy
and start seeing it as justice served.

I wonder what age she'll be when I have to tell her
what nigger means.

I wonder what age she'll be when I have to explain
why the world hates her.
I wonder what age she'll be when she has to learn
what this book has to teach.

FRAGMENT 4

FACET: 1

Age: 15
Location: San Diego, CA
Status: One False Move Away

As my first summer in San Diego waned, I again confronted the world's phantasmagoric imago of blackness as I was walking downtown, somewhere on Park Boulevard. My friend and I were returning to school for football practice. Many of the few privileges that society afforded my blackness came from being an athlete. While I was still vastly overweight—six feet two and a shade over four hundred pounds—that girth came with some power and athleticism and made me a pretty good road-grading offensive guard. If white society could exploit the fruits of my labor for profit or entertainment, then, once they devoured my dignity, they would at least let me nibble the crumbs.

In this case, playing football afforded me a sixth period study hall. My graduation plan required six PE credits, and the school let my after-school practices count as PE. As such, the 1:20 to 2:10 p.m. slot in the school schedule was a study hall for football players. But since I already made good grades, the coaches let me wander wherever I wanted, so long as I wasn't late for practice. So, I'd frequently take a walk downtown before returning around 2:15 to dress for game prep.

On this day, I walked. I walked this walk that I had walked dozens of times before, past the taco shops and pawnbrokers, through the construction dust and tunnels of scaffolding layered with posters of upcoming concerts, movie soundtracks, comedy shows, and graffiti art ranging from simple tags to complex murals.

I was walking, engrossed in a conversation with my friend Jose, who also went by Norenzo. Even though both his birth certificate and state-issued ID said Lorenzo, he demanded people replace the *L* with an *N*. I never thought to ask the origin of his preferred name; even at fifteen years old, I was progressive enough to know that the most basic level of human dignity is to let someone choose what others call them. We were laughing and joking and talking shit like kids do. With Norenzo, it was always about girls. He always talked about "hittin' it" and "smashing," even though I'd never seen him with a girl, and no one I knew would admit to having sex with him. He was one of my best friends—not because of any great connection, but because the cool kids who determine everyone's social status relegated us to the same social sphere. I don't recall ever making friends in high school. Instead, it seemed my friends were made for me. Without planning or discussion, I found myself surrounded by people who would fall within one or two points on society's generic attractiveness scale. None of us were ugly or malformed, but we weren't hot enough to join the court of adolescent royalty. I was too fat. Orlando was too short. Norenzo was—I don't know what Norenzo was. He was tall and lean, with skin the color of golden sand and short waves of hair that he meticulously maintained with a short-bristle brush during the day and gel and a wave cap at night. He should have fit right in at the top. Instead, he found himself with the jesters and ogres on the margins.

As we crossed Park Boulevard no more than six blocks from campus, our world became awash in violent red and blue. Sirens. I had heard them many times before. At night, the sirens would always cause tension. But that tension came hand in hand with living in a first-floor apartment in the North Park neighborhood of San Diego.

Now, North Park has fallen victim to hipster gentrification: coffee shops, yoga studios, and the security of whiteness. When I was in high school, students affectionately and disgracefully referred to North Park as "the Nutty P's." In the Nutty P's, the sirens would often wake me up at night, the staccato red and blue lights invading my bedroom in narrow slivers between the horizontal slats of the cheap blinds. Hearing the siren meant you were or are or will be near a crime. Or so I thought at the time. I would later learn that the sirens just as often created a criminal as they signaled a crime. Regardless, the sirens reminded me that the only thing keeping the world outside from coming inside was a cheap wooden door and some single-paned windows. These windows could barely keep out a breeze, let alone a brick, a rock, or even a fist of someone trying to break in. In my mind, the sirens signaled that the bad guys were out there.

But it wasn't until that day that I knew who the bad guys were.

I heard the sirens, but they are different in the daytime. In day-light, we can see the threats, and we can work to avoid them and remove ourselves from danger. At least most of the time. Some situations are unavoidable. In other situations, the sirens signal that the person controlling them views you as the threat.

The flashing "walk" hand turned solid red as Norenzo and I were halfway across the street. I heard the sirens, but I paid them no mind. I knew they were for someone else. Not for me. Never for me. I hadn't done anything illegal—not in the moment, not in the past. So the sirens couldn't be for me. Sirens are for bad guys. I was an honors student. I was a member of the football team.

I was also black.

The black-and-white patrol car pulled in front of me, and I froze. The world became muffled. The roar of engines and traffic faded into an audible shadow, not quite an echo, but like suddenly being under-water. The flashing lights froze me in the middle distance between myself and my fate. Then, the whole world stopped, frozen alongside me.

The sirens were for me.

As a black man, I know. We all know. Maybe it's innate. Perhaps it's absorbed subliminally through media and popular culture. But as a black man, I know. I know that when the sirens are for me, they could be the last thing I ever encounter.

"Put your hands on the fucking car!"

The words ripped through the *mise-en-scène* of the picturesque late summer day in San Diego. The world around me locked into position for what felt like an eternity. And within this movie still of existence, I was confronted by a hole. The opposite of a camera obscura, this hole was not of light surrounded by darkness but of blackness surrounded by a thin sliver of cold gray that blurred the world around it. My world was a pinpoint of darkness within a frozen glaze of light.

A gun.

The hole was the barrel of a 9mm Beretta pistol that was standard-issue for all law enforcement officers in San Diego. I struggled to regain my thoughts, to reorder the world, and to remember what my father taught me as a child. He always told me, "Show them respect, do exactly what they say, and they won't have a reason to snatch you up." I inhaled slowly, and microscopic slivers splintered the frame, like looking through the windshield after a car crash.

Suddenly, a swift shove in the back forced the air from my lungs and sent my body lurching forward. The world shattered.

"Put your hands on the fucking car! Now!"

The world fell to pieces as I toppled forward, hands outstretched, hoping to catch myself. Expecting the ground, I instead found my fall broken by my hands hitting the hood of his cop car.

"I'm sorry!" I said, my hands splayed on the hood of the police interceptor. Respect authority. Do what they say. I don't know what I was sorry for. Upon reflection, I wasn't sorry for anything. But in the panic of approaching death, I defaulted to deference and submission. "Do what they say, and they won't have a reason to snatch you up." Before I knew it, his hands were all over me. I became newly aware of my body and its relation to white space and white place and the white world—what Frantz Fanon described as the "difficulties in elaborating his bodily schema. The image of one's body is solely negating."[1] My body, my blackness, was no longer my own. Even though America abolished slavery, this officer made damn sure I knew that the state still owned my body. My blackness was his to do with as he pleased. His hands violated my flesh—my flesh being sufficient evidence to justify his intrusion. He checked my shirt, my pockets, reached up, down, around, in, and through my core. He put his hand down the front of my pants and shook my manhood, either attempting to dislodge contraband or to get his jollies. When nothing fell loose, he pulled on the elastic of my underwear all the way around my waist. I can still feel his hands. It gives me chills.

"I'm sorry!" I repeated, more forcefully than before, my voice breaking into a sharp falsetto with fear.

Norenzo was next to me, his silence drawing the ire of the officer. The officer forced Norenzo's entire chest onto the hood and placed a forearm on his back. "You think you hard, or something?" the officer growled, more of a challenge than a question. "Your friend over here is apologizing. What do you got to say?"

I stood hunched over the hood, hoping, praying that Norenzo's next words wouldn't be his last. I prayed that he would offer the officer some reverence, some submission, some reason to hesitate. I silently begged him not to attempt some witty rejoinder, or worse, question or challenge the officer's power. Norenzo inhaled, and my stomach bubbled with bile and terror at the words that would come with his exhale. Time slowed, his mouth captured at one thousand frames per second.

"I'm sorry," he said. "I'm sorry."

Relief. I wanted to cry. I wanted to cry because Norenzo did the right thing.

I wanted to cry because I live in a world where that was the right thing.

"That's what I thought," the officer responded. He then began to violate Norenzo just as he had me. "You think you can disrespect me like that?"

I had no idea to what the officer was referring.

"What did I do?"

BANG

A single shot.

The air exits my lungs. I try to breathe in more, but I choke. Blood flows in irregular spurts from the hole in my chest. I can't breathe. Norenzo drops to his knees by my side. He cradles my head and puts pressure on the gaping wound in my torso.

"He's just a kid, man. He's just a kid."

Traffic stops. A crowd forms. A radio crackles as the cop calls for backup.

The assembly of men and women who had seen enough, heard enough, knew enough, surround the officer. He screams into the radio, "Officer down!"

More police arrive. More citizens arrive. The latter outgrows the former exponentially.

They take the streets. Disband the police.

My life mattered.

So much that my death changed the world.

SLIVER

Close Your Eyes and Count to Fuck

How did I get here?

I wonder how many times "*Put your hands on the fucking car!*" have been the last words someone has ever heard. Police first used a cop car in Akron, Ohio, in 1899. It was a horsecar with the horse replaced with an electric motor, and for all intents and purposes, an automobile the police used, therefore making it a police car. In 1900, the city of Akron only had forty-two thousand people, and while I don't know what percentage was black, it was probably a small proportion. So why does it matter what portion of Akron's population was black in 1899? Simple probability. I can't say how commonly "fuck" was used in the vernacular of 1899, nor can I say how often a white officer uses the exact phrasing "put your hands on the fucking car"

with white citizens. But the conflu-
ence of language, race, and event
required for an officer to utter
"put your hands on the fucking
car" before ending someone's life
probably did not occur in Akron
in 1899.

In the 1940s, automobile manu-
facturers began producing specially
designed police cars. With Ford's
invention of the flathead V-8
engine, producing higher-powered
cars designed as interceptors
became practical and affordable.
These cars had the explicit purpose
of outrunning and catching the
bad guys. So, beginning in the
1940s, it probably became much
more likely that "put your hands
on the fucking car" was the last
thing someone heard.

In the sixty or so years between
the mass distribution of police cars
and my fateful crossing of a street
in downtown San Diego, I imagine
dozens, if not hundreds, of men
and women had the misfortune of
having that command be the last
thing they ever heard.

This phrase, this ugly command
punctuated by unnecessary

profanity, is symptomatic of a more significant national crisis that is just as much part of America's fabric as life, liberty, and the pursuit of happiness: antiblackness. Alongside the more hopeful threads of that tapestry are the threads of antiblackness.

Chattel slavery, convict leasing, Jim Crow, ghettos, and mass incarceration—these five institutions are far older than America's 245 years. Most often, scholars cite 1619 as the beginning of chattel slavery, with Nikole Hannah-Jones's 1619 Project arguing that this year marks the actual birth of America. But the English, whose settlers would rebel and give birth to America, first shipped slaves to the New World in 1562. Queen Elizabeth commissioned naval Captain John Hawkins to sail to the coast of Africa, capture black Africans, and transport them across the Atlantic. As such, chattel slavery of black Africans predates America by 214 years, making the institution almost twice as old as the nation.

On December 18, 1865,

Andrew Johnson proclaimed the
Thirteenth Amendment of the
Constitution ratified and officially
abolished slavery in the United
States. The Civil War was over:
blacks were free. America could
now move beyond its original
sin and begin to heal. Except the
Union allowed traitors to continue
to govern. And while slavery was
now unconstitutional, the amendment included one caveat: as punishment for a crime. So the former
Confederate States immediately
implemented "black Codes,"
which were a series of nefarious
laws designed to criminalize
blackness. With blacks newly freed
but largely uneducated, unskilled,
and without means to buy land
or homes, states made vagrancy
a crime. Some states even made it a
crime for blacks to assemble: three
or more black people together
was illegal. Police would use black
Codes to round up blacks and
imprison them. They would then
sentence them to slavery and sell
them back to their former owners
in a process called convict leasing.
    Alongside convict leasing

came the legalized segregation of Jim Crow. States passed these laws in the 1870s as a method of surveilling and containing the newly freed slaves. In 1896, Homer Plessy, who was one-eighth black, intentionally violated New Orleans' separate car statute by riding in a whites-only car and was arrested. He sued, claiming that the New Orleans statute was unconstitutional. The case made it all the way to the US Supreme Court as *Plessy v. Ferguson.* The court ruled that while the Fourteenth Amendment guaranteed equal treatment of whites and blacks, the amendment didn't *actually* guarantee equal treatment of whites and blacks. It was really just there to make white people feel better about inequality. The final ruling was that the amendment, "could not eliminate all distinctions based on color." This ruling that allowed segregation would last until the *Brown v. Board of Education* ruling in 1954.

So now with slavery abolished, convict leasing outlawed, and Jim Crow struck down, America needed a new way to contain and surveil black bodies, and they found it in the governmental doctrine of eminent domain. Eminent domain allows the government to purchase (steal) any property from private citizens as long as the property is used for public good. In the 1930s, Franklin Delano Roosevelt's New Deal eased the Great Depression and put America to work. One of the primary projects was the Works Progress Administration (WPA), an initiative to advance our country's infrastructure. Highways, dams, a power grid—all built by the WPA.

Much of this infrastructure was built on land stolen from blacks.

Eminent domain abuse was commonplace in the mid-twentieth century. While the marketing campaigns referred to the practice as "urban renewal," internal reports from Chicago more directly called the process "negro removal." According to a report from Dr. Mindy Thompson Fullilove, writing for the Institute for Justice, between 1949 and 1973, eminent domain displaced more than one million Americans nationwide, over two-thirds of whom were black. On top of this, the government paid black citizens less than white citizens for comparable properties, stealing generational wealth under the guise of progress. With blacks forcibly removed from their homes and businesses and left without enough money to buy new ones, they consolidated in ghettos and housing projects.

With blacks again contained in small areas where the state could surveil them, Nixon implemented the War on Drugs to criminalize blackness anew. In a 1994 interview with *Harper's*, which was only uncovered in 2016, Nixon policy advisor John Ehrlichman stated: "The Nixon campaign in 1968, and the Nixon White House after that, had two enemies: the antiwar left and black people. You understand what I'm saying? We knew we couldn't make it illegal to be either against the war or black, but by getting the public to associate the hippies with marijuana and blacks with heroin, and then, criminalizing both

heavily, we could disrupt those
communities. We could arrest their
leaders. Raid their homes, break
up their meetings, and vilify them
night after night on the evening
news. Did we know we were lying
about the drugs? Of course we
did." According to Ehrlichman,
the Nixon administration lied
to justify over-policing and
intentional disruption of black
communities. This criminalization
not of black behavior or politics
but of blackness itself gave birth to
the era of mass incarceration.

Five institutions. Five hundred
years. All to contain, surveil, and
criminalize blackness. All to make
sure that blacks know their place.
To make sure we know that our
place is separate and distinct from
everyone else's.

So how did I get here—spending a picturesque San Diego day
staring down the barrel of a gun
with my hands on the hood of a
police car? By having the audacity
not to be *there*—in the ghetto,
behind bars—the only "theres"
where black people are allowed to
be.

"Put your hands on the fucking car." I cannot say how many men and women and children have heard that command, whose utterance seems to go against police training in de-escalation. The order that cops only give when a muthafucka "wants a reason to." I cannot say how often the command is the last thing someone hears. All I know is, at that moment, I was determined to make sure it wasn't the last thing I ever heard.

SHARD: 1
Status: On the Gridiron

We moved to San Diego in April of 1999, and I hated it. My mother's rash decision to move meant we didn't have time to save or plan appropriately for the endeavor. As such, we took refuge in a transient hotel that offered rates ranging from hourly to monthly. The hotel was constructed in the 1920s, and in its better days, the art-deco facades and rich maroon carpets were classy and exquisite. However, the intervening three-quarters of a century had left the hotel in disrepair and fading into the past. The crisp lines of the art-deco embellishments were weathered by decades exposed to the elements and smoothened by ages of collected dust. Our room was too small for three to share, and it offered only an old squeaky queen bed for us to sleep on. Sitting on the bed created horrible fantasies of the escapades that occurred on the stained mattress, many of which were certainly sexual, criminal, or both. Most nights, I opted for the fold-out cot that the grizzled desk clerk brought to our room.

Our San Diego arrival was in April, which meant I was in town for all of five weeks before school let out. This left me no time to make friends before the summer. I was at the end of my ninth-grade year, and enrolling in school in San Diego was a big endeavor. The school systems on the Pacific coast aligned differently than those I had left behind. In Pennsylvania, middle school was composed of sixth through eighth grades, while high school was grades nine through twelve. In San Diego, grades eight and nine were junior high, and senior high school was ten to twelve. This minor shift in structure meant that my sister and I would have to enroll in separate schools: as a tenth grader, she'd go to San Diego High School. As a ninth grader, I'd be at Roosevelt Junior High.

I couldn't have cared less, but my mother was determined to keep my sister and me together. It was an odd mission considering we would never spend time together at school. However, she managed to find a loophole: ninth graders involved in activities not offered at the junior high could enroll at the high school. My mother pored through the activities that were available at the schools—soccer, chorus, basketball, debate, and dozens of others—before she found two that met the criteria. I had experience in one: marching band. I had played trombone in fifth grade and trumpet in sixth grade, but it was a stretch to say I was involved in band. Regardless, the school bought the excuse and allowed me to enroll.

After two weeks spending all day, every day in a shitty transient hotel, I escaped the worn maroon carpet and lace-lined drapes for my first day of school. First, I went to meet my guidance counselor and set my schedule. When I entered, the secretary directed me to the office of Coach Conner. Yes, *Coach* Conner. My guidance counselor was also the basketball coach and athletic director. He was a small man; he couldn't have been more than five foot five with hair greased to the side in a Hitleresque combover that foreshadowed his militaristic demeanor.

"Come in," he commanded when I appeared in the doorway.

Medals and sports trophies crowded the surfaces around the office. Photos of teams captioned with the school's name and the championship year lined the walls. While the foreshadowing of his hairstyle flew over my head, the nature of his décor did not. His office was a monument to athletic achievement, but it contained no books, no degrees—no recognition of academic life anywhere.

"So, Mr. Chapman," he said, opening a manila file folder. "Just arrived from Pennsylvania."

He only spoke in imperatives. He never introduced himself or asked any questions, so I sat silently awaiting some engagement.

"Gonna be honest with you, Mr. Chapman. It's too late in the year for you to enroll in any required classes and get credit—state law. So how about we get all of your extracurriculars out of the way. Study hall, Auto Shop, Wood Shop, Home Ec, and I have a note here that you're in the band."

"Yes," I stammered. "My mom said I had to if I wanted to be here as a ninth grader."

"You have to have some activity, sure, but we have options," he said. "You should try football."

"I don't think so," I said. I had little interest in organized athletics. Sure, I played pickup games with kids from the neighborhood back in Pennsylvania, but playing school sports wasn't my jam. All the rules and refs and coaches made the game no longer a game.

Just then, his phone rang.

"I gotta take this," Conner said. "Decide. Football or band. You have until I finish the call."

He turned to conduct his conversation. As I sat in the small wooden chair across the desk, staring into the high, grandiose brown leather chairback that was far too large for his frame, I had no idea what I wanted to do. I also had no idea how much time I had to decide.

A gnawing thought at the back of my mind distracted me from the choice at hand—why? Why do I have to choose between band and football, two activities I had no interest in? As I tried to weigh the pros and cons of each option, the gnawing became a chewing, and the chewing metacommentary soon consumed and swallowed the whole of my thoughts. I didn't want to choose between band

and football because it was a choice already made for me by limiting me only to options that others wanted. Yes, I was only fourteen, still technically and legally a child, but I was also a person with thoughts, opinions, and agency.

Or so I wanted to believe. But the fact is, American society still functions very much under outdated axioms of "father knows best" and "children are to be seen and not heard." As a result, this country quickly dismisses the voices of children. Whether asking parents for a treat as they trudge up and down the aisles of a grocery store, or reporting to an authority the unwanted touching from an uncle, a child's voice—their agency—is as easily brushed away as the last remnants of dirt that refuse to go into the dustpan. In America, a child has more value before they are born than they do after they exit their mother's womb.

This silencing of a child's voice is proportionate to the density of their skin's melanin. Not only was I a child in the eyes of my mother and of Coach Conner, but I was a black child. My voice had so little weight that they didn't even brush it off with a condescending idiom, but rather the words drifted straight past them, rustling their clothes less than a light summer breeze. I remembered the officer from my childhood, "Did your dad ever hurt your mom?" And how my answer went completely unacknowledged when it didn't meet his predetermined assessment of the situation. Suddenly, I imagined my mother and Coach Conner wearing those same black uniforms with yellow and gold embellishments.

The black uniform in my mind was replaced by the blue polo before my eyes as Coach Conner spun back in his chair. "All right, let's go see the coach."

I was beginning to learn that a lot of the time, people only offer a choice when they have already decided the outcome.

He launched from his chair with incredible energy that shook me in my seat. I paused for a second as he hurried out the door, only to quickly realize that he had no intention of waiting for me to follow. I nabbed my backpack and sprinted after him.

By the time I reached the main door of the building, Coach Conner had already crossed the courtyard and was halfway up the stairs to the athletics building. San Diego High School was unlike any school I'd seen up to that point. Instead of being one large building, the high school was akin to a college campus with ten separate smaller buildings, each housing a different discipline: arts, science, math, languages, and my destination—athletics.

We followed the long, elevated, concrete walkway around the perimeter of the building until it again touched the ground outside the school's weight room. Coach Conner stopped at the door and shouted within, "Hey, Coach, I got a new one for ya!" Then he marched back the way we came.

I stood in the doorway, trying to catch my breath and cajole my thoughts to catch up with my body. What the hell just happened? Before I could figure it out, another voice joined the conversation.

"Well, don't just stand there, come on in, son." The voice came from Coach Ramirez, a young, lean, Latino man who couldn't have been older than thirty-five—a man who was the opposite of the one who'd just left. He wore sunglasses so dark that I couldn't see his eyes and a wide-brimmed bucket hat, even though he was indoors. He was evidently proud of his body, as the seams of the gray San Diego High School T-shirt he wore were screaming in pain, being stretched to their limits from containing his biceps. Yet, despite his intimidating physique, his voice was warm and soothing.

"So, you wanna play football," he said.

"Actually, I want to be in band," I responded, having made my choice on the trek over.

"Oh, well then, why are you here?" he asked.

"I don't know." I was afraid to tattle on Coach Conner. Even though he had since left the vicinity, I was not willing to risk being overheard crossing him.

"Well, I know," he said. "God gave you that body for a reason. Now you can use it to march around and blow things, or you can come out and kick some ass for me. What are you, six two? Three plus? And still growing? There are only so many six feet two, three-hundred-pound guys on the planet. So, if you want to be in band, I'll walk you over right now. But if you want to play football, we'll get you in shape, get you into college, and who knows, maybe even get you a girlfriend."

He winked at me. I wondered how many times he'd made this pitch before. I didn't care for getting in shape, and I didn't care for college. But a girlfriend? I was fourteen years old and had never even kissed a girl. So with that line, he hooked me.

Coach Ramirez put me in sixth period Phys Ed, and I started practicing that day. I had no idea what to expect. I returned to the athletics building for class, and a short Latino man named Henry—who I'd later learn was the equipment manager—directed me to the football team room for pre-practice instructions.

As I sat on the blue wooden risers awaiting direction in the middle of the stale concrete-floored room lined with lockers, two of the players approached me.

"You new?" one of them said.

"Of course he's new, dumbass. You ever seen him before?" replied the other.

The first of this new age black Laurel and Hardy was James Newton. James was neither what you would call tall nor what you would call slim, but he was proportionate enough that his girth didn't read as fat. He was what today's youth would call "thicc." He was of Afro-Latin heritage, with light brown skin with yellow undertones and wavy hair. The other was Terrell Johnson: a short, rotund dude two shades darker than James with a voice that was oddly gruff and nasally at the same time.

"Yeah, I'm new," I said, unsure of what I could say or how I could say it so that Terrell wouldn't call me dumbass next.

"Damn, you big," said Terrell.

"Dude, that's how you greet the man?" admonished James. "That's fucked up."

"He is big," said Terrell. "What would you call it?"

"Instead of calling it anything, I'd ask his name," said James.

"Then ask his name instead of talkin' shit to me. Checkmate, bitch." Terrell was a real cutup.

"Yo, what's your name, man?" asked James.

"Matt," I said.

"I'm James, and this is Terrell."

"Fat Matt!" Terrell exclaimed. James just dropped his head and shook it slowly from side to side. Over the following two years we'd share on the team, I would come to appreciate their routine, but I had no idea what I had gotten myself into in the moment.

"Where you from, Matt?" asked James.

"Pennsylvania," I said.

As soon as I completed the sentence, Terrell's voice chimed in, "Ugh . . . do they have vampires there?"

As I said, I had no idea what I had gotten myself into.

Before I could respond, Coach Ramirez entered and blew his whistle. The shrill, high-pitched ring echoed off the concrete and reverberated uncomfortably at the back of my teeth.

"All right, gentlemen, let's get to business."

Coach's business was discipline and suffering, and business was good. While I wouldn't dare compare football to the horrors of chattel slavery, the latter institution certainly echoes in the former.

Each day, eighty predominantly black and brown bodies toiled under the hot sun, moving in synchronization at the orders of our overseer coaches for the pleasure and enrichment of other, primarily lighter-skinned, people. Discipline, punishment, and humiliation are a part of both institutions, the "yes, massas" of the plantation replaced with "yes, sirs" of the gridiron. If we didn't move fast enough, not only within but also between plays, coach would punish us with more physical labor—if he were feeling generous, we'd have push-ups; if feeling more sadistic, gassers. Coach punished all of us for the crimes of any of us; if one man jumped offsides, everyone ran. Vomiting wasn't a cause for concern but celebration; it meant that you had pushed through a plateau and gotten better.

Although practices were torturous affairs, I loved game time. I didn't love it for the teamwork or the victory. I didn't love it for the bright lights or the screaming fans.

I loved it because it made sense.

Football is a game full of objective measures: the playing field is 120 yards long and 53.3 yards wide. At each end is a set of goalposts, and these goalposts never move. The obstacles are clear on the field—I have a blocking assignment, and my job is to move that man. I could measure success or failure on every play relative to the distance to those posts—if we moved closer, victory; farther away, defeat. Those games are some of the most stable times in my life.

But even so, I hated football. I hated the politics and exploitation. As players, the school, the coaches, and the fans each expected us to sacrifice our bodies for nothing more than the thrill of victory while our coaches parlayed those same victories into raises and bonuses. And I do not mean sacrifice lightly. I played the sport for three years at the amateur level, and twenty years later, my body creaks and groans from the repetitive stress of constant collisions. I have an ankle that pops every time I walk down a stair, a shoulder that required surgery in my twenties, and multiple concussions that no doubt contributed to my later depression. Thankfully, unlike the slavery of my ancestors, football had a time limit; I could spend each second of each practice counting the seconds until I could go home.

I hated every second I counted.

But it was how the school valued me. My blackness had no value. My brain had no value. But my size did, so I endured the whistles and the sun and the sprints and the vomit. Why? Because I could line up across from just about anyone and move them out of the way. I had never lifted weights and never trained athletically. Still, I had an innate control of my body and leverage that provided me some semblances of recognition and community. So even though I hated it, I stuck with it because in those moments on the field, I was a football player. I was an athlete. I was an offensive guard and a teammate. I had a place and a purpose.

All of which allowed me to forget for brief moments that I was also black.

Such was life in San Diego.

SLIVER

A Liberal Facade

I can hear it now. "It can't happen here," they'll say. "Not in San Diego."

San Diego is too diverse. San Diego is too liberal. San Diego is too—not this. San Diego doesn't have this problem.

No one wishes that were true more than me.

San Diego, like all of California, has a reputation as a liberal hippie wonderland. Movies and TV shows love to remember the Summer of Love in San Francisco and the Free Love culture of peace and pot that originated in the state. They point to the LGBTQ enclaves of the Hillcrest in San Diego and the Castro district of San Francisco. One of my all-time favorite TV shows, *King of the Hill*, often positioned California as the antithesis of the homegrown, conservative family values of the great state of Texas, with the titular character Hank Hill once dreaming of taking a "forty-seven state tour of our great nation. Not California."

But California is more than upscale coastal bastions of the rich and celebrious such as Beverly Hills, Santa Monica, Pacific Beach, and Santa Cruz. The majority of the state is farmland and forests. Most of the state's counties belie this liberal reputation by voting Republican. Even within counties, the demographics compose a broad spectrum. In San Diego County, the wealth deteriorates alongside the coastal breeze the farther you move inland.

La Jolla, one of the richest (and whitest) cities in the country, sits atop magnificent beachside bluffs, and the home values easily cross into the eight figures. Move ten miles inland, and you hit areas such as La Mesa and Mission Valley, where the occupants are still largely professional class, however, the cost of living is a bit more modest, though still well above the national average. Another ten miles in, and you reach El Cajon and Santee, the latter of which is often referred to as "Klan-tee," the more upper-class coastal elites making fun of their less educated and less lucky racial brethren.

As you move inland, the overall wealth decreases, and the proportion of minorities increases. Even so, minority neighborhoods are segregated by race, just as white neighborhoods are segregated by wealth. For example, just south of downtown—literally separated from the white communities by the construction of a freeway, now Route 163—are Logan Heights and Chicano Park, two of the oldest Latinx neighborhoods in the state. Move a little farther north of the white neighborhoods, again across a freeway, and you hit Mira Mesa and Miramar, which are largely Vietnamese and Thai.

The black neighborhoods, however, are disappearing. Gentrification has overrun places that white people once feared— the predominantly black areas such as North Park and Skyline. White people move in and drive

up property values, which raises
taxes and drives out the more
impoverished black citizens;
eminent domain enacted by the
market. As such, the black citizens
of San Diego are forced farther
and farther into ghettos and public
housing projects.

Despite the liberal reputation
of the city, San Diego is also home
to two of the country's largest
military bases: the 32nd Street
Naval Station and Marine Corps
Base Camp Pendleton. The military and conservatism are closely
linked—although these branches
of the military are composed of
people of all races, they tend to
be united in their America-first
ethos. The willingness to die for
America is something I will never
understand. How could any black
person, whose history in America
is a compendium of violence
inflicted against their flesh and
their being, be willing to die for
it? What cognitive dissonance
must occur for a black person to be
willing to fight and die for a nation
that thrives on the incarceration of
their flesh and the destruction of

their communities? While all races appear in the military, joining up voluntarily requires vastly different sacrifices.

This unique blend of thousands of soldiers and extreme white wealth has made San Diego a "closet conservative" city. Despite the liberal reputation, the majority of the voting population doesn't vote for progress and change. They vote against resolutions to end homelessness and police violence. They vote against higher property taxes to fund social programs. They install bench barriers and doorway spikes to keep the homeless away. The citizens know how violent their city is to the poor, the black, the Mexican.

They just don't want to hear about the violence.

They don't want to have real discussions with their other rich, white, privileged friends about how rich, white, and privileged they are. They want to stay in a bubble where they can assume everyone is just like them.

So, it can happen there. It does happen there. But San Diego is very concerned with making sure no one thinks it happens there. They are a "sanctuary city." They call themselves "America's Finest City."

I can't help but ask, for whom?

"Put your hands on the fucking car!"

As I stared down the barrel of that cop's gun, I know the answer now is "not me."

FACET: 2

Age: 15
Location: San Diego, CA
Status: One False Move Away

"You think you can disrespect me like that and get away with it?"

What had I done? I began retracing my steps. It was an utterly unextraordinary day: I woke up in the morning and took the #7 bus down University Avenue until it made the left on Park, through Balboa Park, across the 163 freeway, dropping me off in front of the school. I went through my classes: English, Algebra, Auto Shop, American History, and Chemistry. I had Arby's for lunch. I left campus with Norenzo and headed down to Horton Plaza during our free period. We began walking back. We crossed at the flashing red hand. The flashing red hand? Was that considered jaywalking? Had I jaywalked? The light was flashing, but I can still cross when it's flashing, right? Had jaywalking become a capital crime? An act so heinous that I could skip judge and jury and head directly to executioner?

At that moment, I realized that I had nothing to apologize for. I had perpetrated no transgression. I had committed no crime. But none of that matters: the world views my actions in this moment and this space—their space—alongside the phantasmagoric imago of blackness that haunts both black and nonblack life alike. All that was necessary for this officer of the law—this defender of truth and justice, this man whose own car was emblazoned with the motto of "Serve and Protect"—to draw his weapon, deny my agency, invade my body, and shatter my life was the fact of my blackness. I was grasping for an explanation but afraid to ask for clarity. All I could do was hope to survive. And my only chance for survival was to appeal to his ego, to submit to his violence. To admit to him, then and there, that I knew my place.

I apologized, but not for any acts I had committed. I apologized for not being in my place. I apologized for making him feel threatened. I apologized for the miscarriage of justice that my body and my existence represented. I apologized for the fact that when you are black, no one is looking for justice; they are only looking for an excuse, for a reason, to pull the trigger.

I apologized for not giving him one.

And just as soon as it had begun, it was over. The officer let us off of his car and holstered his weapon. He moved toward the driver's side of the car and opened the door, his chest puffed with toxic masculine pride. Before sitting behind the wheel, he uttered the two-word lesson that still makes my heart stop and my chest quiver at the sight of a police officer.

"You're lucky."

I'll never forget that day because that day is not over for me. I live that day every day. That day is my past, my present, and my future. There is no escaping that day because that day was a spectacular instance of my perpetual existence. There is no moving past it because I am always moving, living, breathing through it.

At this moment, I realized that I had no life of my own. My life was also theirs. The world would use expectations, standards, and terms to contain, surveil, and police me not as an individual but as just another fungible black body. They would never recognize or judge me as an individual. I learned that my achievements would not reflect my ability but rather serve as a commentary on all of us—past, present, and future—whose blood derives from the hold of the ship.

I was fifteen years old when the world again confronted me with their horrible perceptions of blackness. I was fifteen years old when the me I thought I was—the 4.0 student, the high school football player—was ripped away. I was fifteen years old when the potential I thought I had—the 99th percentile test scores and the budding writer—became nothing but a breathing, moving corpse. I was fifteen years old when I died. That cop killed all of me in that instance. Now, twenty years later, I continue to die every day—never physically dead but unable to fully live. Wandering, scrambling, fighting to put the pieces back together.

ABSENCE
Status: Close call.

"Put your hands on the fucking car!"

"What did i do?"

BANG

A single shot.

The air exits my lungs. I try to breathe in more, but I choke. Blood
flows in irregular spurts from the
hole in my chest. I can't breathe.

The officer clicks his radio.

"Sir, calm down!" he shouts.

BANG

No cell phone video.

No outrage.

No trial.

Just two more dead black kids.

How close were we to this?

How close will I be again?

FRAGMENT 5

Facet: 1

Age: 16
Location: Mr. Wilson's Classroom
Status: Head of the Class

Mr. Wilson was frustrated. He had left his position at the front of the room to take up post just above my desk. I always hated the chair desks in his classroom. I was a big kid, so I had trouble squeezing my overly large frame into a school desk made for the average-sized teenager. Between the compact desk crunching my joints into unnaturally acute angles and the heat that arose from my overlapping flesh making me uncomfortably warm, I often fell asleep in Mr. Wilson's class. Why couldn't every room have couches like Mr. Peterson's?

"Who was the president that helped form the League of Nations?" he boomed from just above my head.

His voice shook me from my sleep. I peeled my perspiring head from the desk. He was standing so close that I struggled to make eye contact over his protruding belly.

"Woodrow Wilson," I slurred, answering correctly.

The rest of the class involved themselves in our encounter, and they released a long, low, "oooooohhhh" to egg us on. The sound transported the classroom to the playground with Mr. Wilson playing the role of bully. Only this time, the target of his bullying had struck back, leaving Mr. Wilson with two choices: back down or fight back.

But he wasn't a bully. He was an educator.

"Man, just put your head back down," he said.

I didn't mean to insult Mr. Wilson, but sleeping in American History had become a regular occurrence as the year dragged on. Despite being unable to stay awake in his class, I liked Mr. Wilson. He was a good lecturer: he was engaging, charismatic, and intelligent. He would often speak in character voices and perform comically modified versions of scenes from American history: Washington crossing the Delaware and Lee's surrender at Appomattox were a few of his greatest hits. His humorous performances of history's great white men were made more comical because he was black. The juxtaposition of his black body with the white characters drew attention to the erasure of his ancestors from the curriculum. Most students considered him a great teacher, myself included.

Like me, Mr. Wilson was a big black dude. Our attitudes, however, could not have been more opposite—while I was apathetic and frustrated most of the time, Mr. Wilson was always engaged. His tone and tenor bordered on jolly. He wore his hair in a small afro with sideburns that connected down into a graying beard. But he was the first black man I had as a teacher other than gym class and, even though I didn't know why, that mattered to me.

American History during junior year of high school was part of the state-mandated history curriculum: World History in tenth grade, American History in eleventh, and Government and Civics as a senior. While the bookends to this sequence were largely forgettable—a polished, depoliticized mishmash of facts and figures that began with American ingenuity and ended with America kicking every country's ass, even its own (America really kicked America's ass in that whole Civil War thing), the middle course provided me with a subversive curriculum on navigating black life that, as far as I knew, was only taught to me. Mr. Wilson's class was far from rigorous, and he designed it to be so. The assignments mainly were textbook-company-supplied worksheets for homework with the same company's tests given in class. He graded the courses on a modified curve: each nine-week period included 1000 points' worth of assignments. If the highest student in the class got a 780, then all of the 700s would be As, the 600 Bs, the 500 Cs, etc. In some ways, this grading method incentivized failure: if everyone got a zero, then, theoretically, everyone would get an A.

The students, however, never discussed gaming the system. We did not need to. In addition to using 100 percent of the materials provided by the textbook company, Mr. Wilson made the in-class exams both open book and open notes. I never understood why you would need both since the textbook contained 100 percent of the exam material, often with the answers to the test questions coming in sequence with the text. His exams were less about testing our knowledge than they were about our ability to skim the book, making them nothing more than a glorified word search.

He designed the course to make sure every student who put in even an ounce of effort would earn a passing grade. Perhaps he made it this way because he just decided to mail it in at some point in his thirty-plus years of teaching. If the school is paying for these textbooks and supplemental materials, and the company provides answer keys, why not use them and save time grading? Maybe he realized that the stakes attached to grades were too high. In our hypercompetitive, capitalist society, grades can be the difference between college and a job and struggling to make ends meet on America's minimum wage. Maybe the ease of the class was his way of rebelling against the system that forced him, a black man, to indoctrinate students into the white supremacist, America-first wet dream that we call high school history class. I don't know why he designed his class this way, although the longer I remain in higher education, the more I am starting to see the appeal.

"Mr. Chapman, do you have a minute?" he asked in the way that authority figures do, creating the appearance of a choice when there is only one acceptable option.

"I have to meet with coach," I lied. I expected Mr. Wilson to give me the same lecture about applying myself that I had heard from dozens of teachers and guidance counselors in the past, and I had no desire to listen to it again.

"It'll only take a second," he said, barely registering my lie, swatting it away like a fly. "This is important."

"Coach'll kill me if I'm late," I offered weakly, knowing it wouldn't work but trying anyway.

"You won't be," he assured me, as though he certainly knew I had no meeting.

I huffed. My shoulders dropped, and my eyes rose to the ceiling in a teenage tantrum that did nothing but make me look like a petulant child. I slowly turned back into the classroom and approached his desk. I didn't want to hear this again. "Work harder, apply yourself, go to college, the sky's the limit . . ." All the bullshit drivel adults tell children because if children found out the truth about life, the suicide rate for adolescents would skyrocket.

"Take a seat," he said, offering me a chair next to his desk. "Do you know why I asked you to stay?"

I didn't so much sit as deflate, the air exiting my nose in a slow, audible hiss. Finally, I plopped my backpack down with enough force to disrespect both the books inside and Mr. Wilson.

"No." The response was much terser than I intended, but rather than relent and apologize, I maintained my defiant posture. I knew why I was there; he knew why I was there. I didn't want to hear it again. I didn't want to go to college. I didn't want to apply myself. I didn't want to be a credit to my race. Mostly, I just wanted to sleep. Sixteen years as a black man in America, and I was already tired.

But Mr. Wilson didn't give me the same vacuous, pointless speech that everyone else did. He knew it was empty. Instead, he pulled out his grade book and laid it down with the scores facing me. I looked at it blankly.

"Do you see the problem?" he asked.

"No."

"Look harder," he said.

I scanned up and down the list: 484, 653, 545, 500, 360, 987, 570, 690, 713 . . .

987.

I got a 987 out of 1000. I was less proud of my marks than confused about why he felt the need to discuss them with me.

"I don't get it," I confessed.

"You got a nine hundred eighty-seven," he responded. "The highest in the class."

"So?" I felt my eyes narrow and my head pull back in an expression that revealed how perplexing I found our conversation. Who cares if it's the highest? There was no excuse for it being that low with all the tools he provided us.

"It's the highest by over two hundred points."

I still didn't understand.

"You got a nine hundred eighty-seven. Two scored in the seven hundreds. Everyone else was in the six hundreds or lower. Do you know what that means?" he asked.

"I got an A?"

"*Only* you got an A," he said. "In fact, your score is so high that if I count it, only two of your classmates will pass, and everyone else will fail."

Mr. Wilson continued, "Would it be okay with you if I removed your score from the curve, so the seven hundreds are As and the curve is bumped two hundred points. That way, the majority will pass?"

I was not expecting this. When he asked to meet with me, I had no idea he would put me in a position to determine the grades of my entire class. I also don't know why he felt the need to discuss this with me. It was his class, only he had access to the grades; had he just not counted my score and never told me, I would have been none the wiser. We'd have all passed, moved on to the twelfth grade, and been done with it.

But he didn't do that. Instead, he took it upon himself to offer me the choice, to decide the fate of the entire class.

He took it upon himself to teach me an important lesson about the world's expectations of black people.

SLIVER
Two Americas

Every black person in America gets
two educations.

The first comes in public
school. The three Rs—reading,
writing, 'rithmetic. Ever since
the Supreme Court outlawed the
separate-is-never-equal segregation
of the races with their decision
in *Brown v. Board of Education*
in 1964, black Americans have,
in theory, had access to the same
public school education as their
white counterparts. However, any
American who spends more than
two seconds researching the topic
will find school districts drawn
to resemble a Picasso painting,
redlining just as bad as during Jim
Crow, and the policy of funding
education through property
taxes ensuring that richer (read:
whiter) neighborhoods have
better schools. These practices
combine to make our schools just

as segregated and the education
just as unequal as any point in
history. But landmark events like
Brown v. Board of Education and
the Civil Rights Act allow white
citizens to ostrich their heads up
their asses while the less-privileged,
more melanin-rich of us get buried
in the shit. While the facilities may
be better, the instructors more
experienced, and the educational
tools newer in predominantly
white schools, in the eyes of the
law, all students, whether they
be black, white, Latinx, Asian,
or Native American, receive an
equal education in the American
public school system. Sure, many
of the extracurricular activities and
volunteer opportunities that elite
colleges require are only accessible
to the privileged few, but that's an
issue for another time. As far as the
government is concerned, as long
as we had the same books and
the teachers had the minimum
required credentials, the education
was the same.

The second education comes, if
you are fortunate, in school as well.

But it could come through

the criminal justice system. Some black people learn who they are when they are thirteen years old, and they get tried as adults for nonviolent crimes such as petty theft or possession of marijuana. Or maybe it comes at their job—when they arrive for their first day at work to learn they are the only black employee and are replacing the previous lone black employee. Or maybe it comes through the TV—when the only roles we see of ourselves are drug dealers and judges, the echoes of the lazy Negro of minstrel shows and the magical Negro who saves the day for white folks. All of these instances, these moments of bias and degradation, these moments of exclusion and isolation, serve the same purpose: to communicate to the world—both blacks and non-blacks—the spaces and roles that blacks can safely occupy.

"Safely" is critical here: black potential is limitless. We are as infinite and powerful as the universe: blacks can and have done and been everything from billionaire to president.

But the world has set limits for blackness.

Unfortunately, we live in a world that defines blackness as antagonistic to humanity. And in this world, blacks face unique obstacles to achievement. We also face unique obstacles once we achieve. White mediocrity and white villainy will tear down any black person who goes too far outside the lanes society prescribes.

Why do you think Oprah was on every tabloid in the 1980s?

Why do you think Obama got ripped worldwide for wearing a tan suit?

Why do you think MLB let steroids run rampant until a black dude started breaking records?

Narrow lanes. Nonblacks get the I-805 from San Diego to Los Angeles while black folks get the two-lane back road.

I learned the safe limits of black achievement through a school system ill-equipped to deal with black excellence. The modifier *black* serves multiple purposes in this phrase, *black excellence*. Upon the first instance, black is typically

interpreted as a term that modifies
the person achieving excellence—
excellence is absolute, and in this
case, the source happens to be
black. Upon further analysis, a
second, more insidious interpretation becomes clear—black can
also modify the word excellence.
Despite the supposed good intentions in distinguishing it from
other types of excellence, black excellence also serves to contextual-
ize the excellence through lowered
expectations created by historical
dominance and contemporary
oppression: black excellence exists
in the world as a denigrated form
of excellence, which positions
those who achieve it as a credit
to blackness but undeserving of
recognition by those who are not
black, as black excellence has a
narrow range. It signifies one's
position as the best of his kind but
still of another kind. And once a
black person reaches a threshold
of excellence that demands the
world drop the modifier black,
or if the nonblack world can no
longer exploit that excellence for
profit, then that excellence will

be challenged. Not through fair
competition, mind you, but by any
means necessary. As a black man,
you must always be good enough
to rise above your kind but never
good enough to rise above it in the
eyes of nonblacks.

I wallowed in this liminal
space—this treacherous sea—
between black excellence and
absolute excellence. The churning
waters relentlessly thrashed my
body, leaving me clutching desperately for a safe shore on either
side of the liquid abyss. On the
one side was black excellence: a
pedestal constructed by whiteness,
waiting for me to ascend its steep
pillar to serve as a shining example
of the Negro race. Achieving black
excellence allows nonblacks to
disregard their role in the struggle
that was my climb, to displace
their role in black oppression and
place the onus for black under-
achievement on those same backs
whose slave labor built this nation.
On the other side was the peak of
my abilities, rising like Vesuvius
above Pompeii, simultaneously an
awe-inspiring sight and ripe for

destruction. If I sought that shore, the world would have to confront the bad faith logic of black inferiority. Approaching Vesuvius was enough to make people question if maybe, just maybe, hey, maybe we aren't intrinsically different. Maybe there are socioeconomic and political barriers to stop blacks from equal achievement. Those questions, I knew, would not be answered with the sudden, concurrent enlightenment of the whole of humanity that needed antiblackness to survive. No. The world would answer those questions with my destruction. They would bomb Vesuvius, forcing the eruption inward, destroying black life and sparing Pompeii.

So I stay in the sea. But even the sea is treacherous. The current is strong, forcing me to fight twice as hard to not get ripped into the undertow. But if I push too hard and break through the surface, I get pummeled by the waves. As the tide surges, I have to kick harder to avoid being lost in the swirling eddy. But the breakers only gain in amplitude, their force felt deeper

and deeper into the sea, narrowing
the already thin flow where survival is possible. Such is black life
in this antiblack world.

Swimming in this sea, I learned
that there are no safe shores. There
is no safe space. Both coasts presented greater danger than simply
drowning, so I remained in the
sea of doubt, fighting the waves,
struggling to keep my head above
troubled waters. I still tread in this
liminal space where I have to be
better than everyone else to get
a shot and better than no one to
survive.

And you wonder why black folx
be tired all the time.

SHARD: 1
Status: Higher Learning

I experienced the reality of the unforgiving sea when I was twenty years old. I took the lessons learned in phase one, and I kicked and kicked as hard as I could against the currents. But even when I managed to break free from the tide and begin to make progress, the world tossed more flotsam and jetsam into my path, making the swim more difficult the closer I got to the shore. I knew I could go to college, but coming from inner-city San Diego High, my grades, test scores, and the few extracurricular activities which I had accessed would be unremarkable to any blue-chip undergraduate institution. On top of that, college applications are expensive—the first barrier to underprivileged students. It costs sixty to one hundred dollars for each application—a week of groceries for some families—to even take a shot at college.

The cost meant I had one bullet: Do I aim high and risk missing, leaving me aimless and unprotected going into the future? Or do I aim low, ensure myself a hit, and figure out the rest later? I chose the latter and fired my single seventy-five dollar bullet at San Diego State University whose admission equation dictated the acceptance of local students and guaranteed my entry.

I was woefully unprepared to attend college. Neither of my parents went to college, and my high school focused more on just getting students out of its doors than advancing them to a university. So I spent two years wandering aimlessly through a hastily assembled curriculum of whatever courses had room. After two years of college, I was closer to being kicked out for poor academic performance than I was to earning a degree. Before the clock on my academic probation struck midnight, however, I finally found a path. I found a reason to care and to continue in the university. I found what I thought would be my calling, or rather it found me.

In addition to my courses, I was working a shitty, minimum wage job at an on-campus sandwich shop. I don't say shitty to disparage the labor that millions of service employees engage in every day. I have had a couple of decent minimum wage jobs. But let's face it, the fight for a living wage implies that what these jobs currently pay is a dying wage, and no one should have to work forty hours a week to die. No, this job was particularly shitty because serving my fellow students had social consequences. In a place where I already felt out of place, reperforming the Confederate fantasy of black servile labor within the confines of this highly segregated institution was intolerable. I will never forget the shock that overtook each of my friends' faces whenever they would see me behind the counter slapping meat onto bread: "You work here?" They always spoke those three words, while their inflection informed me exactly how they valued the labor—and the people who performed it—that allowed their lives to function.

This job, however, is where my future path found me. One day, my direct supervisor, Ana, ask me an unexpected and peculiar question: "Have you ever considered, like, acting?"

I had not. At that point, at nineteen years old, I had never even read a play, let alone thought of performing in one. So I responded with a curt but not quite rude, "No."

Despite my apparent disinterest, Ana continued, "I'm a theater major, and I'm in this show, and the director needs a really big guy for a role. I told him I worked with this guy, and that I would ask you, so . . . I'm asking you."

At nineteen years old, I was close to my full-grown height of six feet five, and at the time I was topping four hundred pounds. I verbalized my disinterest more directly. "Not interested." A retort not forceful enough to knock her off track.

"Well, if I gave you the script, would you read it? And if you like it, at least come talk to him?" she pleaded. The tone of her voice triggered in me a primordial urge filtered through centuries of civility, causing me to relent for the most chauvinistic and objectifying of reasons: she was hot, and I thought if I said yes, she'd fuck me.

That never happened. Nonetheless, the play was like nothing I had ever read before. The work was an adaptation of Georg Büchner's *Woyzeck* by a woman named Naomi Iizuka, although, at the time, not a single word of that description held any meaning for me. But the play spoke to me; its narrative distorted by a fractured structure, much in the same way I had come to know myself. The play knew what it was. It also understood what audiences expected it to be. As such, it was smart enough to hide the work it was doing under levels of plausible deniability and interpretation. Its existence seemed to mirror my own in that both myself and this text recognized we were capable of great things while always remaining cognizant of the potential consequences of that greatness. It was a beautifully crafted work, right down to its title that aligned the play's metaconflicts with my own: *Skin*.

I agreed to meet with the director, Peter Cruz. I met Ana outside the back door of the Don Powell Theatre, and we walked in so she could introduce me. As Ana led me across the large proscenium stage, I was transported to a new world. Even though the stage had no set, I was surrounded by kinesthetic scenery in the form of the twenty plus members of the cast doing physical and vocal warm-ups. The empty auditorium echoed with the haunting sounds of vibratos and over-annunciated tongue twisters designed to stretch and relax the vocal apparatus. The diverse bodies swung and flailed through space with a freedom and lightness far from the droning repetition I encountered in my science classes and at the sandwich shop.

When we finally made it to Peter, Ana offered an introduction. "Hey, Peter! This is my friend Matt I was telling you about." Peter Cruz was a bear of a man, easily surpassing six feet in height with a stocky build hardened from years of labor and life. He, like me, was a former football player who decided that the wear and tear on his body was not worth the minuscule chance of a life-changing paycheck. On the day we met, as on most days, he was wearing a short-sleeve gingham shirt—the last remnants of his cholo days—and bracelets covering his forearms from his wrist to his elbows—an odd amalgam of his punk-rock past and his fatherhood present. His hair was age-inappropriate length, not because older people shouldn't have long hair, but because even though he was barely forty, the hair on top could no longer keep pace in length or thickness with that on the sides.

Peter unfolded himself from the thin, metal chair that sat behind a cheap plywood table serving as his director's perch, looked me dead in the eye, and said, "You're beautiful, man. If I was a dog, I'd hump your leg."

Before the shock of these words dissipated, Peter had begun maneuvering me across the room, making a beeline for a young woman who, although approaching graduation, betrayed her age with her lithe, slight frame. He positioned me behind her and stepped back, taking in the image like a sculptor who had just laid the last touches on his greatest masterpiece.

"That's perfect," he said, words that had never been uttered about my engorged frame and melanin-tainted skin.

"Hi," I sheepishly said to the young woman whose personal space I was suddenly invading, "I'm Matt."

"Hi, Matt. I'm Xochitl," she said.

"You're perfect, man," Peter said. "Why don't you stay for tonight, and if you like it, we'll get you in the show?"

"I don't know. I've never, like, acted or whatever *this* is," I said, signaling to the bodies flailing and flexing around me in conjunction with the machine-gun rhythm of "what a to-do to die today at a minute or two to two."

Xochitl placed her hand on my arm and gave me a kind smile. "I had never done it either, the first time," she said with a chuckle, proud of her double entendre.

With that smile and that chuckle, my icy uncertainty didn't melt away, but it certainly thawed.

"Okay," I said, "what do I do?"

What we did was a lot of running around an empty stage and pressing our bodies into the theater's walls in odd poses while imagining ourselves becoming a part of the architecture.

I still have no idea what we did at that rehearsal, but I fell in love. The constant unknowing of the situation. That was more challenging than anything I had encountered. I was great at school because 90 percent of what America considers "intelligence" is just memorization. I could read a book once and regurgitate with no problem the facts within. But exploring, risking—purposefully *not knowing* so that you were free to explore—that was the real challenge. Engaging the world and myself with no intent toward answers, but instead finding pleasure in the search. Acting was a better reflection of how I had come to understand my own life and my struggles with blackness than anything I had ever encountered.

I returned to that theater every night for the next six weeks, even when I wasn't called to rehearsal. I would just sit and watch and learn. And not from some book. And not what someone thought I should know. But instead, I sat in the theater and moved closer to understanding who and what I was.

More than anything, I craved the belonging. I would sit in the ancient, fold-down Don Powell Theatre seats and watch my cast-mates work scenes and ask questions, constantly aware that if I waited long enough, someone's scene work would end, and they'd come to sit next to me. We'd whisper together about our days and our lives and the work being done onstage. From the lead actor to the assistant stage manager, everyone made me feel welcome and accepted, a feeling that had so often eluded me growing up in predominantly white Appalachia. Although many of these relationships lasted no longer than the span of the show we were working on, the momentary connections forced upon us by casting choices felt more complete and more real than the hollow performances of family that permeated my childhood.

Finally, in my fourth semester of undergrad, I was ready to declare a major: acting. Little did I know that my theater education would be so *educational*—although a brief look at a list of mainstream films should have been more than enough to prepare me for the challenges my skin would present in my newly chosen profession. I didn't know, however, that the same structures that create roadblocks to media representation would be an obstacle in my classrooms.

The same director who provided my first foray into theater would also offer my next important lesson on black life in America. In addition to teaching acting and directing, Peter also taught a class ridiculously named "Theatre of Diversity." Just the name alone signals to academia's reluctance to engage with nonwhite, nonmale voices. I can imagine how it came to be:

Lights up. The PROVOST's office.
The PROVOST sits behind a desk made of the cash
being hoarded in the endowment instead of being given
to improve the educational experience of the students.

MINORITY PROFESSORS enter.

> MINORITY PROFESSORS
> Every class focuses on white men.

> PROVOST
> Not every class. Math focuses on numbers.

The MINORITY PROFESSORS stand in stupefied silence at the pure caucasity of the PROVOST's response.

> PROVOST
> Check. Mate.

An ASSISTANT VICE PROVOST IN CHARGE OF DIVERSITY, EQUITY, AND INCLUSION enters stage left and sweeps the MINORITY PROFESSORS off the stage with a broom made of red tape and shredded diversity reports.

WHITE PROFESSORS enter.

> WHITE PROFESSORS
> Hey, Provost, the fact that our classes are full of white men, both as students and materials, is starting to make us feel bad because it reveals our role in maintaining systemic oppression.

> PROVOST
> You're right. How do we fix it?

> WHITE PROFESSORS
> Let's make a class with black, Latinx, Indigenous, LGBTQ, and Asian voices.

PROVOST

Okay. We will balance that curriculum, giving every voice equal weight.

WHITE PROFESSORS

Whoa, now! Let's not be hasty. We said "*a* class." We want just enough to make us feel good, not enough to help them.

PROVOST

That's brilliant! We can look progressive and woke to those outside these hallowed halls while continuing to reinforce white cisgender patriarchy inside. So let it be written, so let it be done.

The all-white collection of the PROVOST and the WHITE PROFESSORS hold up a banner that says "DIVERSITY MAKES THE WORLD GO ROUND." They then face the audience and bow to rapturous applause.

And that was what SDSU did. The theater curriculum included dozens of courses that only read plays and performed plays by white playwrights and only showed films by white directors with white actors. The department had zero black faculty members. Both of these features are standard for college theater departments around the country. The sole blemish of nonwhite thoughts and bodies and experiences was consolidated indistinctly as "Theatre of Diversity." Despite the ridiculous name, the content was expansive and engaging. For the first time, I took a class where the materials we read came from people whose origins were closer to my own. The readings were far more relatable than the standard repetition of the "Great White Men of History" the previous thirteen years of my education had force-fed me. I read works by Cherríe Moraga, Langston Hughes,

Suzan-Lori Parks, David Henry Hwang—artists and visionaries whose excellence was so immense that it precluded the possibility of any racial modifier. I took to these works and produced the most thought-provoking, politically challenging, and intellectually engaging work I ever created. I looked forward to getting assignments back with comments and discussions of where I could take them next. A after A after A-plus on every single project.

My final grade in the course was an A-minus.

When you are black, the equation changes: A-plus A-plus A-plus A-plus equals . . . A-minus? I had never before in my life questioned a grade: who cares if I am only average at learning another people's history and another people's knowledge? I approached the professor, Peter, with a mixture of rage and confusion. Although he is Chicano and I am black, we ran many of the same races and jumped many of the same hurdles, so why was he making them higher? Shouldn't he know what it's like to have the system put up obstacles to your success?

"How did I get an A-minus?" I demanded.

He responded with life-changing truth. "You did some of the best work in the class," Peter said. "But I feel like you didn't push yourself hard enough, and in this industry, as a minority, just being better isn't enough. You gotta work twice as hard for half the opportunities."

He had moved the goalposts because of my skin. The dream, myths, and narratives of America—bootstraps and land of opportunity—ceased being motivation and became obstacles. I thought I was playing the game correctly. But the game is not so simple for blacks. I thought my obstacles were being a first-generation student and from a lower-class family, but I was fighting to overcome these roadblocks to access an opportunity and the world changed the playing field. But not for everyone. Although we all began playing the same game and striving for the same goalposts, the goalposts moved farther and farther into the distance as I got closer. Soon, I found that although I had left my classmates in the dust, they had all reached the end zone and I was no closer to the goal line. The dimensions stretched farther into the distance with each step I took. The obstacle, I came to realize, was not my place in the world—the obstacle was not systemic inequality and access—the obstacle was the world itself: an antiblack world that pathologizes blackness to the point that it will alter itself to keep us in our place. I came to realize I had been resisting the wrong things.

I had no response.

I stormed out of Peter's office, filled with a rage that lasted down the hallway and the stairs and out past the green benches where theater students would gather for lunch and between classes. My anger clashed with the joyous cacophony of performative exuberance produced by classmates who took Shakespeare's proclamation that "all the world's a stage" a bit too literally and would dance and sing and recite monologues for no one in particular but for anyone and everyone in general. I never broke stride as the wake of my egress thrust a pall over the usual energy of the benches, bringing it all to a standstill, their performative joy no match for my legitimate anger.

I was halfway across campus before the anger began to subside. As the raw emotion started to drain, the heat left my face, and I was newly filled, at first with calm rationality and later with gratefulness. Peter was right. I knew he was right. "Twice as hard for half the opportunities." The words rattled through my head and down my spine, eventually settling in my feet and bringing them to a halt on the newly constructed footbridge over College Avenue. Standing there, on the pristine white concrete above the used book store and taco shop that catered to the predominantly white student population with its "American Guacamole," I realized I wasn't angry at him. Peter Cruz had done nothing outside of the world's truth. No, I wasn't mad at him. I wasn't even mad at the world that always qualified my experience and dismissed my accomplishments. Instead, I was angry at myself, disappointed in myself, for needing the lesson spelled out for me like I was a child.

Every black person receives two educations. The first is in the facts and figures derived from and describing the Great White Men of History: Thomas Jefferson, Henry Ford, Dwight Eisenhower. The second is where we, as blacks, exist for and in relation to antiblackness. These two curricula work hand in hand: the first informs us of what is possible, and the second tells us for whom it is possible.

America taught me my place even earlier, but I was too young to
fully learn the lesson it was teaching.

I was in the third grade. We were discussing history.

The Civil War.

The birth of the state.

1861.

West Virginia breaks from Virginia and joins the Union.

They fight against the Confederacy.

They fight against slavery.

Yet, within this context, the teacher felt it necessary to say,

"Not all slaves were treated poorly. Some slaves appreciated being
taken care of by their masters."

I was one of two black kids in the class.

We looked at each other, unsure of what we heard, but knowing
innately it wasn't right.

Now I know what I heard:

"If they can be happy being slaves, isn't not being a slave enough?"

Isn't the progress enough?

Don't you have enough?

The question often goes unspoken in discussions of black progress.

"You have to acknowledge the progress."

"You have to acknowledge things are better."

"Don't you have enough?"

No.

I don't.

Progress is not enough.

Better is not enough.

I want what you have.

And as long as there is a difference, I will never have enough.

FACET: 2

Age: 16
Location: Mr. Wilson's Classroom
Status: Head of the Class

I wonder if Mr. Wilson remembers my response.

"Would it be okay with you if I removed your score from the curve, so the seven hundreds are As and the curve is bumped two hundred points? That way, the majority will pass?" he asked.

With great power comes great responsibility. At that moment, Mr. Wilson had given me great power. He gave me the ability to decide my classmates' futures. San Diego High School is an ethnically diverse, although economically less so, inner-city school. And like many inner-city schools, many of its students teetered on the brink. From my experience there, many of them live with the impression that they will never amount to anything and that the purpose of their time in school is primarily to allow their parents time to work. During my three plus years at San Diego High, I saw friends leave and not come back for too many reasons to remember. From teen pregnancy to quitting school to working so they could support a drug-addicted father or their little brothers and sisters to being stabbed at a McDonald's in a gang-related incident, I saw countless friends not return to class. A single F would be excuse enough to lean into their insecurities and out of their education for many of my classmates.

I was one of the lucky few who began his education on what it meant to be black while in school, relatively late to the lesson, where the stakes for refusing to accept the lesson were devoid of actual consequence. Now, with twenty years of life and experience to reflect on the moment, I realize that Mr. Wilson was teaching me about black life. About community. About sacrifice. But also about how to protect myself in an antiblack world. He taught me that, as a black man, I could only be good enough not to make white people uncomfortable.

This time, the shattering was not instantaneous. I did not splinter and crumble into thousands of pieces immediately upon impact. No. This time, the rending was slow and torturous as the burden shifted onto me. Now, I navigated the sea, the weight of my classmates on my shoulders, forced to choose at which ports to leave pieces of myself. Although Mr. Wilson aided me in charting a course before the journey began, ultimately, the decision between holding on to my achievements, my capabilities, myself, and choosing to set them adrift in the ether for the benefit of others was mine alone. It was a choice where both options made the "me" that remained less than the "me" that began. Either in my eyes or in the eyes of my teacher and classmates, I would be less than when I began.

With the fate of my entire class resting on my shoulders, I made the only choice I could.

"Let them fail," I said.

Like a Roman emperor standing over the gladiator pit at the end of a contest, I chose blood over mercy. By doing so, I stayed true to myself. The world should recognize my accomplishments for what they were, and maybe knowledge of them would inspire my classmates to give half a damn about their education. I chose to let them fail. I could see that this response was unexpected; Mr. Wilson expected compassion and mercy. He expected sacrifice. He expected me to pass his test, to choose community over accolades. He didn't try to hide his disappointment. His head dropped and slowly shook from side to side.

"Okay. If that's what you want," he sighed disappointedly.

But Mr. Wilson had one more lesson to teach me.

When report cards came out the following week, most of the class had passed. Despite offering me the choice, Mr. Wilson disregarded my wishes and discounted my score. I was livid. I looked at Mr. Wilson with disgust. Why would he do this? At the moment, I thought Mr. Wilson was a coward, afraid to give out well-deserved Fs. He was scared to explain to students that they failed.

Regardless of his intentions, Mr. Wilson taught me more in that one moment than all my other high school teachers combined taught me over four years. Mr. Wilson taught me that society didn't care what I wanted. He taught me that if I am too much better than my peers, the world will ignore my work to spare the feelings of others. He taught me that the world values the feelings of nonblacks over the actions done by and to blackness. He also taught me that as a black man, the world expects me to sacrifice myself for the good of the community, a community that thrives on my exile. At that moment, Mr. Wilson taught me a lesson that I have carried for decades.

Mr. Wilson taught me the place of blackness in an antiblack world.

Looking back, I am not so sure I took the correct lessons from the moment. Perhaps, Mr. Wilson made a choice not to be the nail in so many educational coffins. Maybe, he wanted to teach me humility and leadership and selflessness—letting my classmates pass would cost me nothing—my A didn't mean less because others got them as well. My work didn't change. My value didn't change. Nothing changed except others would have an opportunity to succeed. Perhaps he was trying to teach me that I can be a credit to the black race without leaving behind the black race. Perhaps he was trying to introduce the notion of the Talented Tenth into my world view, trying to teach me that I need to use my excellence to uplift others, not put them down.

Perhaps, he was teaching me how to take steps to make the black world and the antiblack world into one world.

Perhaps, the lessons on antiblackness that I took in the moment were not so black and white.

FRAGMENT 6

FACET: 1

Age: 20
Location: San Diego State University
Status: Hard Truths

"Lose a hundred pounds."
    That was not the answer I was expecting.

FACET: 2

Age: 20
Location: San Diego State University
Status: Lemme Back Up a Sec

Once I changed my major to theater, I began introducing myself to
department faculty, asking each of them the same question: "What
do I need to do to make it in this industry?"

The responses I received were strangely reminiscent of a video
game quest. Each professor offered their unique take on the question that matched their personality. The first professor I asked was
the department's undergraduate advisor. She was an amazing woman,
not only for her professional credits but also for her ability to advise
dozens of young adult drama students. She would have been well
within her rights to strangle any one of us for the ridiculous troubles
we brought to her doorstep, but she was far too graceful and patient
ever to offer anything more than sound advice and a smile. Her grace
was almost intimidating. I had a sense that if she ever did reach the
end of her rope, she could destroy us all. My advisor offered practical means for pursuing a career in performance by introducing me to
resources such as ARTSEARCH and *Backstage West*.

The next professor on my journey offered wisdom that matched
his age and his philosophical approach to life. He was the son of
an Englishman, raised in an African colony. This worldly experience instilled in him a perspective that was an odd combination of
thoughtful optimism and naive pessimism: "Don't worry about it,"

he said in his British accent. "No one makes it in this industry. So don't worry about making it—worry about making art. Be guided by passion, not money."

My journey of inquiry was becoming a strange fairy tale. Knowledge and passion. A brain and a heart. All I needed were ruby slippers, and I'd be off to the other side of the rainbow. But I soon learned that this building was concrete, not emerald, and the road to it was black asphalt and not yellow brick. And the man who sat in the corner office on the exterior wall overlooking the small, gravel courtyard with its green benches and trees was no Wizard of Oz.

As I sat crammed into the thin-framed metal chair, feeling its structural integrity bow under my weight, I asked the same question of the Oz-like professor that I posed to the others for what I later discovered would be the last time. "What do I need to do to make it in this industry?"

Instead of offering a way home, this wizard pointed out that my desire to make it wouldn't be as easy as clicking my heels together, as the real world offered no ruby slippers.

"Here's a question—how many people like you do you see on TV? Outside of bouncers and henchmen?" they asked.

Loads, I thought. Will Smith, Malcolm Jamal Warner, Chris Tucker, Eddie Murphy, Morgan Freeman, Don Cheadle—dozens of black men were in leading roles, and hundreds more were making a living in the background.

However, their comments were not racial but instead referred to my other distinguishing characteristic: my weight. "If you want me to be completely honest," they said, "you need to lose a hundred pounds or so."

The fantasy of emerald cities organized by a grid of golden brick disappeared in a puff of cold, hard reality. This was no wizard—this was the formerly Cowardly Lion who'd found the courage to give me the truth. Not only would the color of my flesh mean I had to work twice as hard for half the opportunities, but the volume of my flesh meant that the remaining half of opportunities would be bifurcated further. The girth that had been an asset on the football field would be detrimental to a career onstage and on-screen.

I was shocked. I didn't expect this level of candor in an academic setting, but I also recognized that they were right. There weren't, and still aren't, four hundred something pound people on TV or in film.

I don't wish to incriminate the professor who made these comments, so I won't use their name or gender their pronouns. But, this was a different time. A time where this type of "honesty," although fatphobic in any era, was all a part of the process. "Break them down before you build them up," "prepare them for the real world," and all the other bullshit clichés society uses to justify and normalize students bullying students. Now, twenty years later, our society is finally recognizing that these comments and methods are actually abuse, and theater programs nationwide are rightfully raked through the coals for body-shaming young men and women. But at the time, I didn't know enough to take offense, and I remain in contact with this individual to this day.

You could even say they saved my life.

SLIVER

The Great White Way

Theater saved my life.

I don't mean that metaphorically. I don't mean in an "I found myself and my passion and a reason to live" bullshit way that narratives of underdogs and outcasts often moralize about. I did not find a home in the theater. Sure, I found some friends, and sure, I found a career, but the two institutions that provide both my fiscal and communal support are so antiblack that I don't know if a black man can ever truly find a home.

Theater as a discipline and industry likes to consider itself a bastion of liberal inclusivity. In this place, the tired and poor outcasts, yearning for inclusion, can find a home. And while the theater can be an island of misfit toys, it is, for the most part, exclusive of nonwhite races. And while all

nonwhite races suffer in this primarily white institution, theater is
particularly harsh for black artists.

While American theater is so
much more than the hallowed
boards of the Broadway houses,
that monument to consumerism
in performance offers data that re-
flects the industry as a whole. The
first Broadway musical premiered
in 1866, and since then, 11,328
shows have graced its stages.
Across all of these productions,
there have been only twenty-one
black directors. And there have
been more black directors than
any of the other creator or designer
roles.

The "Great White Way" is de-
scriptive in more ways than one.

FACET: 3

Age: 20–21
Location: San Diego State University
Status: Losing It

I took this professor's advice as a challenge. One hundred pounds. At the time of that meeting, I assumed I weighed between four hundred thirty and four hundred fifty pounds. I assumed because I couldn't find a scale that measured above four hundred. When I stood on it, the scale returned a hurtful "error" message, as though my body was some grotesque mistake not worthy of measuring.

But one hundred pounds wouldn't be enough. Twice as good for half the opportunities. To prove to myself and everyone else that I was serious about this industry, I determined to surpass one hundred pounds.

But I knew very little about dieting and fitness. I knew how to lift weights from my days playing football, and I learned about cardio, but I didn't know any of the science. I didn't understand macronutrients or calorie counters. I didn't know the different effects of various exercise protocols on the human body—steady-state cardio versus weights versus high intensity interval training. I just knew that to lose weight, I had to burn more than I consumed.

That knowledge was just enough to be dangerous. I started going to the gym twice a day. I would do an hour of weights and an hour of cardio in the morning, followed by two hours of cardio in the gap between work and rehearsals. Add this to my classes and my job at the sandwich shop, and I managed to get about three hours of sleep a night.

During this time of four-hour workouts, a part-time job, rehearsal, and eighteen class units, I limited my calorie intake to two protein shakes and a bowl of cereal each day—about eight hundred calories total. My body and my brain couldn't handle it, and I shouldn't have tried. But I fought through, even though I was a wracked, tired mess constantly. I was an exhausted, anxious, irritable zombie, shuffling from space to space, thinking of nothing but all the food I couldn't eat. I would sit in my classes, unable to pay attention, literally shaking from hunger. I found myself falling asleep during rehearsals. I knew this was unhealthy, but instead of asking for help or advice from friends, I sought help from a pharmacy. I began taking caffeine pills, often popping three or four at a time like Tic Tac. They didn't help my focus, but they at least kept me awake and allowed me to function.

Before I could cause irreparable damage to my body, the calendar saved me. The school year came to an end. With a path and a passion in the theater, I raised the previous semester's borderline dropout 1.7 GPA to a spot on the Dean's List. Not because theater lacked intellectual rigor, far from it, but because theater was the first thing I found interesting enough to give my full attention and energy.

That summer, I got my first job that was neither servile nor custodial. On the advice of the theater department's new office manager, Mark, I applied at a temp agency, who placed me in an office job within the health-care industry. I processed documents for ISO 9000 certification. I had no idea what any of it meant. All I know is that it was my job to copyedit and format papers for laboratory processes, place them in a blue envelope with a circulation order, then route those documents to the correct people for approval. Once they made their comments, I would reformat the documents accordingly, place them in a red folder, and circulate them to the same people for final approval. It was precisely as mindless, tedious, and insufferable as the previous four sentences. For this, they paid me eighteen dollars per hour, more than double the eight dollars I had made at the sandwich shop.

The mindless nature of the job was perfect. It allowed me to focus more energy on my weight loss. I began doing research. I talked to friends, one of whom was an amateur bodybuilder, and he helped me plan a diet. I was shocked at how much food I should have been eating this whole time. Granted, it was bland, repetitive food as, when contest prepping, bodybuilders tend to subsist purely on boiled chicken, plain oatmeal, and broccoli, with only small amounts of olive oil or peanut butter for fats. But six days a week, I joylessly shoveled down pounds of this tasteless, pleasureless sustenance and dreamed of my coming cheat day—visions of carne asada fries and ice cream dancing in my head. I began working out each morning with my friend, Arnold, who would later be involved in a police encounter with me, serve as a groomsman at my wedding, and is still one of my best friends. I kept going to the gym twice a day, but I decreased the time and upped the intensity, replacing my long, steady slogs on the treadmill with interval training and plyometrics.

Throughout my training, I never measured my progress on a scale. I didn't need to. I could find all the evidence of progress that I needed in my wardrobe and my body. I saw my 4XL shirts and fifty-six-inch-waist pants begin to hang off me. Day by day, little by little, I noticed changes in my body. One month in, I had to buy a new belt as the old one didn't have a hole that would allow me to fasten it and maintain its purpose. Three months in, the rolls of fat that hung from the sides of my chest had melted away enough that I had actual armpits for the first time in my life. Six months in, I needed to purchase new clothes in unmodified large and sub-forty-inch pants.

Six months after being told to lose one hundred pounds, I stepped on a scale at the gym for the first time. A number flashed twice then solidified. The machine had to be broken. I stepped off, unplugged it, plugged it back in, and stepped again. Two flashes, solid, a mistake. I sheepishly approached Jamal, a high-energy black man that Arnold and I would have brief conversations with between sets, and asked if he would test the scale for me. He agreed, stepped on, and ensured its accuracy.

I stepped again. Two hundred forty-two pounds.

I had lost close to two hundred pounds.

I returned to school in the fall a new man.

My weight no longer limited my acting roles to background roles and character work. At six feet five, two hundred forty-two pounds, I was similar in build to Will Smith and Vince Vaughan. I could now be a leading man. I wasn't the only one who noticed my transformation. I was the talk of the department. More than once, I walked down the hall, and my passing presence would bring conversations to an abrupt halt. They were talking about me. While I received my fair share of genuine compliments and congratulations, I was also subject to rumors ranging from surgery to illness to drug use.

None of it mattered. I had proved all of my silent doubters wrong. I did twice the work, and with it, the opportunities increased. I appeared in numerous main-stage shows at the university, from Warren Leight's *Side Man* to the title role in *Macbeth*. People invited me to parties. I had friends. I had a direction. For the first time in my life, everything was going my way.

I made my first suicide attempt during that school year.

ABSENCE
Status: Too much.

In October 2020, the *Los Angeles Times* asked forty black
playwrights to discuss their experiences in theater.
I don't know what is sadder:
That they only found forty willing to talk,
Or that so many of these forty had similar stories.

"'We love your work, but we can't produce it. What else do you
have?' I heard that over and over again; it was so frustrating and
made me doubt myself. What I think they meant was, 'Do you have
any plays with white people in them? Or will help our white patrons
feel better about being white?'"—Radha Blank

"'I love your work, but I just don't have the courage to do it.' This
white man . . . was othering me and essentially saying, 'I like black
people, but you can't work here because I'm too afraid of your
blackness.'"—Robert O'Hara

"They asked me, 'Which one do you really want to do?' I picked the
latter, which centered on the black southern female experience.
They said, 'We think what's best for us—and possibly for you—is
the play about the white woman. It sounds hilarious! We could get
Julia Louis-Dreyfus!'"—Katori Hall

"I'll never forget one of my first meetings about my play, when I was
told by a white producer, 'I don't know if a story about seven black

men is commercial enough . . . ' In that moment, I was told that the black voice is not the standard, that stories from my community are not human stories. And we have to water down our blackness to cross over to a 'wider audience' because being authentically us is not enough to do so."—Keenan Scott II

"It was my senior year at New York University; I had a playwriting thesis class with one of my best friends, also a black femme playwright. Our professor, a white woman, often confused us for each other, and even went so far as to email us the other's script notes. We look nothing alike, nor were our plays similar in terms of theme, structure or story.
But none of that seemed to matter.
"Reflecting back, I realized we were being lumped together into the monolith that is 'the black play.'"—Francisca Da Silveira

Over and over: too much, too authentic.
Too black.
Real black.
Not the black that white producers sell to audiences.
Not the black that white publishers sell to readers.
Not the black the world wants, but all of the ways we can be black in this world.
Too much of us, and the world doesn't want it.
Or can't believe it.
Or is afraid of it.
The world wants black flesh.
Not black voices.

Not black minds.
Not black life.
Not blackness.

Now, think about what I had to go through for you
to be able to read this book.

SHARD: 1
Status: Going Home

I love the ocean. From the time I got my first car at the age of twenty, I would often drive to the beach. Dead of night, dead of winter—it didn't matter. I love the feel: the gentle heat of the sun; the raising of the hairs on my arms with the passing of the wind; the light buoyancy of the water; the coarse, shifting firmness of the sand—no other location provides such a diverse and all-consuming sensory immersion. I love the sound, the way the breeze and the crashing of the waves combine to transform the world into a living white noise machine. I love the smell, the salt in the air, the blend of plant life and sunscreen. I embraced everything the ocean offered: I learned to swim, kayak, surf, and, most importantly, relax.

I don't know what triggered it. Perhaps it was just the growing dis-ease and disease of living. What was the point? I got in shape. I got the roles I wanted. I got friends. I got everything I had worked for. And I still wasn't happy. I knew what depression was, but black folks learn from a young age not to discuss mental health. "We're strong. We're survivors. We resist. The overwhelming sadness and exhaustion is just a part of livin', and to make it in this world, you gotta be stronger than that." In addition to the cultural stigma around mental health, I feared discussing the topic because of the horrid interactions I had with my mother around the subject. So instead, I got my education on depression from popular culture. I knew it from after-school specials and teen dramas as the quiet boy dressed in black who sat at the back of the class. I knew it as songs by the Cure and My Chemical

Romance, as poetry and paintings and lyrics. Each of those portrayals contains an overwhelming malaise and sadness.

I didn't think I was depressed because instead of feeling overwhelming sadness, I felt nothing at all. I wasn't quite numb. Numb implies that I was not capable of feeling. I recognized where emotions should be and what I should feel, but I didn't care enough to feel them. Instead, an overwhelming apathy governed my world, replacing my joy, my pain, my love, my sorrow—everything—with shades of gray. I wasn't sad; I was empty. I was so hollow that I could feel my guts sink on every exhale, falling deeper and deeper while trying to remain close to my heart. Every waking second had become a blend of panic and despair that accompanies an unexpected 2:00 a.m. phone call from a family member—probably not good news, but was it so bad that it couldn't wait till later?

I had nights like this before—nights where I was too restless to sleep but too tired to be productive. Most of these nights, I'd lie in bed with my eyes closed, concocting strange scenarios in my head, trying to lull myself back into sleep. I'd pretend to be in a coma. Or, perhaps, hiding under the bed from robbers. Anything enough to give my mind a focus away from the evil thoughts and to encourage myself not to toss and turn. On some nights, I would get out of bed seeking distraction, usually by writing or walking. This night, however, I got in my car and drove nowhere in particular.

In high school, before the Southern California gas prices soared above four dollars and ended our endeavors, my friends and I would often engage in what we called "Zen Driving." When we were bored, we would get in the car, and wherever we ended up is where we were meant to be. Of course, I didn't have a car at that time. So all of us football players—Brent, Frankie, Cruz, and Sumu—would cram ourselves into Philip's old white Ford Taurus, which we affectionately called "Lunchbox," and blast Sublime or Hoobastank through the car's three working speakers. If all of us were present, Brent would have to ride in the trunk, the rest of us too large to fit three in the back seat. Sometimes, we'd hear an ad on the radio, or we'd drive past a sign that would suddenly inspire us with a destination. Other times, we'd just go down roads we'd never been down before and see where they took us.

This night, however, I was alone. Brent, Frankie, Philip, Cruz, and Sumu were all younger than me by at least a year. Some of them were still in high school, and others had gone off to jobs or other colleges. I hopped into my blueberry Honda Accord alone, turned on Fuel's "Hemorrhage (In My Hands)," and started driving.

This night, as it turns out, I was meant to be at the beach. I parked my car next to the rollercoaster at Mission Beach, and my senses became overstimulated. My subconscious was trying to take in as much of life as possible before the ending that my conscious mind couldn't fully comprehend. My mouth watered as I crossed the parking lot, the smell of burritos emanating from the taco shop on the corner. To my right were the bright colors and cheesy slogans of San Diego tourist T-shirts and the dull browns and grays of trinkets covered in seashells. I walked across the concrete boardwalk that separated the city from the beach, through the sand, and into the ocean.

I waded until my feet couldn't touch the bottom. An overwhelming apathy overtook my senses, and I could not feel if the water was cold or warm. I only know that it was more blissful and more accepting than anything I left behind on the land. I began to float, drifting in the surf, waiting for the sea to take me. Finally, a wave came and dragged me under the surface, foreclosing on what I thought would be my last breath. And as I hovered beneath the surface, not knowing up from down, I closed my eyes in the loving embrace of the sea.

I didn't want to die that night, but I no longer wanted to live. I can't speak for anyone else, but I never found that the psychological survey to test for depression addressed how I felt or what I experienced. The survey asks if you have thoughts that you would be better off dead. I don't recall ever thinking that I would be better off dead, but rather the opposite—I often found myself not caring if I lived.

However, the panic I felt in that brief moment, not knowing if I would die, made me feel alive.

The air left my lungs. I was suddenly kicking and thrashing against the tide, but I had no idea in what direction I should push. My chest began to burn as my arms and legs pulled the last bits of oxygen from my lungs.

I went back to school the following week as though nothing had happened. I went to my classes. I went to work and rehearsal. I hung out at the green benches outside the building, cracked jokes, laughed, and made stupid videos. I went back to my life as though everything was okay.

But it wasn't.

Theater saved my life, but it didn't make me alive.

FRAGMENT 7

FACET: 1

Age: 28
Location: La Jolla, CA
Status: Token

Everything came at once. Rage. Confusion. Arguments. Questions. I had cruised through the first year of my doctoral program, but now, suddenly, the brakes of my soul engaged. My spine shivered. My stomach became a bottomless pit as my insides lurched, attempting to stop the emotions and thoughts that were careening wildly through my mind. The screeching tires froze me in my tracks, and I gritted my teeth, hoping that the inevitable would not come.

Crrrsssshhhhh-sshhnnnkkkk

And there it was. Blindsided. A metaphorical collision at highway speeds between who I was and what I had accomplished and *this* professor's prejudice and assumptions of blackness. He stepped from the devastation unscathed. I found myself once again picking up the pieces.

I had just begun my second year at UC San Diego. Because their academic calendar used quarters instead of semesters, the school year started later than I was used to. From kindergarten through my master's, I always returned to class long before the calendar flipped to September. But here at UCSD, the start of the fall term came in late September. The beautiful, crisp coastal air drifted up the seaside cliffs from La Jolla Shores and over the campus of UCSD. However, this ocean breeze could not break the stale, stuffy air of Professor

Bosch's office. Despite the floor-to-ceiling windows, the office still managed to be dim. Hundreds and hundreds of books filled with dated, faded pages refused to be a reflective accomplice to the sun-lined walls. Their slow decay contributed to the mustiness of the space.

We were discussing my teaching assignment for the upcoming quarter. For the first time, I would not be one of a group of teaching assistants for the undergraduate theater history sequence. Instead, I would begin progressing through the teacher training sequence most PhD students followed, and I would be teaching my own section of TDHT 10—Introduction to Script Analysis. I still don't know why the department called it "Introduction," as there was no subsequent advanced course.

I would teach twenty students how to analyze the structures of four plays from the Western canon: Beckett's *Waiting for Godot*, Ibsen's *A Doll House*, Suzan-Lori Parks's *The America Play*, and Shakespeare's *Much Ado About Nothing*. While being a theater history TA was a valuable experience, my primary responsibility was grading papers. Play Analysis would afford me some freedom and the opportunity to develop as a teacher. But not too much liberty—the department meticulously curated the course content into a forty-page handbook that included detailed daily lesson plans, lecture outlines, and all of the in-class activities, assignments, and grading rubrics.

"So," Dr. Bosch said, "when you teach *Godot*, we have two film versions that you can show clips of—and we also have two for *A Doll House*; one is this really cool avant-garde version!"

"Awesome!" I said, externally mimicking his enthusiasm, but in all truth, not caring a lick about our current conversation. Honestly, I didn't see the need—I had the handbook, I could read, and I knew his email and office number if I had questions.

"And we don't really like teaching *Much Ado*, but it has the double plot we need to teach, plus, we have to teach a Shakespeare."

"Of course," I echoed, hoping to end the meeting as soon as possible. The day was beautiful, and I wanted to get to the beach before the after-work crowd showed up to vulture the parking spots and the waves.

"And then we do *The America Play*. I bet you'll have something to say about that!"

For just a flash, less than a blink, I swear I saw the sunlight streaming into the overstuffed office from the lofty windows of his office dim. Why *The America Play*? Why would *I* have something to say about that? *I* was a Shakespearean. *I* had two master's degrees in Shakespeare studies. *I* had played Macbeth and Aaron. *I* had written a thesis on black actors in the Renaissance, the meat of which I would publish as an article. *I* was a Shakespeare scholar.

But Dr. Bosch didn't assume I'd have something to say about *Much Ado About Nothing*. No, at this moment, in this professor's eyes, my experience said far less about my knowledge than my skin tone ever could. Instead, he assumed I'd have something to say about *The America Play* by Suzan-Lori Parks, the only script of the four studied in the course by a nonwhite playwright, who in this case was black.

I began to rationalize his words in the way the world trains us to—to give the white man the benefit of the doubt. The thoughts overlapped as I justified his prejudice to myself:

He isn't racist; this is nothing more than a man of a certain age whose entire upbringing occurred in the shadow of civil rights; he meant nothing by it; this is his best, although admittedly sad, attempt to relate to me as a black man.

But a question gnawed at my generosity. At first, the inquiry just took beastly little nibbles. As our conversation continued, however, the bites became bigger and began eating away at my dissonance. Afraid that Dr. Bosch might see this creature flickering in my iris, I turned my gaze to the books on the shelves. I had to silence the monster before the question escaped my lips: Would I be here without the *Compton Cookout*?

SLIVER
Sho Good Eatin'

Ah, the Compton Cookout. In the spring before I enrolled at UCSD, a fraternity hosted a derogatorily themed party that displayed the antiblack underpinnings of the entire collegiate Greek system to the world. This entirely white fraternal institution thought it would be funny to advertise and conduct a party in modern-day blackface: the invitation called for participants to wear ghetto clothing (whatever that means), bring fried chicken and watermelon, and drink forty-ounce bottles of "black" malt liquors: Colt 45, Steel Reserve, and Mickey's. Upon learning of this racist fiasco, black students at UCSD (about two hundred among the student body of thirty thousand) organized in opposition to the party and the university's toothless response to it. In lieu of an apology, the black students received threats such as the Dr. Seuss statue outside of the famous Geisel Library donning a noose.

So how could the university maintain its reputation while also maintaining its racism? Not by doing the obvious—punishing the white perpetrators for their crimes against blackness. Of course not. Instead, the university increased recruitment and admissions for minority students. Instead of dealing with the danger, the university decided to put more black people in the line of fire.

"Would I be here without the Compton Cookout?" Of course, it was not this exact question that gnawed at my mind in moments and places where I questioned my belonging, but always some variation of the phylum within which that question is classified: What am I doing here? Do I belong?

I knew I didn't belong. Not here. Not in this institution built by colonizers and slaveowners on top of land colonized and stolen from the Kumeyaay people. This institution, like all American universities, is a concrete thresher designed to separate blacks from blackness. Not to make them nonblack. Not to incorporate them into civil society. But instead to isolate them from their communities—to make them into the "educated black man [who] feels at some point in time that his race no longer understands him. Or that he no longer understands his race."[1] So no, I didn't belong here. I didn't belong here any more than the homeless citizens displaced from the surrounding community or the crack addicts who I encountered in Orchard Manor as a child.

But is there anywhere in this world where blacks can belong? This world, joined together in its declaration that our ancestors are unworthy of engagement as a human culture but instead commodified us as human property? This world that decided blacks exist to be stolen from their homelands and brought to a new land? This world that still, centuries later, steals the progeny of these captives from their homes—only now it's by the police whose supposed mission is to serve and protect? How can

blacks belong when in all spaces
and all places our flesh is always
already stolen: from our homelands, from our heritage, and from
ourselves? How can we belong anywhere when we don't even belong
to ourselves?

Indeed, at this moment, I didn't
belong to myself. My knowledge
and experience were disregarded,
flushed away like the refuse of
last night's dinner and replaced
by the fungibility of my flesh. My
self didn't matter here. In this
beaten, worn, brown leather chair,
inhaling the particulate matter of
colonizer knowledge that floated
in minuscule specks through the
diffuse sunlight, I was not a man. I
was currency. I was the dollar bill,
the greenback—but brown. I was
the most nonthreatening version
of blackness they could find. No
matter what I did, no matter what I
learned or how I fought, my blackness precedes and precludes my humanity. My passions and my training didn't affect Dr. Bosch's opinion
of where I would have something
to say, only my skin. Frantz Fanon
describes existing triply as a black

man, of being "responsible at the same time for my body, for my race, for my ancestors,"[2] and for the first time, I understood what it meant to have a past that you were not a part of speak for you.

Dr. Bosch was smart enough to know that his words could not be contained within this moment. He was aware of the Compton Cookout incident; we had discussed it during my admissions interview. His words were shocking, but by the time the emotions rising in my gut reached my brain, the shock had dissipated to a dull thud. This thud mimicked my heartbeat and drove into the base of my skull. It's the same dull thud that arises when trying to teach a temperamental four-year-old a new skill, the frustration experienced repeatedly slamming against a crumbling facade of patience and responsibility. I'd been through this before, I told myself, and I was sure I'd go through it again.

As I had so many times before in my life, I asked myself, "How did I get here?"

SHARD: 1

Status: Haply, for I Am black

After I graduated from San Diego State University, I spent three years in the beating heart of the America that racists want to make great again. Sadly, I came here to engross myself in the thickest blood of white culture. I knew I wanted to be an actor and eventually a teacher. When I told my mentors this, each offered the same advice: if you want to act or teach in the American theater, you have to be able to do Shakespeare. Upon this advice, I applied and was accepted into the recently formed Shakespeare and Renaissance Literature in Performance Program offered by Mary Baldwin College and the American Shakespeare Center. I didn't do this because I loved Shakespeare. Hell, I still don't. But I needed to find out why American theater decided to make itself in his image if I wanted to have a career in the field.

When I enrolled, I just flat out didn't get Shakespeare. For all the talk of his work being universal, I never understood how anyone could connect with a four-hundred-year-old story of a Danish Prince who takes a ridiculously convoluted path to revenge. Why not just stab the motherfucker at the beginning? Why subject us to four hours of bullshit first? But my mentors all said if I wanted to work in this industry, I had to learn it. My mentors said so.

I never questioned if the "you" in that advice was a universal "you," a royal "you" that made the advice applicable to all. At the time, I had no reason to. Now, as I was sitting in this office, my professor assuming my knowledge based on my skin tone, I wondered if the "you" was meant just for me—as in:

1. "if *you* (as a six-foot-five black man)
2. want to act (an occupation that engages with a minimal range of representation) or
3. teach (a profession in which blacks are less represented than acting) in the
4. American theater (an industry where people of color held only 6 of 148 executive-level leadership positions),
5. *you* (to diffuse the threat that your very being entails)
6. have to be able to do Shakespeare (to show your willingness to conform to whiteness)."

Yes, that's a lot of subtexts. But by the time I was sitting in this office at the age of twenty-five, I had more than enough experience to know that all speech between races is coded, recoded, and decoded, filtered through a four-hundred-year history of domination and segregation.

I was, as I would find to be the situation more and more often as I rose through the ranks of the academy, the only one. I was the only black person in this program. I was the only black student. There were no black faculty. The program was three years long, allowing me to earn both a master of letters and a master of fine arts in that time. My three years overlapped with five cohorts of students, approximately one hundred twenty-five students, and I was the only black one. One. I wish this were more of an anomaly, but sadly it is the status quo. I was alone, here, in the gateway to the South, with all that entails.

Although the program was isolating, I was able to find fellowship in a place that continues to feel more and more my home: the gym.

With Mary Baldwin College's fitness facilities sorely lacking, I joined the local YMCA. Many of the locals embraced me, and I joined them in workout programs, basketball games, and even the occasional church picnic. In some ways, these connections allowed me to balance the isolation I felt in my education. But these connections were also all white. However, in the gym, we were just regular people who had a common interest. While on a basic level, the same was true of the program—we each came to study the Bard—graduate education is the epitome of elitism. As the only black person, every moment served as a constant reminder of how the world at large views my kind.

But if you want to teach or act in American theater, you have to be able to do Shakespeare.

So, I persisted.

I persisted through my movement teacher telling me I was in danger of failing his class. I am not sure how you fail movement. I showed up every day and participated in the exercises, which primarily consisted of floating and flicking through space. I did what the professor instructed us to do day in and day out.

But that wasn't enough. When we met for our midsemester progress meeting, he told me I was in danger of failing. I asked why, and this professor told me something I never expected to hear uttered on a college campus: "I can tell you are thinking."

I was floored.

I was in danger of failing because he assumed I was thinking?

"I can tell you're thinking," he said, "and you don't trust me as a teacher. I need you to let go and trust me." I did not trust him? I was not aware that trust was part of the curriculum. How exactly does one evaluate trust in a manner that is neither arbitrary nor capricious? But also, this professor and I had no relationship outside of the humid gymnasium where we held the course. How the hell would he know if I trusted him or not?

Or perhaps more apropos: how could I show him that I trusted him? What would it take for him to either believe or disregard trust in my grade? While my experiences in education had taught me that the goalposts for blackness can always move, this was something entirely new. This professor didn't just move the goalposts; he made them invisible. How could I meet his standard when it exists neither on paper nor in policy but instead as an abstract? Despite appearing in class and participating in every exercise, this professor projected onto me mistrust and saddled me with the burden of proof for a feeling over which I had no control.

But this professor—and most nonblack professors in this anti-black liberal discipline that prides itself on its inclusivity—will never understand the barriers to "letting go" that blacks face. Our success and our mobility—hell, our very lives—each intersect with our ability to perform, confirm, and submit to the expectations of an antiblack world.

Yes, we can absolutely be ourselves: we are capable of breathing and loving and living as much as anyone. But we are not always free to be ourselves.

To be ourselves is to invite danger into our lives and violence to our flesh. To be ourselves—if we can even remember what we truly are in these modern lives birthed from the hold, the plantations, the coloreds-only lunch counters, and the prison system—is to give the world an excuse to obliterate us. Simply standing up to oppression and declaring "I am a man" has been a capital crime for blacks in America. The distance between being ourselves and putting on a performance is equal to the distance between getting home safely and a judicially justified bullet in the head because the officer "had reason to believe his life was in danger."

Let go.

Between the intersection of our races and the coercion inherent in student/teacher relationships in a capitalist society, I could not help but travel back in time to when education was a death sentence for blacks. In the pre-bellum South and on slave plantations in the North, the Master would whip a slave to death for knowing how to read. And here again, that history echoed—"Don't think, nigger. Work!"

Even if I remove race from the equation, the conceit failed to make better sense. I was failing for thinking. How could a concept so absurd even exist, especially in what marketed itself as an institute of higher learning? I had no choice except capitulating to his demand that I stop thinking—a task that I had no idea how to accomplish. How can I follow his directions without thinking? How can I engage without thinking? How can I be black in this class, in this institution, in this state, without thinking?

I turned to the only solution I could think of: alcohol. I used the distilled vapor of the most refined grains to dull my inhibitions and frolic through the remaining semester of bullshit. Yes, I put myself in danger. Yes, I left myself open to the most base stereotypes of minstrelsy. But I had no choice. I had to try to turn off my blackness. Since that was an impossibility, I had to turn off my mind. Interestingly enough, my professor never noticed, or at least never commented on, my inebriation. Instead, he complimented me on my improvement in the second half. Right then, I should have begun questioning the education I was receiving, but I put my head down and carried on. This class wouldn't be the last time I turned to the drink to get through my education. Why not? It was the most effective tool for coping with the overwhelming antiblackness of academia.

"If you want to teach or act in American theater, you have to be able to do Shakespeare."

The mantra instilled in me by the white theater establishment echoed in my mind. So still, I persisted.

ABSENCE
Status: How can we be antiracist?

Racism is not simply in actions, institutions, and
systems of oppression.
Our modern world is the product of colonization of nonwhites,
genocide of Indigenous peoples, and slavery of blacks.
These processes are not just about violence toward people and
bodies,
but violence toward being, ways of knowing, and sources of
imagination.
America—
and England before it,
and Spain before it,
and Portugal before it,
and Morocco before it,
and China before it—
did not just take people from Africa to make slaves.
They had to take hearts, minds, epistemologies, and cosmologies
from the land and its inhabitants.
Unwind them, dismantle them.
Replace them with their own.
This violence cannot be undone.

Those universes, destroyed in the name of God and man and
human, cannot be remade.

Our world is now made on that death.

We cannot imagine our world without this violence occurring,

as the imaginings are the product of an imagination built on that
violence.

Tautology? Perhaps.

But how do you explain water to a fish?

To extract the racism from our world is to pull the thread that holds
the fabric together,

leaving nothing but a thought at the tip of our tongues

that we can't remember imagining.

So how can we be antiracist?

Not by banging our heads against the world hoping to fix it.

We do it by dismantling this world

that has dismantled so many before it.

SHARD: 2
Status: Livin' on the Edge

I persisted through my thesis advisor attempting to get me kicked out of the program for being honest with a guest director. My final year in the program coincided with an upheaval in the faculty that left our MFA acting program without an acting teacher or a director for our thesis show. My final year curriculum was piecemeal, thrown together at the last minute with whatever guest artists were available. On the positive end of this jigsaw course plan was Rob Clare, whose acting course was terrific. On the opposite end is someone who shall remain nameless, as the theater is still a small community. The majority of our problems were not the director's fault. In this instance, the responsibility lies with poor bureaucratic processes and a lack of communication with students who diligently paid over $25,000 a year for tuition. On multiple occasions during this fateful final year, the program told students when and where to be—only for us to arrive at an empty space. Plans would change last minute, events would be delayed, and we would be uninformed. By the time our guest director came to audition us for our thesis show, I had become disenchanted with the program and was ready to receive my degree and get out.

The director was a white woman of some reputation who was at that time in her sixties. While she was famous and had been innovative in the past, her techniques and productions had become stale. Rarely able to secure gainful employment in professional theaters, she found a place in academia, as the outdated modes of the institution still held her in high regard.

The Shakespeare and Performance program at Mary Baldwin College was run in conjunction with the American Shakespeare Center. The former Masonic Temple in downtown Staunton was split by the two institutions. The ASC made the fourth floor of the building home to their administrative offices, while the graduate program used the fifth floor for courses and rehearsals. This floor consisted of two large rooms that mirrored most cathedrals in the country: at one end of each room was a raised platform designed to hold an altar, and high, concrete gothic arches filled with stained glass windows lined the exterior walls. Below this stained glass was a line of moveable padded pews that could be placed in rows for meetings and services and moved to the sides for more exciting gatherings such as initiations or parties. We affectionately called the two rooms Masonic Red and Masonic Blue because of the colors of the tattered, stained carpets that covered their floors. I often wondered if the stains came from student high jinks or arcane rituals.

It was January, and the new year had brought snow, ice, and the type of cold that soaks deep into your clothing. Even after hours of class, the coats and scarves we removed when entering the temperature-controlled classrooms maintained the memory of the cold in their fibers. The sun set early at that latitude. And despite Staunton, Virginia, being historically part of the South, it was far enough north that by dinnertime the sun had been gone for hours. With every footfall breaking through the thin layer of ice created by the snow melting under the sun's rays only to refreeze at night, walking to auditions created a symphony of satisfying crunches. Occasionally, that crunch would immediately precede a loss of footing. But the snow provided enough padding that falling only bruised my ego.

I took the stairs up to Masonic Blue, hoping to warm myself

up a bit before my audition. I made it to the top, removed my coat, and revealed a sweat-drenched shirt that stuck to my back. Instead of heading to the bathroom to refresh myself, I stood in the lobby waiting to hear my name. When called, I left my coat and my fucks in the small antechamber we used for props storage and walked onto the blue carpet. I introduced myself and my pieces as is customary in the industry, "Hi. I'm Matthieu Chapman, and I will be performing Benedick from *Much Ado About Nothing* and Aaron from *Titus Andronicus.*"

I launched into my pieces with a freedom and energy that can only come from recognizing that the only conceivable consequences of your actions cannot harm you.

"I do much wonder that one man, seeing how much another man is a fool," I said with an inflection indicating that the fools were on the other side of the audition table.

" . . . when he dedicates his behaviors to *love*,"

I grabbed my dick through my pants, letting our esteemed director know exactly what I thought of the program I was in.

" . . . will, after he hath laughed at such shallow follies in others, become the argument of his own scorn by failing in love: and such a man is Claudio. I have known when there was no music,"

I paused. I paused so long that the director raised her eyebrows to encourage me on.

Just before she interrupted to ask if I forgot the words, I drove on.

" . . . with him but the drum . . ."

I launched into an air drum feature from Rush's "Tom Sawyer": boom-boom, budda-bap, boo-bap, boo-bap, boo-bap . . .

"and the fife!"

Benedick continued for more than my assigned two minutes. Between the air guitar, humping the ground, and acting like a monkey, the action took far longer than the words ever had before, but she let me finish the piece. As I paused to transition into Aaron, she raised a hand.

"Thank you," she said with a slight smile on her face, "I've seen enough." She did not speak angrily or condescendingly. Rather her tone and the slightly upturned corners of her thin lips indicated that she didn't know what to make of me. If she was not amused, she at least appreciated my enthusiasm.

I found myself relieved that she stopped me. I was out of breath and exhausted.

"Please, come take a seat," she said, gracefully princess waving her hand at the chair across from her. Once I was settled, she moved straight into questions with no pleasantries.

"What do you hope to get out of this experience?" she asked.

I probably should have found a couple of the fucks I left in the foyer before coming in to perform because apparently "to get a degree and get out of here" wasn't the response the director wanted.

"You can leave," she said, without thanking me for my time.

I thanked her, stood, then walked out the door. My audition was over.

News of this got back to my thesis advisor, who asked if he could meet with me and the program chair to discuss my audition. About a week later, I walked into the chair's office in Rose Terrace—the large red-brick converted home that now served as the program's administrative offices—not knowing what to expect.

"You wanted to see me?" I asked, as one does when they have been summoned.

"Come in, come in," said Dr. Minter, the head of my graduate program, "have a seat."

Dr. Minter took his seat behind his desk, leaving only one open chair. Seated across the vast mahogany desk from Dr. Minter was my thesis advisor, EJ, who had called the meeting.

I could tell by the way EJ held his hands in front of his face—with fingertips pressed together so tightly that his nails had turned white—that he had been instructed not to speak. "Hi, EJ," I said, taking the seat next to him. My greeting was not only met with silence, but he didn't even look in my direction.

"Tell me what happened." Dr. Minter spoke calmly and clearly, as he always did. But at this moment, his usual undertone of humor was nowhere to be found.

I explained myself as though on trial, giving only the vaguest, unassailable facts of the situation and volunteering nothing superfluous. "I went to the audition. I did my pieces. Well, one of my pieces. She stopped me before I could do the second. She asked me some questions, and then I left."

"What did she ask you?" Dr. Minter asked though I am sure he already knew the answer.

"She asked what I hoped to get out of the process."

"And what did you tell her?"

"The truth," I argued.

"The truth?" EJ could no longer hold his tongue.

"EJ," Dr. Minter scolded. Just then, I don't know who Dr. Minter's scold was meant to protect. EJ appeared beyond livid, and perhaps Dr. Minter requested his silence to keep him from saying something he would regret.

"The *truth*?" he repeated, the words themselves coming as bile from the darkest pit of his stomach. "Your truth was disrespectful bullshit. She is a professor. She is a professional. She is a guest to this program, and you embarrassed all of us!"

"How? I told the truth," I countered.

"I have been teaching and doing theater for twenty years, and I have never been associated with a program where what you did would be acceptable. What you did was disgraceful. It was petulant. It was disgusting..."

I considered interrupting, but there was no point. Once a white man, especially one with authority of this fashion, gets on a roll, there's no stopping them. So instead, I began to interrogate his anger in my head. Why was my truth so disturbing to him? Did he truthfully find what I said so monstrous? My words were honest. My words were my truth.

To me, at least. But I could see on EJ's face that this was about more than just my words. Perhaps he truly felt that I had disrespected our guest, and maybe I did. But I found his response disproportionate to my crime: I was an A student. I was a runner-up for the Andrew Gurr Award for Outstanding Thesis.

As someone who is now an educator, I see the potential to use this incident as a teachable moment. But EJ wasn't interested in teaching. He was interested in punishment. Could I have lied? Could I have told half-truths to assuage the ego of this guest? Of course. But isn't honesty the best policy? Aren't brutal truths more valuable than comfortable lies? Sometimes. But not across racial lines. I would later learn the idea of "straight talk" that black communities have is foreign to many other cultures.

I cannot help but wonder what other factors played a role in his response—if perhaps it wasn't the disrespect that made him leap directly to expulsion before he heard my side, but instead, if it was about who was disrespectful. I could not help but wonder if this was about my body, my blackness. The director had asked a question, and I had responded with my truth.

But in an antiblack world, do I even own my truth? I had managed to avoid all the world's mechanisms for surveilling and controlling my flesh: I didn't live in the projects and I had avoided prison. On top of that, I infiltrated the whitest of antiblack institutions—Shakespeare Studies. But as Frank Wilderson said, "The structure exceeds and anticipates you." And in this case, when the world could not keep my flesh captive, they took control of my narrative. I told my truth, and this man criminalized me for it. How do we reconcile that my truth—the truth of being and my position in the world—exists within a centuries-old continuum of antiblackness? My truth is their pain. My truth is their guilt. My truth is a reminder of everything the world has done and continues to do to my people. The antiblack world thrives on the control and surveillance of not only black flesh but also black words and black thoughts. And while EJ could not stop me from speaking or thinking my truth, he could punish me for doing so. At that moment, EJ was the police and the overseer. He took control of my story—he needed me to know my place and suffer for it.

It must be exhausting to waste one's whole existence policing and controlling ours. Imagine what the world could be if it would just let blackness be. Imagine what blackness could be if it didn't expend all of its energy resisting.

EJ rolled on, repeating himself and his disdain for me until Dr. Minter raised a hand and stopped him. "Okay, we understand how you feel, EJ," said Dr. Minter. "Matt, do you have anything to say?"

I had loads to say—about how this entire program stands on a foundation of oppression and erasure. About how the only way I could succeed in this program was by getting drunk before class. About how the program excludes minorities through its very epistemological focus. About how the faculty and staff were so busy patting one another on the back for their "inclusivity" and "progressive politics" to notice that everyone in their circle was white.

I had loads to say. But unfortunately, nothing I could say would make my situation better. By this point in my life, I had learned a lot about navigating an antiblack world, and I knew that what they wanted at this point was submission. EJ wanted me to apologize. He wanted me to beg and plead. He wanted me on my knees and at his mercy.

But sorry for them, I still hadn't found my fucks.

So instead of saying loads, I said very little.

"I told the truth, and if the truth isn't acceptable, maybe you should ask yourselves why."

That "very little" said loads.

In this world, a man cannot be black, talented, and proud. He can only be two of the three. I had to be black; I was stamped so at birth. My enrollment in the program meant I had talent. So, when I decided to be prideful, not to bend the knee and kiss the rings, that was the last straw. I'll never forget the look on EJ's face: the blend of confusion, fear, awe, rage, and disbelief was somewhere between a Greek drama mask and a rabid bulldog. I thought he was going to explode. I thought he was going to leap from his chair and strangle me.

But physical violence would make him the bad guy. Instead of following through with his white-knuckled fists, he turned to his colleague in an attempt to deploy the metaphysical violence that was solely his purview. "He should be kicked out of any program in the world for the way he behaved and is behaving. He is petulant [read: talented and black]. He is disrespectful [read: proud and black]. He is a disgrace [read: black and not under our control] to this program and this theater." EJ then struck. "He has to go."

Dr. Minter replied as calmly as ever, even after EJ's tirade, "Thank you for your input, EJ. I'll take it under advisement. You can go."

EJ, with shock on his face and silence from his mouth, stood and left the room.

"Should I go too?" I asked, unsure of where I stood.

"Not yet." Thankfully, Dr. Minter had instructed me in numerous classes and chaired my first thesis. "Did you really say that?"

"Yes," I replied, confirming the story I had just told.

"And was what you said true, that you just want to get a degree and get out?" he asked.

"Yes," I repeated.

While I had always liked Dr. Minter, it was what he said next that has influenced me to this day. "Then here is what we'll do. While I don't necessarily agree with what you said, I think EJ overreacted. I'm not here to police your feelings; I'm here to teach, and kicking you out doesn't do that. You won't be in the MFA thesis show; the director has made quite clear she doesn't want to work with you. But we will find you a role to earn your MFA."

I'm not here to police your feelings.

I wish the rest of the world behaved the same.

I want to teach or act in American theater, so I have to be able to do Shakespeare.

It was becoming my mantra.

And because of Dr. Minter, I can teach and act in American theater.

I persist.

And persist.

And my persistence led to my admission to the doctoral program in theater history, theory, and criticism at UC San Diego. Again, the advice of my mentors paid off.

Every so often, I think back on my time at MBC and UCSD. I think of that advice, and that office, and that day, and the meaning of that "*you*" becomes more and more evident.

SLIVER

A Terrible Thing to Waste

Time for a history lesson.

For as long as blacks have read and written in America without slaveowners executing them for that crime, scholars and intellectuals have promoted education as the key for black equality. In the early twentieth century, eminent wordsmiths and intellectuals such as Booker T. Washington, WEB DuBois, Frederick D. Patterson, and Mary McLeod Bethune were among the primary proponents of this rhetoric. Booker T. Washington, who was among the last generation of black leaders born as slaves, worked in the coal mines and salt furnaces of West Virginia to fund his education as a freedman. After graduating from the Hampton Institute, Washington purchased part of the plantation his ancestors worked and built the Tuskegee Institute on the land. Turning a former plantation into a school to help blacks learn skills that allowed them to earn a living in postbellum America has to be one of the biggest middle fingers a black man has ever given to white America.

Washington was what some would call a realist, what others may call a defeatist, and what WEB DuBois called an accommodationist. Washington believed so strongly in education that he was willing to sacrifice representation to acquire it. His proposed Atlanta compromise of 1895 offered whites total control of the American government in exchange for a free, basic education for all blacks. With over a hundred years of hindsight, this seems like a terrible proposition for blackness. Even when blacks have representation, America finds a way to ensure the education system fails black people.

WEB DuBois also promoted a path to educating black America. DuBois's most recognizable contribution to black intellectual theory was his argument of the "Talented Tenth." This theory argued that the Negro race needed leaders who could rise to the top of the race, the most talented 10 percent, and use their abilities to infiltrate white society. Once the 10 percent had proven their capabilities to whites, they could then open the doors for other blacks. This top 10 percent, however, could not be built without a solid foundation of education, and he argued that: "Men we shall have only as we make manhood the object of the work of the schools—intelligence, broad sympathy, knowledge of the world that was and is, and of the relation of men to it—this is the curriculum of that Higher Education which must underlie true life. On this foundation we may build bread winning, the skill of hand and quickness of brain, with never a fear lest the child and man mistake the means of living for the object of life."[3]

Unlike Washington, who valued a more practical, industrial education designed to provide blacks with economic advancement,

DuBois based his path to education on blacks receiving a classical education in the humanities and empathy. While Washington wanted blacks to have knowledge, DuBois wanted blacks to create knowledge.

Taking the foundation laid by Washington and DuBois, Frederick D. Patterson, Mary McLeod Bethune, and William J. Trent put their own money—as well as other people's—where their mouths were. By playing off white liberal guilt, these three incorporated the United Negro College Fund (UNCF) in 1944. The fund's sole purpose was to provide scholarships and grants for black students to get an education. By approaching presidents of white universities and positioning their donations as a moral responsibility, Trent raised $78 million for black education during his twenty-year tenure as executive director. The UNCF used this money to endow and administer the general scholarship funds for the thirty-seven Historically black Colleges and Universities (HBCU) across

America. The UNCF continued their social justice, moral responsibility-based donation calls into my lifetime with heavy-handed, although effective, advertisements emphasizing the stark situation black youths faced in earning an education. These ads all ended with the iconic slogan "A mind is a terrible thing to waste," subtly shaming its more affluent viewers into donating to quell their guilt.

Washington, DuBois, Patterson, Cookman, and hundreds of others did their best to grant black men, women, and children access to education and made great strides in doing so. But black education has always been an exercise primarily of compromise and secondarily of survival. Actual advancement and enlightenment are, at best, tertiary concerns of the education of black America. These visionaries never anticipated that black thought, black knowledge, and black education could not transcend that damaging racial signifier that precluded their proprietors' potential acceptance and contributions to the academy.

Academia has veered from the road laid out by these visionaries. Now, as a whole, it spins its wheels in the mud, entrenched in a cycle of erasure and exclusion that diminishes black knowledge. At best, the academy begrudgingly accepts black thought with the caveat that its presence must be either whitewashed, marginalized, or, as is most often the case, *both*. At worst, the government intervenes and bans it because it makes white people feel bad. While government intervention only recently became the trend with over twenty states proposing laws to ban teaching critical race theory without even knowing what it is, the resistance to black thought is not new. The question then becomes, what are the forces at play in creating this erasure and exclusion of black knowledge in the academy?

At every level of consideration, higher education is heavily segregated, even to this day. While I will not recount the entire history of slavery, segregation, and Jim Crow in higher education, I will present some of their present manifestations. The antiblackness of the university as a whole is revealed through its relation to a much smaller, even more poorly funded network of universities and colleges who still bear the "black" designation: those thirty-seven Historically black Colleges and Universities. Regarding HBCUs' existence, some more progressive education advocates have begun referring to non-HBCUs as PWIs: primarily white institutions. Suppose you think the difference between PWIs and HBCUs is merely one of heritage and semantics. In that case, I will direct you to a recent study published in the *Journal of Financial Economics* that revealed race-based discrimination in higher education loans.[4] No, I am not talking about individual student debt, although grads of HBCUs have, on average, a 50 percent higher debt burden than their PWI counterparts. I am talking about bond debt. As public funding for education dwindles, most institutions have begun to rely on private loan funding for large-scale infrastructure improvements: everything from maintaining existing heating and cooling systems to constructing new medical schools. This study revealed that HBCUs repay, on average, eleven cents more on the dollar for bond debt.[5] While eleven cents is less than many of us have between the cushions of our couches, when spread out over billions of dollars, this extra interest amounts to hundreds of millions of dollars. HBCUs essentially pay a race tax for existing—a fine for nothing more than being black and seeking an education in an antiblack world.

This debt, however, is symptomatic of a larger cycle of structural violence that disrupts the foundations of black community formation. We have no more significant social crisis confronting America than that surrounding blackness: black Lives Matter protests, racist political rhetoric, and police brutality against blacks have become a nightly occurrence on the evening news. Against the backdrop of this spectacular violence, the insidious acts of violence against black bodies, black minds, and black epistemology on college campuses go unspoken.

In the rare instances when black thought is allowed in the academy, it must take one of two tracks. The first is to filter it through the nonthreatening, assimilationist, distorting Fourteenth Amendment signifier of "African American." If we look beyond blackness as an element of human identity and discuss blackness as a position of incommunicability with civil society, then we can see how universities disarm and deny blackness. They appropriate black flesh while obscuring the onto-logical absence and radical being contained within so that this flesh signals progress to the oppressor and creates plausible deniability and doubt around their continued role as oppressors. The ivory tower cannot risk admitting blackness as it is, but only as they need it to be. If we accept that the world is anti-black, then the black assimilation is an oxymoron. As such, within this frame, incorporating blackness into the fold—either by coercion or by infiltration—is always a revolutionary act. So once black thought has the revolutionary demand stripped away, and only the polished, perfect, "African American" glare of reformist compromise remains, academia cracks open the door.

The segregation of knowledge also impacts academic employment for blacks. According to the national survey of earned doctorates, the number of black PhD earners has shown a steady increase in number and proportion over the last twenty-seven years, rising 73 percent between 1994 and 2020 from 4.1 percent of all PhD earners to 7.1 percent. However, although there has been a steady increase in the number of black doctoral researchers, the percent of black faculty at universities has remained stagnant, rising only 14 percent, from 4.7 percent to 5.4 percent. A study published in 2008 in the *Journal of Higher Education* looked at the actual percentage of black faculty members in various departments and compared it to the expected rate based on the

populations of degree holders
and other factors. Based on the
ratio of terminal degree owners
to faculty hired, only four of the
fifteen disciplines had a higher
number of black faculty than
expected—music, history, English,
and comparative literature. Each
of these disciplines contains a sub-
field specific to the black diaspora,
leading the *Journal for blacks in
Higher Education* to argue that
"there appears to be a prevailing
racial view that black people
are best, and perhaps uniquely,
qualified to teach that part of the
history of our country that relates
to blacks."[6] In other words, universities only hire black professors to
teach black topics. The conclusion
is that the academy views all
knowledge as racially coded. And
if they only hire black professors
to teach black knowledge, they
are subconsciously free only to
hire nonblack professors to teach
nonblack knowledge.

So now we are left with a
conundrum: in a system that
views black professors as capable
of teaching only black subjects

and considers these as only having value to black students, how do we create space for inclusivity?

The university, through the entirety of its conception and evolution, has been segregated. No matter how many slave-owners' names are stripped from their buildings, no matter how many black students they admit and black faculty they hire, the institution itself is the product of epistemological segregation of knowledge. This segregation of knowledge offers new interpretations of universities' efforts toward "inclusivity"—blackness is allowed inside the building but still kept separate (and unequal) from non-black thought. Under the guise of access and opportunity, American universities reenact *Plessy v. Ferguson*, centering whiteness and white feelings in the discussion of diversity, inclusion, and equity.

"To teach or act in America, you need to be able to do Shakespeare." Looking back, I now wonder if that advice was exclusive *to me* as a black man, or exclusive *of me* as a black man.

Shard: 3
Status: Under Attack

With three words, time stopped. I sat, paralyzed, at the front of this small meeting room at the Milwaukee Hyatt Regency. The thin, grotesquely patterned carpet turned to ice, and I sat crystallized in place. In this new glacial world, the frozen moment between the seconds turned the reverberations of those words into icy stalactites. They fell from her mouth and formed a cold prismatic cage around my being. As the piercing shards of language enclosed on my peripheries, I felt each one strike a chord in my soul.

I wanted to crumble. I wanted to surrender my body to gravity and collapse onto the table at which I sat. But I couldn't. To do so would be "unprofessional."

I was at the Mid-America Theatre Conference. MATC is usually one of the less intimidating stops along the academic conference circuit. I was presenting a paper that reread the colonial structures of Shakespeare's *The Tempest*. I was arguing that the colonizer/colonized dynamic offered by post-colonial readings of the play was too simplistic to capture the racialized differences between Prospero, Ariel, and Caliban.

The first half of the paper went smoothly. There were a few nods of recognition and furrowed brows of thought—reactions I had become accustomed to in my experience delivering papers. But when I reached the discussion of the early English conquerors' positioning of Native Americans as ontologically human at the first moment of encounter, a member of the audience shattered the normative standards of conference etiquette.

"That's not true!"

The words crawled from the middle of the crowd. The shriveled feebleness of the voice wore a thick armor of indignation and white fragility. Her words, however, were a sword, and with three words, she disavowed my argument and disemboweled my being. All of my work, my research—my self—shredded. Not with questions or counterarguments, but with the difference in distance between our bodies and the topic at hand. She was white; I am black—and in the world of early modern literature, her flesh gives her credibility that no amount of evidence or rhetoric could ever give mine.

Once I recomposed myself, I began to scan the room for the face that matched the words. I did not immediately identify my assailant. Instead, all I saw was a smorgasbord of white faces made whiter by the shock of the moment.

Again, as I had so many times before in academia, I found myself alone, isolated in my blackness. Some of the faces were shocked at the incivility—one of their own breaking the social contract of the situation. Some of the faces mixed this shock with fear—terrified that the interruption would spark in me a stereotypical media representation of black rage. Some mixed their shock with glee—these faces hid partially behind their programs, but I could see the smile in the corner of their eyes. I broke the world from its standstill and, instead of cowering, engaged the voice.

"What's not true?"

Among these shocked, white faces was one that retained its color. For the first time, I saw my assailant. Aside from the pronoun "she," this person was everything one would expect to have the gall and ego to interrupt an invited speaker with her evidence-free counterargument. She was old. She was white. She dressed in a manner that attempted to convey class and wealth.

Although I invited a debate on the matter, my assailant rejected my attempted engagement. She did not hide in shame, however, nor did she apologize. Instead, she reached deep into her arsenal of whiteness, her history of privilege and colonization and domination, and unleashed a weapon that sought to remove from the gathered company any doubt of who was in charge.

She permitted me to continue speaking.

"Never mind. Continue," she said, with no apology, no recognition of her rudeness, no pleasantries distributed in between that would present her words as anything other than the command they were.

I became livid. I inhaled all the righteous anger of centuries of oppression and I screamed. I leapt over the table and rushed my assailant. I pulled my six-foot-five frame as tall as I could, looming over her sagging one. I began to address the audience, calling out my assailant for performing the very power relations between black and nonblack that I was arguing for in my paper. Instead of my prepared arguments, I used this woman as evidence to show everyone that her denial of my agency, my arguments, and my knowledge—with nothing more than the raising of her white voice—was better evidence than anything to be found in early modern discourse. I positioned this woman as symptomatic of the larger power dynamics imposed by academia as a whole and the conference in particular.

Or at least in my mind, I did.

In reality, I calmly rebutted her initial accusation of untruth with something she never expected my black body could: intelligence and calmness. "Ma'am, nothing any of us says here, either on this panel or at this conference, is true," I said. "The best any of us can do is gather evidence and present an argument, which can be either accepted or resisted. But none of us are right or wrong because none of us are arguing for true."

I saw her wince. By maintaining my composure and undercutting her knowledge, I had cut her deep. Combatting her stereotypes instead of engaging them put her far more effectively in her place than my fantasy of spectacular confrontation ever could. I paused, awaiting her response, but she offered none.

Before the uncomfortable silence and stillness bubbled over into conflict, the moderator, who had remained perplexingly silent during the confrontation, afraid to side with blackness even when it clearly had been wronged, broke the room out of its collective pall.

"Matt, would you like to continue," she asked, "or would you like to conclude?"

I paused for just a second more, evaluating my assailant, trying to judge if she had recognized her faux pas and would allow me to continue uninterrupted, or if she would wait for me to let my guard down and attack again. We locked eyes in cold, steely conflict, and with a breath that said, "you do not own me," I continued my paper.

Defeated, my attacker gathered her belongings and quietly left the session.

After our panel concluded, numerous people in the room approached me to apologize for my assailant's actions, but none of them levied any blame on her.

They instead made weak excuses: "Sometimes she doesn't have a filter."

They spoke in the passive voice: "I'm so sorry that happened to you."

They offered that most common dismissal of antiblack violence that the world gives to distract from the inherent imbalance between our nation's races: "She's just crazy."

None of them would speak on her actions. None of them would

decry her behavior. None of them would name her deed as what it was: antiblack racism.

Truth is such a fickle concept. Truth is never what it claims to be. Truth is always subject to bias, interpretation, and perspective. Truth is not facts and history, but rather the consciousness of those data points and the ability to present them in self-serving ways. Truth is about power. And like so many times in my life before, the power of truth was not on the side of my blackness. Antiblackness distorted the truth to deny the culpability of their entire race in the actions of one rude woman. While the assault of one racist angered me, the response from my supposed "allies" was far worse. Like so many times before, antiblackness denied my pain and her violence, thus unmaking me all over again.

FACET: 2

Age: 28
Location: La Jolla, CA
Status: Token

In his office at UCSD, Dr. Bosch gave me a first-hand demonstration of higher education's racialized division of knowledge, a reaffirmation of my place in the world: in an antiblack world, my blackness precludes my individuality.

Knowing this new rule allowed me to play the game differently. Resisting antiblackness through achievement and education is less effective than through guilt. I would go on to use this to my advantage as best I could. Every February, when theaters around the country produce their one black show, typically an August Wilson, I would emphasize my blackness over my experience in theater. The simple fact of blackness got me my first gig as a dramaturg on a university production as well as my first gig as a dramaturg on a professional production. I was qualified for both posts, but those qualifications were not good enough for other opportunities. Only when the theater needed black flesh to sell to their liberal, nonblack audiences did the door open. The white-lash that our contemporary society deploys in response to black achievement would certainly scream reverse racism at the revelation that I used blackness to my advantage. But, I would counter, although I exploited my blackness in these circumstances, I allowed others to exploit my blackness as well—the nonverbal quid pro quo of America's racial contract.

Despite everything, I am proud to have earned a doctorate. Half of what I learned, I would not trade for the world. The other half, I wish I could forget. I wish I could forget how a potential committee member rejected my dissertation proposal because the work I was doing on blackness (which I eventually published as a well-received monograph) was, in his words, "impossible." I wish I had never learned that education, which for so long theorists and intellectuals positioned as the key for black equality, had no way of accounting for or allowing in my blackness. More than anything, however, I wish I had not sat in that office on that day and heard the unconcealable white excitement in that white voice. The excitement that my presence assuaged any concerns he may have had about departmental racism amid the outcry caused by the Compton Cookout. The program finally had another black body—they had someone who, to them, had a being innately intertwined with black art. Finally, they had my flesh, and that mattered more than my experience, education, and knowledge ever could.

FRAGMENT 8

FACET: 1

Age: 28
Location: Escondido, CA
Status: Could It Be Love?

I thought parties were supposed to be fun. But instead, I found myself sitting in the downstairs bedroom I shared with my fiancée in my future mother-in-law's house. Alone, crying, isolated by more than just physical space, I had excused myself from my soon-to-be family's annual Christmas party.

My mother-in-law's Christmas party was not your typical informal holiday gathering of well-wishers. Instead, it was more akin to a fancy corporate soirée complete with cocktail attire, bartenders, servers, and in some years even valets. She dressed the house meticulously from floor to ceiling in the garments of the holidays: garland imitating snow-dusted fir trees hugged the stair rails; the napkins, rugs, and curtains had been changed from neutral tones to snowmen, reindeer, and Santa Clauses; and bits of holly and mistletoe hung from light fixtures. In the grand entrance to the home stood a fifteen-foot-tall artificial tree that required a ladder to assemble and decorate—the flight of the angel ornaments aided by an A-frame of hollow aluminum.

The whole family worked together to tackle the extraordinary task of hosting this party. We spent weeks shopping and organizing only to then spend days cooking and cleaning. I must have made a dozen trips through the avocado orchards and down the steep hill of

Deer Springs Road to grab "one last thing" or add supplements to "I thought I had enough." At the house, my fiancée presided over the finer details of the cleaning work, and her sisters peeled and crushed and stirred and sprinkled and frosted. My mother-in-law's desire to celebrate and impress made the party a chore as much as celebration, but it's the thought that counts. We all recognized that this party was not for us but our jovial, mixed crowd of loved ones, acquaintances, and my mother-in-law.

My mother-in-law, God bless her, is well-meaning, but she is a product of both her time and her privilege. She grew up in suburban Chicago in the 1960s, protected by a bubble of wealth and distance that separated her from the protests and riots of the civil rights movement happening in the more urban centers of her city. I don't think she ever meant harm in our interactions but, like many white people, she felt the burden of her whiteness in encounters with blackness. Instead of connecting with me as an equal human, she would begin our interactions in one of two ways: either by qualifying her whiteness or relating to my blackness. I call this phenomenon racial credit—the act of white people banking past experiences with blackness in order to cash them in later with other blacks to prove that they aren't racist. It's as though people think that being nice to one black person means they can't be racist to any of them, or that their one minor encounter somehow erases the centuries of systemic racial violence.

This December night, the exhaustion of the preparation week and the cheerful, alcohol-fueled buzz I was nursing muted my typical awareness and caution. I was surrounded by company with whom my relationships varied between polite and personal. This was as safe a space that I could ever find in America: incorporated into the wealth and privilege of white society not in a servile role, but in a legal relation. It turns out, however, that antiblackness never goes away—quite the opposite. When we think we are safe is when antiblackness can be the most destructive.

"Hi, Matt," my mother-in-law approached me with a glass of red wine in her hand. "Are you enjoying the party?"

"Yeah," I replied, "I'm just tired."

"I have someone I'd like you to meet," she said. Then, before I could respond, she turned away and headed me across the dark tile of the kitchen toward the dining nook.

I shrugged and followed. She arrived at her target and began speaking while I was still a few steps away.

"Dr. Charles," she said to a man sitting at one of the high leather barstools lining the tall, narrow windows of the breakfast nook, "this is my son-in-law, Matt."

For a moment, neither my mother-in-law's associate nor I could muster words. Instead, we looked into each other's eyes, and I swear I saw the same shock and disappointment in his that I know I held in mine.

"Hi, Matt," he said, hiding his exasperation, "I'm Raymond."

We held each other's gaze, engaged in a psychic communication in which each of us tried to assure the other while excusing my mother-in-law. I had been here before, and Dr. Charles's face told me he had, too. The safety I had felt only moments ago left me completely blindsided to the fact that death had crept into the room. My mother-in-law had hit the white liberal jackpot: a two-for-one sale where she could show she wasn't racist to two blacks simultaneously. This was the first time I had attended this Christmas party, and although close to one hundred of my mother-in-law's coworkers and business associates attended, she only took the time to introduce me to one. The black one. The *only* black one.

"Hi Raymond," I said, extending my hand. "Nice to meet you."

"I'll leave you two to it," my mother-in-law said. Then, she turned

away to laugh and bask in compliments about the cocktail menu and
food arrangements.

Leave us to what, I'll never know. I wanted to disappear. I wondered if Dr. Charles felt the same. Finally, after an interminable
second of silence, I broke the tension.

"Nice to meet you," I repeated, not knowing what else to say.
"Will you excuse me?"

I stepped away before hearing his response. I exited the crowded
kitchen and stumbled through the hallway. I searched for air and
freedom from this place, but since this was now my residence, I had
nowhere to go. Not that it would have mattered, anyway. I couldn't
drive, as my blood-alcohol level, while probably not surpassing the
legal limit, was certainly in the range of "the suspect is getting bellig-
erent." So, I went to the bedroom that I shared with my fiancée.

As I had so many times in my life, I asked myself, "How did I
get here?" How did I come to live in this home full of my white fiancée's white family? Steph and I had known each other for less than
a year. I had only met her family a handful of times before agreeing
that I should move in with her, into her parents' home. I didn't know
enough about Steph, let alone the rest of the cohabitants—her parents, her brother, her youngest sister, and another unrelated couple
and two of their daughters—to know what I was getting into. My
life was a rich tapestry of unpleasant interactions with an antiblack
world, and nothing in that history told me that this was the right
choice.

But my history and experience conflicted with my present. As the
old saying goes: "Love is blind." And I was falling in love. I wanted to
see Steph more. Unfortunately, with both Steph and me in school
full-time, working full-time, and living apart, we hadn't gotten to see
much of each other. Depending on the traffic between my apartment
in La Jolla and her parents' home in Escondido, our commute to

one another spanned anywhere between thirty-five minutes and two hours. With our packed schedules and the distance between us, we only saw each other every other week or so. The move was utilitarian for more than just our relationship. The fact is, the house in Escondido required more upkeep than the occupants could manage. I am still pretty handy with tools and carpentry, and I enjoy manual labor whenever my livelihood doesn't depend on it. With me joining the group, it would lessen the burden on everyone. In exchange, I would live rent-free. For a grad student trying to survive on an assistantship stipend and a side gig as an SAT tutor in one of the most expensive cities in America, living rent-free was truly a blessing from the ancestors.

But "love is blind" is more than just a cliché that either denigrates a partner's physical appearance or provides an excuse to ignore a partner's flaws. Love can also blind someone to forthcoming danger by obscuring the red flags with rose-colored glasses. Thankfully, for the most part, it was an amenable situation. I was never victim to any intentional slights or violence from this new family, which made the unintentional, oblivious ones all the more painful.

I don't know how long I laid there before my fiancée noticed my absence and came to check on me.

"Are you okay?" she asked, with a trepidation that informed me she already knew the answer.

I wish I could say the words poured out of me, but pouring implies a flow and gentleness that was utterly absent from my response. My speech was fractured by the violence that always seemed to accompany blackness in any situation. No, I did not let it flow but rather vomited jagged fragments of pain and experience. The vocal shrapnel erupted from a place beyond thinking. The bits and pieces of being emerged from my guts and my soul as a low, guttural whisper punctuated by sharp, sniffling inhales. My chest was tight. My throat was closing in as quickly as the walls around me, leaving me unable to catch enough breath to utter complete sentences without pause.

Steph cautiously but lovingly approached and sat next to me on the bed. She listened intently as I described so much more than the situation that had just occurred with her mother and her mother's colleague. I began a disjointed, incomplete description of the many times the world had not seen me but only my blackness. It had been so long since I had felt heard that as soon as I was able to capture an ear and a heart, I couldn't stop. My thoughts and emotions splintered and tumbled out of my being. The pieces collected momentum and became an unstoppable, chaotic avalanche of past experiences and terrible imaginings.

I described how this one was harrowing because I thought that our marriage and my new family would help to suture the many ruptured pieces of my existence. And while I didn't expect the wounds to heal completely, I hoped that the jigsaw puzzle of my being would at least fit together to form a coherent picture, even if the ruptures still bore my scars. I described how having that fantasy shattered was worse than all the others because, this time, I didn't even get a chance to pretend it was real before it was destroyed.

I am sure she was sympathetic, but I am also confident that she didn't understand. How could she? No one could. At least no one who had lived their life free of the cursed stain that our nation's history has stamped onto black bodies. But still, she sat and listened.

My words splintered into so many trails and paths that they led us to our future children. When we first got together, we had discussed having kids and were on the same page. We would have two, possibly three children. A boy and a girl and, if we wanted to continue after the first two, another boy. Atticus Hadrian, Inara Jane, and Thaddeus Rex, respectively. I still can't believe she was on board with naming our possible third child after the mightiest of dinosaurs, but love produces the strangest things.

But now—I couldn't do it. I couldn't bring myself to imagine having children. How could I justify inflicting the life I had led onto an innocent being who had no choice in the decision? How could I take the jagged pieces of myself, shattered and broken so many times, and suture them together into someone else? How could I pass on these razor-sharp shards of pain and violence and death that would slice away one end of his tapestry while the other was still being knitted by life? How could I spend the rest of my life hoping and praying that the tapestry could be woven faster than it was being cut away? What is a life spent hoping against all hope that she never realizes and experiences her blackness in a world that only values its destruction and consumption?

I spoke until I ran out of the energy to speak. My mouth ran a thousand miles an hour trying to keep up with the eruption pouring from my soul. But my tongue and lips were no match, faltering from exhaustion. My mind was still racing, but my mouth was dry. My eyes burned with tears, and my throat was scratchy and raw. My entire body was shaking, attempting to outrun the avalanche that I had become.

Without my words to distract from the silence, fear and panic encroached on the room. How would Steph respond? How would her first encounter with the world's view of my blackness be received? Would she stay or would she go?

SHARD: 1

Status: The Pass

"How did I get here?"

I was on my knees staring down into a heartless sea. My vision and stomach were equally distorted by vertigo.

"How did I get here?"

I could smell the sea air. The aroma of sand drifted forty feet up the sea cliff and mixed with the acrid stench of vomit, simultaneously reaching my nostrils and raising new bile from my stomach.

"How did I get here?"

The question rang through my consciousness as it had so many times before. This time, however, the context was unfamiliar—the question was sincere as opposed to rhetorical. I tried to piece together my morning: I got on my bike, I saw a coyote, I locked up my bike—and then I was here. How many steps could I not retrace? How many blanks needed to be filled?

I fumbled through my pockets, searching for tokens to help ground me in reality. Finally, I found my keys and my phone. I flipped open my black plastic Motorola and saw the time—6:46 a.m. I had left my house at 5:00 a.m., rode my bike, then I was here—a gap of over an hour. My clothes were soaked with sweat, so I must have been in the middle of a workout.

Panic began to creep up my spine. What in the hell happened? I sat on the cool ground and gathered my bearings. The wind rushing up the cliff filled my lungs and suppressed the fear rising in my chest. I got up and began to walk, focusing intently on my breath. I walked to the only place that made sense at the moment: campus psychological services. The office didn't open until nine, and it was only seven thirty. I didn't know what to do, so I folded myself onto the cool concrete next to the door. I sat, holding my knees, trying to hold off my tears and panic until the first practitioner arrived.

I failed on both counts.

As soon as I saw someone with a name tag that included the title "doctor," I assaulted them with a barrage of raw emotion. This unfortunate young resident nearly dropped his coffee at the sight of me—a six-foot-five, two-hundred-sixty-pound tower of a man crumbling in front of him. I was crying and shaking and stuttering. I was babbling incoherently, trying to make logical sense of an illogical, terrifying situation. I am surprised I was not met with pepper spray or police intervention.

"Hold on, slow down," he said, raising his hands in a gesture somewhere between comforting and defensive. "What's going on?"

I mustered all my strength to say something that made sense. "I need help."

"Okay, okay, please come in," he said. "I'll take care of you."

I took a deep breath and stepped through the door he was holding open. He sat me down in a small, dark interior office with no windows and only one entry. Horrible gray office carpet covered the floor—the tough, scratchy type that has no pile but is the favorite of capitalists for its extended warranty. Instead of sitting me across the desk from him, he pulled his chair to my side and sat facing me with no barrier between us.

"Okay," he said, "take a deep breath, and start from the beginning."

I told him my story. I woke up. I rode my bike to the gym. I blacked out. I came to at the glider port. I had just vomited at the top of the cliff.

"I think I was going to kill myself," I said.

He told me that the medical term for what I experienced was a "fugue state." While they are not uncommon, they are treated seriously. He began administering diagnostic surveys for a whole host of conditions: major depressive disorder, anxiety disorder, borderline personality disorder, bipolar disorder, schizophrenia—more tests than I can remember. I spent hours in his office filling out page after page of vague questions:

"Have you ever considered hurting yourself or others?" Yes. I mean, isn't that part of the human experience? Who doesn't at times get frustrated enough that they want to kill someone else? Who doesn't sometimes wonder what death is like—if there's anything after all of this?

"Does your energy level fluctuate?" Yes. Isn't this true for everyone? Isn't this why coffee and wine are both billion-dollar industries?

"Do you ever wonder if the world would be better off without you?" Isn't that literally the plot of one of the most well-known Christmas movies of all time?

If you couldn't tell from my frenetic, disjointed overanalysis of the surveys, the first condition with which I was diagnosed was attention deficit hyperactivity disorder, ADHD.

I was also diagnosed with major depression and anxiety.

The campus doctor wrote me prescriptions for Prozac and Trazadone. But the university does not manage long-term care, only crisis intervention. So he wrote me a referral for outside psychiatric medication management and psychological therapy.

At that time, I had no idea what mental health care entailed. It's not like managing physical diagnoses, where a doctor identifies an ailment, makes a diagnosis, applies treatment, and, boom! Done. You're healed.

No.

Addressing mental health is more akin to blindly throwing darts at a moving target. Eventually, I found a doctor for medication management who, in addition to my previous doctor's diagnoses, made her own. Along with major depressive disorder and anxiety, she also diagnosed me with schizophrenia. The schizophrenia diagnosis was odd. While my mind was often racing, I had never experienced hallucinations, at least not to my knowledge. But then again, how do you know if what you see or hear is real all of the time?

What I didn't know at the time but came to learn later is that the pseudoscience theories of black people that came about during slavery continue to influence mental health care for blacks today. As a result, when black people seek mental health care, they are more likely than nonblacks to face one of two scenarios. First, blacks are at risk of having their issue downplayed to the point where they receive no treatment. Or, second, the opposite: blacks are misdiagnosed with diseases that have criminal connotations, such as schizophrenia, sociopathy, and others.

At this point, however, I was willing to do whatever she said. I recognized that I had run out of options for self-care, so I needed her help. She immediately upped my Prozac and replaced my Trazadone with Seroquel—a fairly potent, highly addictive, antipsychotic drug. The Seroquel helped to slow my mind and improve my sleep almost immediately, although the effects of the Prozac were nonexistent. She informed me that it could take up to eight weeks for Prozac to produce any therapeutic effects and advised me to up the dosage and give it more time. After suffering for another two months with the Prozac offering no respite, we began the arduous process of weaning me off the drug so that we could attempt something new. This is not a unique experience: more than two-thirds of the time, an adult patient with major depressive disorder requires more than one clinical intervention before achieving relief. Learning this startled me—when a patient reaches a crisis state, it can sometimes take six months to find a way to return to their everyday life. Once the Prozac exited my system, she switched me to Zoloft combined with Wellbutrin. This combination worked for about eighteen months before subsiding, another common outcome in mental health treatment. So we began exploring new options. Since I first began taking medication for my depression ten years ago, I have been subject to six different medication protocols.

FACET: 2

Age: 27
Location: Escondido, CA
Status: Could It Be Love?

I met Stephanie Kwan Kelly on Match.com. We connected almost immediately and on the strangest of characteristics: she was only tangentially American. While she was an American citizen, Steph was the daughter of missionary parents. She was born in Thailand, raised in Nepal and India, and spent years volunteering in South Africa and Nigeria. She had only returned to America to attend nursing school, after which she planned to return to Africa.

I found her worldliness and unselfishness appealing.

I was also attracted to the fact that she didn't think of me as black.

I mean this in two senses. With dark eyes and bronzy, coppery skin, people who have a broader understanding of the world's diversity than the stereotypical divide of "white, black, Chinese, or Mexican" often struggle to identify my race. My particular ethnic ambiguity has led me to be mistaken for Latinx, Egyptian, and North African. Also, with how blackness exists in the American mind, people often struggle to reconcile my grasp of the English language, taste in music, and lack of a criminal record with my racial identity. On more than one occasion, friends and colleagues have been shocked beyond the point of speech to discover that I am black, preferring to think of me as not black rather than assume that a black man could have a doctorate.

But having spent so much time in South Africa—which has different intersections of color and social status than the US—Steph considered me a person before she considered my race.

In the second sense, I am not ashamed to be black—quite the contrary. I love being black.

I hate how the world views blackness.

Being black is exhausting. blackness in an antiblack world is only partially tied to one's skin. No human being is "black" in the visual sense. The descendants of slaves are brown, tan, copper, bronze, taupe, umber—even getting as dark as ebony. But none are black: blackness in America is a concept. A position. A politics. A history of domination. A present of disenfranchisement. In America, black is born of slaves, sentient flesh, less than human.

But Steph's more global experiences with the intersections of race, politics, and power created space for us to explore a relationship outside of the dynamics of America's history with race and antiblackness. Sure, she recognized that she had certain privileges and protections based on her skin—antiblackness is a global phenomenon, after all. But she was not raised in a nation where those privileges and protections are predicated purely on my destruction. Her whiteness and my blackness both certainly exist, but our histories allow us to remove them from direct binary opposition.

Or at least that is what I told myself. I had to rationalize my attraction to Steph in some way beyond Fanon's insistence that I wanted her to make me white. I had to somehow separate my interest in her from America's history of illegal miscegenation and interracial rape. From my own family history of interracial psychological and sexual trauma.

"She's not white," I kept telling myself. "She's not *American* white."

We had corresponded through email and spoken on the phone

for two months before we met in person. Even though we had this connection, the prospect of our first rendezvous made my stomach churn—the butterflies of excitement battling the waves of dread.

"What if she is *American* white?"

"What if, in person, I am too black?"

We planned to meet one morning in early March to hike up Roosevelt Mountain, famous for the well-known San Diego landmark, Potato Chip Rock, which stands at its peak. The previous day's heatwave outlasted the setting of the sun. So, even with the cool ocean breeze that washed over La Jolla, I could still feel the sweat beading at the small of my back as I sat in my fifteen-year-old white Honda Accord early in the morning. Even though the sun was still rising over the Sierra Nevadas in the eastern distance, the mercury in America's Finest City rose beyond the balmy stereotype of seventy-two and sunny.

The anxiety built as I made the forty-minute drive to meet Steph. I kept wanting to turn around. I was terrified. Not necessarily because of what would happen on our date—what's the worst that could happen? We don't connect in person, have an awkward time together, and go our separate ways. I was terrified of the opposite—what if we fell in love? What if we got married and had kids? And what if we ended up just like my parents? What if she got angry and called me nigger in front of our child? Or worse, called our child nigger?

The conflict between wanting to be loved and being afraid of being loved tore through my consciousness. I was wrestling with the black imago, the phantasm of blackness that echoes and interacts with every black experience. I wanted everything between Steph and me, between us, to be between only us. But nothing in my life is ever just mine. The between "us" also includes all black men who live and have ever lived—my individual experience inextricable from the past experiences. I tried to push these histories from my mind and live in the moment. I didn't want to sabotage myself as I had so many times before on first dates. "She didn't see me as black," I reminded myself. "And she isn't white."

But the reassurances didn't last. All the hours on the phone, the emails, the connections formed over distance would now have to survive in person. Shit. We were going to meet. I was suddenly overcome with terror—the stakes I had previously dismissed came roaring back, doubled in force.

I wanted to vomit as her gold Toyota Corolla appeared around the bend. Once she emerged, she was more beautiful than her photos. Steph was tall with jet-black hair. She wore dark sunglasses that initially covered the beauty of her eyes with the intrigue of mystery. Those glasses were perched on a crooked nose—her imperfection that creates perfection. Her *wabi sabi*—like the Chinese porcelain repaired with gold or Cindy Crawford's mole. She removed her sunglasses to reveal kind eyes that are always smiling, even when filled with tears.

"It's so nice to meet you," she said, wrapping me in a warm but slightly awkward embrace.

"You too," I said.

"Shall we?" she said, indicating the trail.

"Let's." I extended my elbow.

She took my arm in hers, and without so much as a cue, we goofily skipped off in unison like characters in Disney's cartoon *Robin Hood*, where the title character is a fox. The tension melted. The stakes were washed away by her strange mix of confidence and awkwardness.

The hike was far more arduous than we anticipated. The sweat and panting blew away any airs we were putting on to impress each other. Our conversation started light, but we soon exhausted the small talk and pleasantries about the weather and our upcoming school tasks. Eventually, it turned to my studies.

"Tell me again what you study," she asked.

"Performance theory," I said.

"What in the world is that?"

"It's the study of performance," I said, piecing together the vast field into a digestible elevator speech. "Not just stage performance, but social performances, gender performances, race performances. Any twice-behaved behavior is a performance, so brushing your teeth is performing hygiene, dressing in those clothes is performing gender—"

"Oh," she said, with both curiosity and confusion. "Can I just tell people you're getting your PhD in voodoo?"

"Sure," I said. "Half the time, I don't even know what I'm studying. But I did take a seminar on shamans and witch doctors, so I guess technically, part of it is in voodoo."

"Woo!" she responded with a laugh. "You do voodoo, and I'll be a witch doctor. We can't all be acupuncturists."

After close to three hours of laborious walking and even more labored talking, we finally reached the peak. We sat on a flat stone that angled to overlook Poway, California, extending to where the sea formed the horizon at the curve of the earth. We shared a small, unpretentious lunch of CLIF BARs and clementines while waiting for a small crowd of fellow hikers to clear so we could take pictures of ourselves on the Potato Chip. The Chip is so sharp and flat that photos taken at the right angle make it appear as though you and the rock are floating on air thousands of feet above the earth. In all actuality, the stone is only about twelve feet from the ground.

After another two hours or so of descent, we stood hesitantly on the road's soft dirt shoulder. Neither of us quite knew how to say good-bye. I didn't know how to say it because I didn't want to say it—I wanted to stay with her. Throughout our entire day, over five hours of conversation, she never once fell into the stereotypical potholes that black men constantly encounter in their daily interactions with an antiblack world. She didn't try to relate to my blackness through slang or funky handshakes. She didn't hesitate to hug me. She didn't ask what we eat or why we dress that way. She didn't ask about my hair, or O. J., or which Jay-Z album was my favorite.

She made me feel something I had never felt before.

Not love.

Humanity.

I didn't feel the burden of my history. I didn't feel the burden of my blackness. I didn't feel the responsibility of school or money or family.

I felt human.

Eventually, she broke the silence. "It was great to finally meet you."

"You too," I said.

The wind rustled through the sparse desert brush and dry, crisp leaves, underscoring our hesitance. We were like schoolchildren, both afraid to make a move, both worried that being too forward would set us back, possibly forever.

She stuck out her arms, and I wrapped mine around her body so tightly that my hands passed her back and met my elbows around her ribcage. As we embraced, I felt the air rise and fall in her chest, the rhythm of her lungs in harmony with her heartbeat. My blood joined the symphony, bringing my heart in time with hers. As we held each other just a bit too long, the world faded to black, and it was just us.

I was in love.

Not black love.

Just love.

SHARD: 2
Status: Goldilocks

While my medication management was off and running, finding a therapist was an exercise in futility. In the four months it took to find a combination of drugs that helped, I had contacted dozens of therapists with little success in making a connection. I would later learn that this is a problem in the black community; something as simple as a name or a spoken inflection that signals blackness is often enough for a therapist not to return that patient's calls.[1] Despite these setbacks, I knew I was too close to the edge to give up—I never knew if the fugue would return or what would happen if it did.

In addition to the persistence and time required, finding a therapist is a Goldilocks process. My first appointment was with a white woman who couldn't have been older than thirty-five. She was always impeccably dressed, both her body and her office outfitted with the clean lines and classy adornments that signaled she came from money.

"Hi, Matt," she greeted me in the small, secure anteroom of her office designed to protect the identities of her patients. "Can I call you Matt?"

"Sure," I said. I prefer Matt, however her presumptuousness irked me before I even made it to her office.

She shook my hand and walked me down a small wood-paneled hallway. At the end, she held the door and gestured for me to enter. "Sit wherever you'd like," she said.

The office was organized with military precision. The angles of the furniture and the distance between pieces were so precise they could have navigated ships through a maelstrom. On one side was a small gray couch that, although entirely upholstered, still maintained ninety-degree angles on both the arms and the back. Above this couch were bookshelves—the books methodically organized by size to create a consistent, descending slope from left to right. Across from the sofa was a sitting area with a small rectangular wood coffee table and two overstuffed leather chairs placed atop an ornate fringed rug that protected the hardwood floors. Although this was her office, there was neither desk nor filing cabinets, instead she opted to keep those elements elsewhere in an attempt to disarm her clients into feeling at home.

I chose one of the high-back leather chairs, and she took the one next to it. "How are you doing today?" she asked.

"Umm, fine, I guess." The words were stilted. I cringed—this wasn't what I was expecting. I was expecting what I saw in movies—visions of the analysand lying on a couch telling tales of their mother while the therapist sat above their head taking notes. But, instead, it was just a conversation.

"Fine is good. Is fine better or worse than usual?" she asked.

"Worse, I think," I responded, unsure of what she wanted to hear and unsure of what I could say.

"You're uncomfortable, that's okay," she remarked without hesitation. "It can take time to get comfortable doing this. Why don't you tell me what brought you here today?"

I looked at her with trepidation. How honest should I be? If I'm not honest, there's no point in doing this. But if I'm too honest, I might be leaving in a straitjacket. I decided it was better to be frank and not see her again than lie and work with a therapist under false pretenses. I told the truth.

"I'm here because I don't know how to keep living in a world that hates black people," I said.

She recoiled in her seat as fear and confusion spread over her face. She looked offended, as though I had just called her racist. "What do you mean by that?" she challenged as much as asked.

I gave a truncated history of black life in America, both my own and the nation's. I spoke of chattel slavery and its afterlives in police brutality and mass incarceration. I spoke of always being the only black person in the room when I am in academia. I spoke of the fact that our criminal justice systems and economic systems both weighed blackness differently than other races and always to the detriment of the former. I described to her the decision I had to make as a black man in La Jolla every time it rained: do I leave my hood down, risking sickness and cold? Or do I put my hood up, risking being perceived as being in the wrong place at the wrong time, a mistake that often leads to shouting and drawn guns and "hands up, don't shoot" and protests? I discussed the constant tension and stress of being a black instructor for a class full of white students at a university where blacks held no seats of power and made up less than 2 percent of the student body. I was constantly walking on eggshells around my students because I knew they could misinterpret any gesture as a violent transgression due to my skin. I described to her feeling isolated racially within my own department.

As I rattled off all the ways in which my blackness preceded and exceeded my physical being, her face slowly morphed from shock to intent listening to bemusement. I could see her bubble of privilege, of isolated whiteness, begin to collapse. Then, as I approached the closing of my monologue, the facts turned to questions: What am I to do? How do I survive knowing that the distance between life and death is a white person's bad day? How do I navigate waters where I have no recourse to any accusation made by a white person? How do I live when society wants nothing more than for me to die but needs me alive and suffering to confirm their humanity?

When I was all talked out, I looked at this therapist, this white woman whose bubble of privilege had been invaded and destroyed by an encounter with my blackness, who was able, in a moment, to reconstruct her bubble twice as thick.

She looked at me and smiled, "I don't think that's true."

Without facts, without knowledge, rather with nothing more than sentimentality and liberal faith in the system that reproduces both her privilege and my suffering, she dismissed my entire existence. "I don't think that's true" is the rationalized kin of the assumptive logic of "if they are in jail, those people must have done something to deserve it." It is the common refrain from society in instances of spectacular black violence: "If they had just followed orders." In other words, "the system has always worked for me, so I don't believe that it doesn't work the same for others."

But such is the life of blackness—simultaneously hyper visible and invisible. We are always seen, as though the very molecules of the air we breathe are not composed of oxygen and nitrogen but rather spyglasses and cameras. Yet, even with video evidence, we are rarely seen, such as in the cases of Eric Garner or Rodney King—the world renders the pain inflicted on our flesh invisible and unspoken. The anguish builds and builds—each death another brick in the castle of antiblackness. And when our marches go unseen and our protests go unheard, blacks will respond in the same language that the oppressor speaks to us: violence. And when the bulwark of the castle is threatened by black action, when the black people burn down a police station, the system offers two tactics. First, they respond by increasing violence on the black lives. In rare occurrences, this method of quelling the black's demands fails, and the system sacrifices one of its own in the name of maintaining our suffering. "The system works; the cop was convicted," the world says out loud while rolling back our voting rights and comparing black Lives Matter to white supremacists storming the capitol. But this was 2011. Liberal humanism was the zeitgeist, and with the election of Barack Obama, so many white people adopted a smugness of "we did it," as though the guilt that led them to vote for a black man obliterated the history and realigned the present of antiblack racism.

In so many words, she said she didn't see color. And I believed her. I looked to the Harvard degree on her wall and deduced that she probably had an upper-class upbringing in the Northeast. She probably went to some overpriced private school where her parents purchased connections as much as education. Then off to Harvard. With so much overbearing, isolating whiteness contained in that sheet of embossed carbon framed in its own ancestors, there was a real chance she didn't see color. There was a real chance she spent her whole life surrounded by whiteness and the privileges it bestows—most notably, the privilege not to have to see color or consider its circumstances unless some of it enters from the kitchen. She didn't see color because society is designed to keep her safe from it.

And not just literally, but metaphysically. To see color—to look around the world and engage with the multitudes of cultures erased through enslavement, genocide, and oppression for nothing more than their color—would mean to look in the mirror and face a hard truth: that everything she had, everything she was, was a byproduct of the violent eradication of Native Americans and the forced breeding of Negro slaves. To see color was to look in the mirror and see a murderer and a rapist.

So instead, she chose not to see color, and as such, she couldn't possibly see me.

Our first appointment would be our only appointment.

Unfortunately, like Goldilocks with her too-hot porridge, this therapist was too white.

After another two or three months of consistently hounding every therapist who took my school-funded insurance, I was finally able to book another appointment. This time, the therapist was a white man. Dr. Vincent was an older gentleman, likely in his seventies. He had attended medical school in the wake of *Brown v. Board of Education* when many med schools first allowed black students. In his prime, he would have been tall and well-built. But in the present, age chipped away at both his height and musculature.

He welcomed me into his office with a clap on the shoulder that, although inappropriate for a first meeting, was more welcoming than off-putting. I sat on the faded, fabric couch beneath the window. His office was thick with the scent of pipe tobacco, Old Spice, and peppermint, conjuring in my head images of old-school masculinity. The aroma made me think Dr. Vincent would have been right at home riding horses through Monument Valley and engaging in shootouts with bandits.

"How are you doing today?" he began.

"I'm not sure," I replied, hesitant to deliver the evaluation of my blackness's inextricable relationship with my mental health that I gave to the last therapist.

"That's okay," he replied with both sincerity and interest. "Is there anything in particular that you're not sure about?"

The question was honest. I felt like he was genuinely interested in learning about me.

Dr. Vincent was a great listener, and as the conversation turned to blackness, he remained engaged. This time my monologue became a Platonic seminar, with the two of us engaged and questioning each other on our perspectives of the world.

"I just feel so isolated," I said. "I'm the only black person I ever see at school. I feel like if I actually act black, they'll kick me out."

"What does 'acting black' mean?" he asked.

"I don't know," I said honestly, "but not acting black feels like I have to perform to some standard they have of me constantly, but I don't know what the standard is."

"That's interesting," he said. "There were two black students in my class at medical school. I never thought of it as *only* two. I never thought how they had to alter their behavior for us."

"Two out of how many?" I asked.

"There were seventy of us who started together," he said.

"And with blacks making up about fifteen percent of the population, all things being equal, there should have been ten."

"So why weren't there ten?" he asked.

"There are two options," I answered. "Either blacks are naturally inferior, and only two were good enough to get in, or there is some systemic obstacle to them getting in."

"And for you, these obstacles still exist?" he asked.

"Yes, they do. But the problem is," I admitted, "I don't know what and where they are. I only find out about them when I fail to get over one."

"I see. That must be stressful," he said, seemingly understanding my predicament. "So the issue of being black is causing you trouble, but you don't know what the trouble is or when it will happen?"

While this understanding was simplistic and reductive, it was the most a white person had ever listened and the closest a white person had ever come to understanding.

"Sure," I said, "but it's bigger than that. I want to be clear: I don't have a problem with being black—the world has a problem with me being black."

"Ah." His eyes widened as his head rose in a slight nod of enlightenment.

Our first hour-long session flew by, and I was comfortable with him for the first fifty-nine minutes. We continued to discuss blackness, my blackness, and its position in the world. All the while, he took notes on a yellow legal pad. Oddly enough, his note-taking didn't trigger my persecution complex—the spider-sense never tingled as he audibly scribbled minor remarks. For fifty-nine minutes, I thought I had found a therapist.

I should have left at fifty-nine minutes.

As we both stood, he extended his hand. I grasped it, and as we shook, he enclosed our handshake with his left hand.

"I would like to invite you to my church," he said. "I think it will help."

"No, thank you," I responded. "I was raised in the church, and it's not really my thing."

While still grasping my hand, his kind eyes found mine, and he spoke with a sincere sentence that shook me to my core. "I can help treat your depression," he said, "but only Jesus can cure it."

Paralysis set in. What in this man was comfortable enough that he would evoke Christianity as the cure for my mental illness in our first session? While studies have shown that the fellowship of a church does have positive effects on well-being, at that moment, my mind turned to the plantation. I imagined my suffering alongside that of my ancestors. I imagined having the master look me in the eyes and tell me that the suffering he inflicted was for my own good. I imagined what it must have been like to have the master whip and beat you six days a week only to tell you that he is saving you on the seventh. The contemporary rhetoric of "how much is enough" merged with the religious rhetoric of obedience and the meek inheriting the earth. At that moment, Dr. Vincent reminded me that the world had no intention or interest in ending my suffering. Instead, the world would prefer to dismiss black suffering—bury and obscure it—under a ruse of hope and metaphysical futurity. Jesus couldn't cure me. Jesus wasn't there to end my suffering. Instead, his role is to make me okay with my suffering with promises of a place in a heavenly kingdom.

I did not see Dr. Vincent again.

In this instance, the porridge was too—well, this wasn't porridge. I had no interest in drinking this Kool-Aid.

Truths and secrets are the fundamental basis for psychotherapy. Effective therapy requires delving into things that the patient has never shared with anyone, often even themselves. As such, both the patient and the doctor have to be comfortable for the therapy to work. I saw three other therapists during my search. One of them I wasn't comfortable with. Two of them broke up with me; they said they didn't think they could help with my specific issues. But none of them seemed comfortable with my open attitude toward the role blackness played in my mental health. Some of these doctors would offer referrals, while others just offered dismissals. The mental health profession is either shamefully homogeneous or shamefully segregated; even though each of these therapists admitted they were ill-equipped to deal with the intersection of race and mental illness, none provided me with the contact information for a therapist who was. Hell, none of them could even offer me the name and number of a black therapist, which was a request I began making after having the doors to help closed to me by so many white faces. After trying for over a year with no success, I ceased seeking therapy and focused on my medication.

SLIVER
Let's Go Crazy

"And there is reason to think that
the sensibilities, both of their minds
and bodies, are much less exquisite
than our own; as they are able to
endure, with few expressions of
pain, the accidents of nature, which
agonize white people. It is difficult
to account for this otherwise than
by supposing (which is probably the
case) that animal sufferings derive
a great part of their activity from
the operations of the intellect. If so,
uncivilized man is not without his
advantages . . . it is certainly a very
great one, to be able to face death
. . . not only without dismay, but
with indifference."
— Dr. Collins, *Practical
Rules for the Management and
Medical Care of Negro Slaves in the
Sugar Colonies*

This quotation comes from
one of the earliest treatises, first

published in 1803, on managing
the health care of black slaves.
Despite the dehumanization of
slaves that runs rampant throughout the text, Dr. Collins's work
is progressive in that he proposes
better health care for slaves. Not
for the slaves' well-being, mind
you, but because proper treatment
will result in fewer deaths and
more births, thus saving slaveowners money in the long run.
Throughout the text, Dr. Collins
describes at length the many differences not only between whites and
Negroes, but also between varying
types of Negroes. And while Dr.
Collins did not invent the tropes
linking blacks to animals and
placing them in a position as less
than human, his work is among
the first to attempt to use these
distinctions to improve the health
care and lifespan of Negroes.

"Why are you bringing up
slavery? Slavery ended one hundred
fifty years ago! Can't you just get
over it?"

Honestly, I wish I could.

Unfortunately, these assumptions that blacks are somehow

less than human and should be
treated as such in health care
continue to impact the lives of
black Americans today. A survey
of medical students published in
a 2016 issue of the *Proceedings of
the National Academy of Sciences
of the United States of America* revealed that half of current medical
students still believed at least one
pre-bellum myth of physiological
differences between blacks and
nonblacks. Most commonly, 40
percent of students believe that
blacks had thicker skin than
nonblacks. Many also believe that
blacks are less sensitive to pain.
As a result, doctors are less likely
to prescribe black patients pain
medicine than other races.

These beliefs are not limited to
individuals. As the world becomes
more dependent on artificial
intelligence and machine learning
to manage patient health care,
these biases become encoded into
algorithms that determine proper
treatments and procedures. On
October 24, 2019, *Science* maga-
zine published a comprehensive
analysis of health-care computer

programs used by US hospitals. The study analyzed the algorithms that health-care systems use to manage close to two hundred million US patients and found that black patients were less likely to receive referrals to specialists and costly medical treatments. Despite having equal health-care costs in the previous year, the algorithm routinely assessed blacks with lower risk scores, resulting in blacks receiving, on average, $1,800 less health care annually than whites. In total, the algorithm only assigned 17.7 percent of black patients extra care. Researchers estimate that the actual number needing extra care was 46.6 percent. The disparity is a result of biases built into the program.

The disparities caused by myths about black people extend beyond physical medicine: black mental health care in America also suffers from centuries-old pseudoscience on black slaves. In 1851, Samuel Cartwright published one of the earliest treatises on slaves' mental health, *Diseases and Peculiarities of the Negro*

Race. In the work, Cartwright argues that if white men oppose the Deity's will by trying to make the negro anything else than the submissive knee-bender, then the slave will develop a malady known as drapetomania. This disorder causes slaves to defy their natural state and desire freedom, which leads to sulking, dissatisfaction, and, ultimately, attempts to escape. Cartwright argues that the disease can be cured by "whipping the devil out of them" as a "preventative measure." Thomas Lathrop Stedman included the disorder in his 1914 third edition of the *Practical Medical Dictionary.*

In other words, black slaves who wanted freedom were mentally ill. While many abolitionists mocked Cartwright's work, the underlying premise that slavery was the natural state of blacks continued to influence black mental health care. Before the civil rights movement, medical practitioners primarily considered schizophrenia a harmless form of neurosis experienced mainly by white, middle-class housewives. In the 1960s, however,

magazines began to describe
schizophrenia as a violent social
disease manifesting in rage and
aggression. Interestingly, with this
change in description came a shift
in the population the disease afflicted. Now considered a violent,
criminal disorder, schizophrenia
was primarily diagnosed in black
men—specifically those aligned
with black Power movements.
A 1968 article published in the
Archives of General Psychiatry described schizophrenia as a "protest
psychosis" with symptoms that included "hostile and aggressive feelings" and "delusional anti-white-
ness." As recently as the 1970s,
American medicine considered it a
mental illness for a black person to
want to be free. Even today, black
men are five times more likely to be
diagnosed with schizophrenia than
white men.

Unfortunately, the trend of
criminalizing black mental health
issues shows no signs of ending.
The mental health-care field still
lags woefully behind the general
population in terms of black
representation. In 2019, less than

4 percent of psychologists nationwide were black. Furthermore, this
percentage gets cut in half when
looking at black psychiatrists,
as less than one hundred of the
forty-one thousand psychiatrists in
America are black.

I wanted to end this sliver with
something hopeful, or at least
pithy and petty, but I was too depressed. I was worried if I went too
far, I might get misdiagnosed with
schizophrenia again.

FACET: 3

Age: 27
Location: Escondido, CA
Status: Could It Be Love?

My beat-ass Honda Accord struggled to ascend the steep hill to Steph's home in Hidden Meadows. It was pouring rain, and the wheels would spin when I tried to accelerate from a stop at an intersection. The signal on my newly purchased smartphone died, killing my maps app and leaving me to take a wrong turn down a dirt road that I was certain led to my death.

"This is it," I thought, imagining a plot similar to *Get Out* years before the film debuted, "I've been lured to my death by freaky cult people." I held my breath, worried that the sound of my own breathing may drown out the approaching banjos that would undoubtedly spell my doom.

But, thankfully, no banjos came. No rabid hill people from a 1970s horror movie descended on my vehicle. After a few more wrong turns, I reversed course and found the street sign that signaled I was on the right path: Alps Way.

As I made the left turn up another steep asphalt drive, I couldn't believe what I saw. I had to be in the wrong place. Steph was so humble, so grounded, so—ordinary. There was no way that this automatic iron gate with a call box stood sentry to her home. I pressed the combination of keys that dialed from the perimeter to the house phone.

"Hello," said an unfamiliar voice. "Who is it?"

"Uhh, I'm not sure I'm in the right place," I said. "I'm looking for Steph Kelly."

There was no response. I must be in the wrong place. I shifted the car into reverse to back down the narrow path when I heard a click. Then, a massive iron gate emitted a grinding squeal and began to swing open.

As I snaked up and down their driveway, I couldn't help but be confused. The home was a 5,500 square foot house nestled on eight acres of land in the hills of Escondido. The landscape blossomed with dozens of plant species that rivalled the local nursery. Silhouetted palm and eucalyptus trees peaked from behind the roofline. Finally, I pulled up to the white plaster-coated three-car garage trimmed in light blue painted wood eaves and large finials with bewilderment on my face. Just then, Steph emerged from the house to greet me with a kiss and a warning.

"Don't be alarmed, but my family's a little weird," she said.

I had no idea what she meant by this, but I responded with confidence. "No worries." How weird could they be?

While the individuals each had their own quirks, nothing about her family was beyond the pale. I met her father, Stan, a six-foot-eight former college basketball player with a peculiar sense of humor who punctuates his speech with non sequitur "hallelujahs." I also met her two younger sisters. Her youngest sister, Raquel, is a six-foot-two ball of goofy energy whose mannerisms would be right at home in the body of the vulture henchman of a cartoon sorceress. Her next youngest sister, June, is the tall one. At just over six feet five, her height surpasses my own. Last, I met their mother, Tracy, who at five feet eleven was the shortest of the bunch and the most accomplished. Tracy was the medical director for a Veterans Affairs Hospital in

Barstow, which meant that she made a four-hour weekly commute home on the weekends.

We spent most of the night engaged in the textbook introductory conversations and questions demanded by our social contract. After making the cycle of "Where are you from?" "What do you do?" and "Lovely weather we're having" three or four times with the various members of her clan, I finally got to have my first conversation with Steph's mother. However, Tracy decided to skip the typical pleasantries and launched straight into a story from her childhood.

"Have you ever been to Chicago?" she asked.

"Yes, actually," I said, "a couple of times. We had a long stopover there when I first moved out here from Pennsylvania."

"Oh, I grew up there," she said. I was uncertain where this was going. We were in Escondido; why was she bringing up Chicago?

"Well, in the suburbs just outside of there," she said. "When I was a kid, I remember my dad taking us to the city once. I was probably eight or nine; I don't really remember. But I remember seeing these huge skyscrapers."

"Was the Sears Tower built then?" I asked.

"Oh, I don't know which one it was," she said, "but I had never seen buildings like this before. And he took us inside of one, and these were the days when elevators had operators. And I remember going into this elevator, and the guy operating it was black."

"Okay?" I said, waiting for her to continue.

And just like that, the story was over. There was no climax, no button, no moral, at least not that I could see. I imagine that for a child in the 1960s, whose senses had not yet been dulled by a world of screens, visiting this skyscraper would have been a memorable event. From its height to its architectural features to the details of its interior, everything about the building would be new to the child's young eyes. Chances are she had never even seen one on TV, let alone in real life.

But Tracy didn't tell me any of the details of the building. The only adjective she seemed to deploy in any part of her anecdote was about the elevator operator: she made sure to tell me he was black.

Perhaps this was the weirdness Steph had warned me of? While Steph was born overseas and spent most of her life outside of America, her mother was born in Chicago and raised in the city's largely segregated suburbs. But this encounter was not weird. It was a fact of black life. I had lived long enough to know that the white liberal mind will, at its first encounter with a new black body, roll out their antiracist credentials—spend some of their racial credit. In Tracy's case, however, the resume was woefully thin; she did not point to a friend or coworker or favorite author who was black as most do in this situation. The best she could muster was a solitary man from her childhood whose name she did not know—only his job and his skin tone.

Was Steph worried her mom was racist? Tracy couldn't be racist. No way. She had started clinics in Nepal and Mexico, and her children did service all over the world. Perhaps all of her goodwill was the performance of white guilt that manifests in a savior complex? Maybe she was doing her best to show me that she accepted black people, even though their injection into her life was minimal?

No, Tracy wasn't racist. She was just *American*.

But I understand why these trips to the bank of racial credit would give nonblack observers pause. Yes, they can be cringey. Yes, they can be gauche. But all nonblack people do them, and all black people experience them. They are the small moments where nonblack people feel the burden of the systemic difference that they are responsible for. The socially acceptable responses to the presence of black people have changed in the liberal psyche. Still, along with that change, they never bothered to create the tools to deal with the structural differences between nonblack and black. Why would they? The ideology of post-race Obama voters was always about looking good to other nonblack people—blacks were never part of the deliberations.

SLIVER

Wake Up

In the age of social media, these formerly small-scale racial credit exchanges have expanded into a full-blown Economy of Wokeness. Using *woke* in regard to racial progress and social justice originated in the early twentieth century, as a new era of black radicals in the immediate afterlives of chattel slavery urged black freedman to "wake up" to their new reality and engage in the new era of activism. In 1923, revolutionary activist and businessman Marcus Garvey coined the phrase "Wake up, Ethiopia! Wake up, Africa!" as a call to the global black diaspora to join together in a new age of social and political consciousness.

Now, woke is a buzzword that right-wing pundits and internet trolls use to demean and insult anyone who cares about anything. Tired of doing backbreaking labor

for starvation wages? You must be
woke. Tired of your boss sexually
harassing you? Pipe down, member
of the woke brigade. Think a
Supreme Court justice shouldn't
have sexual assault allegations
on his record? What is this, the
woke-pocalypse?

But not all of these examples
engage in the Economy of
Wokeness. The exchanges of racial
credit that circulate violence in
exchange for good will occur exclusively between nonblacks—businesses and social media activists
and schools showing each other
how much black Lives Matter
to them without ever engaging
black folks in the interactions.
Some common exchanges in the
Economy of Wokeness include:
  1. Multinational corporations
tweeting black power fists and
pledging millions of dollars to
help uplift black communities and
black causes, but then never paying
because only black people check
the receipts.
  2. Universities, theaters, and
other institutions publicly issuing

statements of their own volition, promising to move forward with an antiracist mindset, only to return to business as usual as soon as the fire at the police station is put out.

3. Cities like Washington, DC, painting "black Lives Matter" on the streets during the day while teargassing protestors at night.

4. The federal government voting to make Juneteenth a holiday while doing nothing to stop states from stealing our right to vote, end police violence, or discuss reparations.

Each of these instances functions to make nonblacks feel better about the world—to make a big spectacle out of the idea of progress without making any actual progress for black people. As Claudia Rankine wrote in the *New York Times*, "the white liberal imagination likes to feel temporarily bad about black suffering," and they trade these bad feelings for social capital with other nonblacks to feel better about the detestable mistreatment of blacks.

Now, as the antiblack world

uses wokeness to trade in and profit off our suffering, woke takes on new meanings for blackness. Woke is no longer a rallying cry. Woke is mourning. Woke is being trapped in the past tense of our own funeral, our own wake— cursed to forever stand vigil for our own who the world kills and kills again for the pleasure of others. Cursed to never bear witness to these deaths, only to care and mourn for those who remain. "In the wake," Christina Sharpe argues, "the past that is not past reappears, always, to rupture the present."[2] Each moment of wokeness, each exchange in the economy, is the past reappearing to rupture black presents. The Economy of Wokeness is the stock exchange of the wake—the antiblack world's method for profit off black consciousness while avoiding black empathy.

The Economy of Wokeness exists alongside police brutality and mass incarceration as another afterlife of chattel slavery. Chattel slavery denied black humanity through physical

violence—accumulate our flesh
and profit from dominating our
labor. The Economy of Wokeness
denies black humanity through
metaphysical violence—accumulate our deaths and profit from
trading in our pain.

While blacks aren't found
hanging from trees as often
anymore (thank you kindly), the
absence of spectacular violence
does not equal the presence of
human relations. In this antiblack
world, liberal nonblacks perform
antiracism almost exclusively for
other nonblacks. Meanwhile,
blacks are left watching and
wondering when they are going
to be antiracist toward us. Maybe
antiracism isn't the answer. How
can we be pro-black?

But what can we do? Imagine
if I were to ask this woman, this
American white woman, my
girlfriend's mother, what her role
was in oppressing or liberating my
people. Imagine how she would
have interpreted that exchange
both in the moment and in the
culture. In that moment, I am
the brute, the inciter, the uppity

one who can't just leave well
enough alone. Best-case scenario,
she admits that she hasn't done
anything and half-heartedly asks
what she can do moving forward.
She has no intention of acting on
my suggestions, mind you. Instead,
her contrition is performative, an
attempt to exit the conversation in
a way that makes me think she isn't
racist. But as black people know,
that best case is a fantasy as distant
from reality as liberation. In the
worst-case scenario, she displays
what she has done in perpetuating
the violent oppression of my
people and calls the police. As a
black man in this white woman's
home, the police would justify any
violence she inflicted. In the eyes
of the world and those who police
its varying lines of race and class,
my blackness alone is reason for
her to believe her life is in danger.
And her belief is enough to absolve
her of the sins of my flesh.

But the most likely scenario
is she plays the played out and
overplayed "I marched with Dr.
King" card that black people are
all too familiar with. If everyone

who claims to have marched with
Dr. King actually marched, the
streets would have worn to dust.
But, of course, that line of thinking
isn't always so literal. Maybe they
donated to the United Negro
College Fund or black Lives
Matter. Perhaps they hired a black
employee or took an African-
American Studies course in
college. Maybe they shared a meme
that challenges the notion of All
Lives Matter, joined a Facebook
group that claims to be progressive,
or stopped donating to the police
brotherhood association. But
they always have a reason that
they aren't racist, and this reason
never involves actual interaction
with other races. Instead, it shows
just how far they are from understanding, leaving them completely
unaware that their reasoning only
serves to prove their racism—the
accounting of one's antiracism is
itself the racist act.

So we don't ask the tough questions of white people in personal
relationships. We can never ask.
We can't even ask simple questions
such as "When are you going to

ask what we need?" or "When
are you going to stop deciding
you know best and just let us be?"
We can't even ask "What do you
mean by that?" in these individual
moments of racial disconnect
because questioning a human in an
antiblack world, questioning their
intent, is perceived as rage. As a
being composed of violence, every
thought, every word, every action
is less than a breath away from
being interpreted as such. And
while we have no recourse to the
violence we experience every day,
the distance between a polite interaction and the cold steel of handcuffs and the taste of concrete and
a black leather-covered foot driven
between our shoulder blades is less
than a syllable. The space between
"don't shoot" and "hands up" is the
distance between life and death for
every black person every second of
every day.

ABSENCE

Status: Letters from the Editor, Part 2
On black Joy

"I am interested in these ideas, but as a book of essays.
I want a book that talks about how black Joy
thrives in spite of all this violence,"
said the editor.
black Joy.
This book isn't about black Joy.
This book is about why we differentiate black joy from the
fundamental human emotion of joy.
Joy.
Great pleasure or happiness.
Human beings take joy in . . .
In things
like living
and loving
and in not having to overcome, but in already being there:
black joy
blacks take joy in . . .
In spite of things.
In spite of the violence.
In spite of antiblackness.

In spite of everything the world tries to make us.

Like excellence, joy needs a qualifier to account for black ontology:

black joy is anathema to an antiblack world.

black joy is their new minstrelsy.

Our pain is their joy.

Our joy is their anger.

And frustration.

And rage.

That even with their foot on our necks,

and even though we can't breathe

we can still laugh

and love

and live

with a passion that they will never experience.

FACET: 4

Age: 28
Location: Escondido, CA
Status: Could It Be Love?

I sat collapsed next to the bed, waiting for her reply. I couldn't help but wonder if our engagement would have a lifespan of less than a month. I couldn't help but wonder if I'd have to spend the next era of my life explaining to all of the friends to whom we had just shown off her ring why we were no longer getting married. I dug my fingers into the carpet the color of an overcast sky, and felt the pile as it slowly slid passed my fingertips. I pressed so hard that I could feel the plasticized weave of the carpet's underlayment. Thoughts of where I would live next crept into my mind; my residence in her parents' home was entirely dependent on our being together, which was entirely dependent on her response.

I tried to fight off the encroaching panic by counting my breath: One . . . in . . .

Maybe I could crash with Matt and his weird new roommate who only ate bananas.

Two . . . out . . .

Or Eric and Jess? I know they just had a baby, but . . .

Three . . . in . . .

Worse come to worse, I can sleep in my car until I finish school . . .

Four . . . out . . . five . . . in . . .

I can shower at the gym . . .

Six out . . . seven in . . .

. . . and park at the school . . .

Eightoutnineintenout . . .

How much is a parking permit?

Eleven, twelve, thirteen, fourteenfifteensixteenseventeen . . .

As the numbers grew higher, I became confident I'd never see Steph again. I had broken the social contract—I had let out my truth, and our love could not cross the boundary between civil life and social death. Even the decision of *Loving v. Virginia* that allowed interracial marriage could not transcend time, space, and ontology.

My inhales and exhales lost distinction, and the air stopped in my throat. My breath was trapped in the space between my life and hers. This moment contained all the infinite scenarios and countless possibilities of our future. She had to decide whether it would be ours together or mine alone.

I was frozen. Paralyzed. My mind echoed with my mother's voice—"I told that nigger to have you home by seven." I wondered if I had crossed the line and become black or if she had crossed the line and become American. Deep from the darkest recesses of my mind came a thought, an outcome I knew I couldn't survive—"I knew I shouldn't have gotten engaged to a nigger."

When she finally began to respond, her first move was not to open her mouth. Instead, she scooted in close and laid her head on my shoulder. Then, after a brief moment, her mouth opened and formed six simple and life-changing words:

"It's okay. I still love you."

I collapsed onto her chest in a mix of exhaustion and relief. She had encountered my blackness, stepped into the shadow that hovers over every waking moment of my life. But instead of coming out the other side, she stayed in that shadow with me and held me.

And from then on, my life was just a little bit brighter.
And I fell in love with her all over again.

FRAGMENT 9

FACET: 1

Age: 26
Location: UC Irvine
Status: Resistance

I met Frank B. Wilderson III in the spring of 2011. Frank is a true revolutionary, one whose impulses extended beyond rhetoric and into actual practice. A well-known writer who spent many years in South Africa fighting against apartheid, Frank's story is truly remarkable. So remarkable that his first memoir, *Incognegro*, won the American Book Award. His second memoir, *Afropessimism*, was long-listed for the National Book Award. He is also professor of black studies and drama at UC Irvine, which conducted a joint doctoral program in theater with my own at UC San Diego. By this point, his revolutionary tactics had been tempered from prosecutable actions into powerful rhetoric of black structural positioning.

The first critical theory course I ever took was Frank's Afropessimism course. Having come from a background in acting, I had no idea how to approach the dense theoretical texts he exposed us to. Orlando Patterson, David Marriott, Jared Sexton, Saidiya Hartman[1]—nothing I had learned in college taught me how to translate this level of thinking. Their vocabularies are intimidating and mind-boggling; critical theory speaks its own language, and at times, it is as obtuse and indecipherable as Cretan hieroglyphics. Ontology, paradigmatic structure, a priori, always already, Gramsci,

Marx, scales of coercion and consent[2], the narcissistic slave[3]—I didn't grasp anything.

Of course, the drive to the class didn't help either. Being part of a joint program between UC San Diego and UC Irvine meant that students enrolled in either program had to take courses at the opposite campus at least once a year. While San Diego and Irvine are only eighty-five miles apart as the crow flies, that eighty-five miles could take anywhere from just over an hour to just under four hours depending on whether the traffic in the outskirts of San Diego and Los Angeles decided to cooperate. Each week, I would meet my fellow PhD students from UCSD—Julie, Sonia, and Lily—in La Jolla at 7:30 a.m. so we could carpool to Irvine for class. Sonia and I also had a three-hour Introduction to Theory course sandwiched between the commute and Frank's seminar. So, while Julie and Lily could go off and work on the week's reading or other assignments while waiting for class, Sonia and I were stuck in a classroom listening to a three-hour-long dissection of one sentence of some long-dead white philosopher whom I didn't care about.

By the time I got to Frank's seminar, my back and knees ached due to the hours spent curled in Sonia's Honda Fit, and my head hurt from the hours spent in Intro to Theory. Each week after the theory class, I was utterly exhausted and ready to go either home or to the bar. Instead, I went to Frank's class and the most daunting and complex thinkers and theories I had ever encountered. Even in my most rested, most willing states of mind, the works that Frank assigned us were challenging and required multiple readings to understand and many more to synthesize. The readings and discussion ceased to be informative or profound in my exhausted state and mostly just pissed me off.

One of the first texts we read was from a sociologist named Orlando Patterson titled *Slavery and Social Death*. This exceedingly optimistic tome uses over three hundred pages to address the basic question, "What is slavery?" To do so, Patterson evaluates thirty-odd slave-owning cultures throughout history. The title alone left me disenchanted with the topic. We all know what slavery is—forcing people to work without pay—and no amount of big words and obtuse theories were going to make me buy into crap about natal alienation, general dishonor, and subjectivity to gratuitous violence prior to an act of transgression. According to Patterson, meeting these three conditions constitutes slavery, and together they create the condition of social death. Social death, Patterson argues, defines the "slave in civil society." Part of my resistance to this notion of slavery was that it ignores the particular experience of chattel slaves in America—the experience of my ancestors. While slavery has been a part of civilizations ranging from ancient Greece to Yamato Period Japan to eleventh century Britain—but those slaveholding practices weren't like the slavery of blacks in America. None of those slave systems abducted people from their homelands and shipped them across an ocean. None of those cultures made slavery an inheritable trait. None of those institutions engaged in the forced breeding of slaves to enrich the slaveowner. Each of these is unique to chattel slavery in America. To equate black slavery with these other systems elides the specifics and diminishes the magnitude of the violence inflicted on black flesh in America.

Another part of my resistance was that I had no idea what any of those things meant.

My understanding at the time was that this notion of slavery is foundational to Afropessimism, which was the topic of the course. My superficial reading of the field was that Afropessimism argues that, for blacks, Patterson's articulation of slavery is inextricable from black being—for nonblacks, slavery is something they *do*; for blacks, slavery is what they *are*. As a black man in our modern world, I am supposed to be "natally alienated"? Okay, so I don't have a place to call home? I'm somehow separated from and unable to return to my homeland? That's not true—I'm from West Virginia, and I was there about a year ago. "Generally dishonored"? Bro, I'm in a PhD program. "Subject to gratuitous violence"—we have laws that protect me from violence. I didn't understand much, but what I did understand made it sound like blackness was worthless. I had heard enough of that from my mother, my past professors, and the police. The last person I needed to hear it from was this educated black man who in my mind should have been doing more to uplift blackness than to destroy it.

"Fuck this shit," I thought. "I'm not a fucking slave."

I shut down. I wasn't buying this bullshit. It was just some shit that people wrote to sound smart and get jobs. In academia, the most esoteric work is often the most praised, and I was sure Frank didn't believe this stuff. How could he? He fought against apartheid in South Africa and saw blackness rise up and take a country. He was just out to get a check; he had to be. No way a slave could ascend to the rank of full professor in this whitest of institutions.

I continued to try and make sense of the reading, but nothing worked. The more I read, the less I understood, but the more I consumed, the angrier I got. I didn't understand 80 percent of it, and the 20 percent I did understand I had almost thirty years of life, of experience, of not being a slave, with which to refute it. I was black. I was proud to be black most of the time, regardless of how painful being black could be. I wasn't going to let anyone call me a slave—let alone a dead slave. But fuck it, if I'm dead, I may as well act like a corpse. So I sat quietly in the seminar as the discussions between Frank and my classmates washed over my zombified head.

While most of my professors would let their theory train rumble on unabated, crushing the souls and minds of those tied to tracks and unable to hop on board, Frank was not most professors. Despite the theoretical underpinnings of his work, Frank was more human than the majority of his colleagues. Four weeks into his seminar, he entered the room in his standard dark-colored, long-sleeve shirt and took his usual seat at the head of the ring of tables. But instead of launching into his lecture, he offered an evaluation of the room.

"I feel like some of you aren't fully grasping the material," he said. "So I would like to take this time to answer any questions you may have that will help you going forward in this seminar."

The room was dead silent. I looked around and saw the same tension on each of my classmates' faces that I felt on my own. This was a PhD program, one of the country's elite performance studies PhD programs, and Frank just called us out for not getting it. He had issued the academic version of the prisoner's dilemma, only in academia, you are ratting on yourself for a sentence of being forever looked down upon by your colleagues. Asking us to admit our lack of understanding was akin to asking us to confess to murder.

After an interminable pause, Frank broke the silence. "So there are no questions?" he asked incredulously.

"Fuck it," I thought, "I can either look like a fool or actually be a failure."

I sheepishly raised my hand. I felt every set of eyes turn to me with pity, offering a silent prayer to forgive my soul for the intellectual suicide I was about to commit.

"Honestly," I began, "I don't even know what questions to ask to get me to questions that will help this make sense."

There was a gasp throughout the room that was silent but palpable. I had done too much—not only did I not understand the theory, but I had also admitted to not even knowing how to verbalize my misunderstanding.

The room froze with bated breath, awaiting Frank's response, while I awaited the academic punishment to come. Would he accuse me of not doing the work? Would he kick me out of the class? Would he remove me from the program, relegating me to nothing more than a cautionary tale for future students? I was sure he would in some way demean me.

After what was probably only seconds but felt like days, I saw Frank's eyebrows rise. His lips slowly parted.

He chuckled.

"Okay, I get that," he said with a smile. "I forget how new to this some of you are, and sometimes I move through this stuff too quick. Let's start from the beginning, and I will take more time to engage questions as they come up."

As I am sure Frank would agree, I resisted Afropessimism as strongly as I could, as strongly as any student he'd had before me. I know that my incessant, often childish, and underdeveloped questions tested his patience. But Frank's revolutionary past informs not only his politics and theory, but his teaching as well. Regardless of how many questions I asked, he never dismissed them and never responded condescendingly. He listened, truly heard what I was saying, and rather than offering counterarguments, offered questions.

"How can I be dead?" I asked. "I am here, talking, breathing . . ."

"Is that what indicates life?" he would respond.

"Yes," I would say, "I can still die, so I can't be dead."

"Is it possible for life to exist at varying levels of abstraction?" he asked.

I had no idea what he meant. "Levels of abstraction?" No. Life was life. Death was death. White was white. And black was black. I had no idea how close my binary dismissal of his theory was to the metaphysical realities of my situation. I left this conversation feeling that I had wasted a quarter in this seminar. I should have taken Post-Colonial Theory instead. At least that dealt with actual history and not some bullshit about social death. All I had to do was submit the required paper, and I'd never have to think about Afropessimism again.

Or so I thought.

But Frank's a different kind of professor. Every other seminar ended with me submitting a paper to the professor and sometimes receiving written feedback and sometimes never hearing from the professor again. Instead, Frank asked each student to have a phone call with him to discuss not only their final paper but also their experience in the class. I dreaded this phone call. I just wanted to be done with this man and this theory and this antiblack thinking.

SLIVER

The Voice of Reason

No one believed Cassandra.

In Greek mythology, Cassandra was the daughter of King Priam and Queen Hecuba of Troy. The god Apollo favored Cassandra, and he offered her the gift of prophecy. Cassandra accepted Apollo's present. What Apollo did not tell Cassandra is that he gave it to her to win her love. And when she did not love him for it, Apollo turned into a classical men's rights activist. He punished Cassandra for not giving him the love he felt he deserved because he was a "nice guy." Apollo cursed Cassandra to always share the truth about the future, but for no one to ever believe her. She tried to warn Troy about the Greeks hiding in the horse, but they didn't believe her. So everyone died. Then Agamemnon died. Then she died.

All because people ignored her and called her a liar.

Cassandra refused Apollo's love, so he told the whole world she was crazy, and they believed him. And even after a whole bunch of people died because they ignored her prophecies, they still didn't believe her.

Facts. The basis of truth. Objective. Observable.

But not equally.

Facts. A measure of power. A story told by the winners.

Facts are a product of white male hegemony. What is history and what is folklore, what is truth and what is rumor, what is belief and what is myth—each of these distinctions tells us more about those doing the analyzing than about the object being analyzed. For centuries, everyone whose genitalia or skin tone fell outside of the Euro-American patriarchal ideal had their ways of knowing become subject to one of two fates: either be relegated to the realm of magic, myth, and heresy; or be violently destroyed. These two fates allowed for one outcome: the epistemologies that served the overinflated egos of white men would survive.

Even within the academy, opinions and perspectives are taught through the limited range of Eurocentric, Western knowledge. There is a range of acceptable ideas that the current liberal university is willing to support and disseminate. In 2019, President Trump issued an executive order protecting free speech on college campuses in response to claims that universities refused to book or allow space for speakers who wished to espouse rhetoric that fell too far to the right on the political spectrum.

That "fact" is one side of the story. The other side is that these speakers and groups had moved so far right that they posed a clear and present danger to nonwhite and nonmale students, faculty, and staff. However, since race- and gender-based hatred has always been an acceptable political position in America, we call them "alt-right" and not "White Terrorists."

These canceled bookings and the subsequent executive order

received national attention. However, what receives far less attention is how the university deploys this same impulse to limit the range of left-wing discourse that is allowed. While the 2021 wave of laws banning critical race theory in classrooms garnered a national spotlight, academia has a long tradition of silencing voices that speak too far from the left. There is no need to ban critical race theory; the university already restricts liberal speech to the sphere of social reform. Go too far left, past integrationist desires and into revolutionary demand, and you reach a space where the work disrupts and challenges whiteness's position as the normative subject. Some fields even challenge the notion of humanity itself.

Once you reach this space, the space of revolution, the mechanisms of censorship engage and bind and gag the renegades. If you don't believe me, ask Ward Churchill, who lost his tenure and his job at a prominent university for his critique of 9/11. Reform is acceptable; revolution is not.

Being happy with your oppression is acceptable—challenging your oppressor, overthrowing your oppressor is not.

Cassandra didn't need Apollo's curse for the world to disregard her knowledge. She was a woman. The circumstances of her birth and her genitalia already rendered her unable to produce knowledge that the patriarchy would accept as truth. She was a woman trying to speak the truth, trying to spread knowledge, trying to warn the world, and like the mad scientist in any disaster movie who turns out to be correct, the world deemed her a lunatic and a liar. She became the archetype of the crazy woman, a cautionary tale of what happens when women step out of line and try to engage with a man's world.

The "alt-right" cancellations revealed that the university limits the range of acceptable speech for the white male voices by whom the academy is constructed and continues to serve. How do you think it treats those who are even further from that center? Those for whom the university was never intended?

The women? The Latinos? The disabled? The blacks?

Particularly blacks, whose history of subjection and domination provides every justifiable cause for them to perpetrate the most spectacular of violences against the institutions that were built and continue to thrive thanks to their slave labor. What restrictions do primarily white institutions place on the speech of black students, faculty, and staff? What space remains that could possibly exceed this censorship and exclusion?

While still relegated to margins, the African-American, Fourteenth Amendment, assimilation-based rhetoric can access the university. Its role, however, is not to educate students in any way. Instead, these bodies and thoughts confirm the university's progress and assuage its guilt. The primary role of these professors is not to disseminate black knowledge but rather to serve as examples of how the university's employees and the system itself are not racist. While many of these professors are doing important work, the university exploits

their work and their bodies for
racial capital. This is not the fault
of the individuals, mind you. This
is a violent system displaying black
flesh as evidence that the university allows and supports "black
excellence."

My experience has taught me
that this is the acceptable place
for blackness in the American
university. Stay in line and kneel
at the altar of antiblackness—or
at least keep your head down and
your mouth shut—and you might
survive as a black professor. Step
outside of that place and into
another position for blackness at
your own risk.

But if even a small step invites
violence, why not make a giant
leap? Some voices go so far left
they advocate for dismantling the
structure in which the political
scale exists. The university also
censors these voices, although the
censorship of these voices is more
structural than spectacular. While
the right-wing voices of hate are
often met with rallies and coun-
terprotests when they arrive on
campus, the radical revolutionary

voice is rarely even allowed on the grounds.

However, this revolutionary thought is not entirely absent in the academy. Those universities who strive to claim their place as the brightest beacons of enlightenment—the Harvards, the Stanfords, the University of Californias—will always allow one radical black voice within their walls. And in times of racial strife, these universities will use this black thinker as a shield to deflect any accusations of the school's lack of progress regarding racial diversity. In doing so, however, the universities inadvertently display their racial homogeneity, rendering the lone radical black professor the exception that not only proves but also enforces the rule of antiblackness.

I support professors in both positions, and I stand for all methods of survival and self-care.

But these black revolutionaries are my influences. My path is guided by those whose work seeks to dismantle the world. On occasion, the university offers a

black revolutionary a position—
Angela Davis, Frank Wilderson,
and Kathleen Cleaver, to name a
few—and when this black intellectual stands up and challenges the
norms, the violence comes. The
university punishes the ungrateful
black professor as Apollo cursed
Cassandra, to serve as an example
that implicitly teaches the student
body what is unacceptable. In an
institution with dozens, if not hundreds, of voices clamoring through
the grammar of antiblack epistemology, the black revolutionary
mind becomes an example made
flesh, a physical manifestation
of the unspoken rules of civility
that order polite society. Within a
framework of antiblackness, black
voices of dissent that challenge the
superiority of such a biased epistemology are akin to the homeless
man with a sandwich board shouting that the end is nigh. They are
the voices of madness and insanity
that are, although correct in their
prophesies, cursed to never be
believed.

Although stated perhaps more
explicitly and with more pessimism

than one is accustomed to, this view is not unique. The assumptive logic of that critique exists on the same scale as any academic field whose name carries a raced or gendered modifier: black studies, ethnic studies, women's studies, gender studies—each is a way of knowing that the university qualifies to center and normalizes white maleness. In more specific terms, the racially coded knowledge that serves as the foundation for the American university system is one of the primary critiques of black radical theory. Take bell hooks, Hortense Spillers, Fred Moten, Joy James, and countless others who have each wielded their intellects as pickaxes and sledgehammers to chisel away at the alabaster ramparts defending the academy as the "site of social production of conquest denial."[4]

Thankfully, the university as an institution lacked the foresight to anticipate how these more revolutionary, more scandalous intellectuals and theories would appeal to students for whom the university restricts access.

FACET: 2

Age: 26
Location: UC San Diego
Status: A Breakthrough

When my phone rang at 2:00 p.m. the Friday after classes ended, I was resolved to just "yes" and "mm-hmm" my way through the conversation, thus ending it as quickly as I could. But Frank wasn't calling to hear himself talk. And he wasn't calling to pass judgment.

He was calling to have an actual conversation.

"How are you doing, Matt?" Frank asked.

"Fine."

"Okay. How was your experience in the class?" he asked.

"What do you mean?" I responded.

"Well, I know you struggled a bit early on, and I wanted to see if you had any lingering questions?"

"I think I'm good."

"Are you sure?" he asked. "Because I'm a bit concerned about your paper."

Ah, my paper. I wrote about Tiger Woods. Dude is rich and famous. He also suffered one of the most tragic fates (and I mean that in the classical Greek sense) of any modern man. Like Oedipus, his hubris was his downfall. I argued that because he had so far to fall, he couldn't be socially dead. If blackness existed on a flat plane of social death, then Tiger would have been able to neither rise nor fall.

"What about my paper?" I asked.

"I would like you to rewrite it," he requested as much as demanded.

Rewrite it. I hadn't been asked for a rewrite since my very first paper in undergrad for Rhetoric and Writing Studies 101. I had never written an essay before, and I had no idea how to write an argument or use sources to support the argument. So instead, I just gave a book report–level summary of Plato. This phone call with Frank transported me back to that moment in my 101 course—of reading through the professor's remarks and finding on page three, less than halfway through: "I stopped reading here. This is not the level of writing I expect from college students. Please come see me in my office hours." But a rewrite at the doctoral level confirmed all of my fears—I had failed. I wasn't fit to be here. This wasn't a place for me.

"Rewrite it how?" I asked.

"I understand your argument," he said, "and it makes sense at a political level, but it doesn't really engage with the class material. You are writing about Tiger Woods's experience, and the class was about ontology."

"So?" I retorted.

"Well, as Fanon tells us, ontology leaves experience by the wayside."

What do we have other than our experiences? What are we other than the sum of our deeds? I snapped. "I don't know what that means! How can we just ignore experience?!"

But instead of acknowledging my anger, Frank engaged, "That's a great question. I am not saying we should ignore experience, but maybe understand that not all experiences exist within the same context."

Both the calmness and clarity of his words brought both my rage and my mind back to earth. Context. That was something I could work with. "What do you mean by context?" I asked.

"The slave exists in a different context than the human," he said.

"But that's what I don't get—how am I natally alienated? I have a hometown."

"Where are you from?"

"Dunbar, West Virginia."

"Okay, great. You were born in West Virginia. Where are your ancestors from?" he asked.

"Well, my mom's side is German, English, and Irish, and my dad's side is African," I stated.

"Do you see the difference between the two? One side has specific nations and cultures and customs to point to, and the other side is just generalized blackness. So, West Virginia is a part of your history," he continued, "but it is not your heritage. Everything has a history—a rock has a history. But only humans have a heritage. On one side, your heritage goes back to varying distinct human cultures, and the other side only goes back to the slave ship. Anything before that is lost."

This simple explanation floored me.

With that, it all fell into place. I remembered my childhood, my mom calling my dad nigger. Nigger is what remains of the Africans who got off the ship at Jamestown—the African became natally alienated in the hold of the ship. Nigger is the paradox of being owned as human chattel and yet not recognized as a person in your own right—general dishonor. Nigger is being bred, whipped, beaten, and still forced to labor all day, every day for no pay—subject to gratuitous violence prior to an act of transgression:

black is the body gently swaying in the Alabama breeze—subject to gratuitous violence.

black is the police dogs and firehoses of civil rights—general dishonor.

black are the bodies who serve as the prison slaves, not only incarcerated, but ripped from the refugee colonies established on a land and in a world that is not their own—natally alienated. A closed circle of Africa—black—nigger—black—Africa—the distinctions between these concepts collapsing under the weight of slave. A continuum from John Hawkyns to Captain William Tucker to Abraham Lincoln to Lyndon Johnson to Ronald Reagan to George W. Bush to Assata Shakur to WEB DuBois to Frederick Douglass to Olaudah Equiano to Peter the Negro. Afropessimism wasn't about me and my blackness. Afropessimism was about the world that chose to articulate my blackness in this way—more than a racial category of human identity, but rather a position of noncommunicability with civil society. Frank Wilderson's book *Red, White, and Black: Cinema and the Structures of US Antagonisms*, in which he coined the field of Afropessimism, wasn't about me. It was about how the world articulated blackness not as a racial distinction within humanity but as the metaphysical absence through which human presence, with all the rights and privileges that entails, garners coherence. I was not a being of pure nothingness, even though the world functioned on seeing me as such. He brought under this umbrella various theorists who "explore the meaning of blackness not . . . as a variously and unconsciously interpellated identity . . . but as a structural position of noncommunicability in the face of all other positions."[5]

In short, an Afropessimist is someone who believes that all of modern life, not just the actions that occur, but the imagination and desires that lead to those actions, are dependent on black social death. An Afropessimist is someone who does not take the human as a divine, metaphysical constant but instead interrogates the possibility that the human is a social construct in the same ways as race and gender. What if red and yellow and white and brown are the four wings of a house standing on the one foundation, and blackness is the hole in which they poured the concrete? In other words, without the concept and word and embodiment of nigger, the world as we know it couldn't exist.

Afropessimism did something for me that no other discourse could. It explains how my mother could marry and have children with a black man and still call him nigger.

Recognizing that social death was inextricable from the black condition allowed me to speak in a vocabulary that would explain my past. My mother's attitude toward my father, my encounter with the police when I was fifteen, my mother-in-law's attempt to relate to my blackness before my humanity—each of these moments made sense in relation to social death. If the world's coherence requires blacks to exist in a position of social death, as Afropessimism argues, then my white mother could never truly be married to my black father. The world would not honor the relation. The officer pulling his gun is not an aberration—a violent interjection into my being, but a necessary part of maintaining our positionality. I am subject to gratuitous violence. My mother-in-law could not relate to me as a human, as human was not a part of my constitution. So she engaged the part of me that was positioned in her antiblack world: my blackness. In the recognition that Afropessimism had the explanatory power to address my ruptured existence, I shattered again.

But this shattering was unlike the others.

This shattering allowed the pieces of me to slip through the chains in which civil society had bound my existence. Afropessimism, despite its name, can actually be quite liberating for blackness. The theory has the explanatory power to unleash unbridled hope, not a hope contained by reformist compromise and white fragility, not a hope of changing this world, but a hope of a new world. A hope beyond the realm of imagined possibilities—a hope beyond hope. It allowed me to see the world and my place in it in a whole new light.

The problem was not me. The problem was not my blackness. The problem was the world—the world that had pathologized my blackness as an illness, a defect, an abject humanity. The world that limits itself out of a sadomasochistic urge to dominate blackness. The limits were the problem of the world.

Afropessimism reframed my entire existence, and I became limitless.

During that phone call, I realized Frank's revolutionary flame had not been tempered, but rather, he had focused its fire on a new objective. He would revolutionize the world not only by challenging its prevailing knowledge, but also by challenging young minds such as mine to create new knowledge.

During that phone call, I became an Afropessimist.

"Afropessimism is too defeatist."

A common critique

of Afropessimism

is that the field of thought is

nihilistic.

Giving up.

Hopeless.

Quite the contrary.

Afropessimism is all about hope:

Hope that we will look beyond the surface,

hope that we can move past the symbolic and to the substantive,

hope that we will move from reformist compromise to revolutionary
demand,

hope that we can engage a metaphysics of absence instead of
always assuming presence,

hope that someone will prove the theory wrong.

I am hopeful that in my lifetime I will see

a world in which blackness is not antagonistic to humanity,

where our being is not always already composed of and subject to
gratuitous violence,

where words like excellence, joy, and resistance won't need

qualifiers because of my flesh.
I am hopeful that I will see that world
for all of our sakes—black and nonblack alike.
I am hopeful that world exists.
I am also certain that world is not this world.
This world uses
incarceration
subjugation
legislation
litigation
to strangle the hope from black flesh.
The strange fruit does not fall far from the lynching tree.
And I hope this world will stop,
but I fear that to do so we must stop the world.
Afropessimism is all about hope—
just not hope for this world.

FRAGMENT 10

FACET: 1

Age: 26
Location: San Diego, CA
Status: To All the Girls . . .

"Ya wanna go rolla skatin'?" I yelled in a fake Bronx accent from my friend's car as we sat in the game day traffic exiting Qualcomm Stadium.

I saw her face light up. "Shuh thang," she yelled back from her car in a fake accent as bad as my own. "Lemme give ya mah numbah."

That was how I asked out Angela Davis. No, not that Angela Davis, but I took the name as a sign.

It was the first time I ever asked out a black woman.

SHARD: 1

Status: Where Have All the black Women Gone?

Growing up as a young child in West Virginia, I had many black women in my life. When we lived closer geographically to my dad's side of the family, I got to spend time with my grandmother and aunties and cousins. Kay, Nika, B, Kim—we'd go to their houses for cookouts, birthdays, and just to visit. I also had my first-grade teacher, Mrs. Meriwether, a fifty-something black woman who recognized my intellect and suggested I get tested for gifted classes. Even my grade school principal at Ford Elementary, Miss Sanders, was black. While I wasn't particularly close to any of them individually, they were still a part of my life—grounded counterbalances to the over-the-top caricatures of black women on TV and in movies.

But at every phase of my life, I found myself exposed to fewer and fewer black women. Once we left West Virginia for Pennsylvania, I saw my dad's family on rare occasions, typically once during the summer and once around the winter holidays. Without my dad's family to fill the void, I became more aware of how few black people were in my life. In West Virginia, we were the only black family in the neighborhood. The same was true in Pennsylvania. All of the kids I played with—Kimmie, Joey, Ashley, Jared, Greg, Matt, Josh, Andrew—were white. While I had black friends at school—Dewey, LaKisha, Carl, Karen, and others—they all lived farther than walking distance from my house. For a ten-year-old, that may as well have put them on another planet. Never once in my six years in Pennsylvania did I ever go to one of my black friends' houses.

When we moved to San Diego, the population became more diverse, but my friendships did not. In truth, I had very few friends in San Diego. Sure, I had classmates and teammates and neighbors, but very few friends, very few people I kicked it with outside of school. Part of this was geography and part of it was financial. But most of it was my awkwardness and anxiety and depression—who wants to hang out with the broke, fat, black kid? I didn't often invite people over, except Philip and Norenzo, who were almost as broke and just as black as I was.

Once I graduated from high school and enrolled in college, systemic and institutional racism washed most of the blackness from my life. As a theater major at SDSU, I only remember two black women enrolled in my department, Brittney and Brittany; the former was an actress and the latter a costume designer.

Graduate school eliminated black women from my academic or professional life almost entirely. During my three years at Mary Baldwin, none of my fellow students nor professors were black, let alone black women. And while I did have some black women in courses during my PhD—amazing, intelligent, black women like Jaye and Sally and Patrice—they were always from different campuses or different departments. No black women enrolled in my PhD program while I was there. I had one black woman as a professor, and she was the first black woman instructor I'd had since Mrs. Meriwether in the first grade.

While I managed to clear all the hurdles to educational advancement that America creates for black people, thousands of others were not so lucky. And, yes, a lot of it is luck. Making the leap from high school to college as a black person is no small task, not with chains of violence pulling you from behind and the winds of oppression and history blowing in your face. Aptitude tests, applications, visits, extracurricular activities—all of these things cost money. While these expenditures are undoubtedly worthwhile, for many black families, who on average have about one-eighth the wealth of the average white family, no amount of budgeting can create the $75 needed for a college application or the $120 to take the SAT. And when black people clear these hurdles and make it to college, we are much more likely to accrue debt and much less likely to graduate than any other race. Even if we earn a bachelor's degree, we are less likely to have the high-profile mentors and recommendations necessary for graduate applications. And that is if we are even aware that graduate school exists. And after climbing the mountain for four years of undergrad, two years of a master's, and five years of a PhD, blacks still do not reach the mountaintop. Even with a terminal degree, blacks are less likely to get academic jobs than their nonblack peers and even less likely to earn tenure and promotion.

And these hurdles are not accidental. Excluding black people is one of the founding principles of the American higher education system. Asher Price of the *Atlantic* recently uncovered documents revealing that the University of Texas only began requiring the SAT for admission after segregation was ruled illegal. They required the exam specifically because they knew it would reduce the number of black applicants who qualified.[1] On top of this, most graduate programs require students to take the Graduate Record Exam (GRE) as part of their application. However, studies have shown that the GRE has little predictive power in gauging one's success in graduate school. Instead, as Victoria Clayton states, the GRE is "a proxy for asking, 'Are you rich?' 'Are you male?' 'Are you white?'"[2]—questions that automatically exclude black women on two of three counts.

Two of three counts. While I encountered these obstacles, despite my blackness, my cisgender maleness offered me advantages in clearing them that black women do not receive. As a black man, I am one identifier away from the normative subject. While that step is a giant leap across an endless chasm, if you squint enough, you can almost imagine I belong. Or you can at least imagine that I am nonthreatening enough to be allowed in. For those who exist further than me from that full-fledged subject—the minorities within minorities, such as black women or black queer men, or minorities within minorities within minorities, such as black queer women—I cannot imagine the obstacles they face.

But my decreased interactions with black women were not solely the product of these systemic hurdles. Rising through the ranks also affected my own psyche. Sometimes, I would look around my classrooms and conferences, and I would begin to feel that I had transcended my blackness. Not that I had become white, but that I had reached a level where everyone was so progressive and enlightened that maybe, just maybe, my blackness didn't matter so much. It wasn't racist that the vast majority of people who met my education and economic standards were white; it was just a quirk in the system. And if I, as a black man, overcame the obstacles, any black person could.

Of course, it was racist. Of course, it is racist. Yes, I overcame the obstacles, but that doesn't mean every black person will get the opportunities. And now, as a black man who has "made it," I feel a profound responsibility to help other black people achieve. But here is where the game of civil society trips me up. I feel trapped in a paradox—I long to engage in black communities and black culture, but I am so removed from them that I feel like a tourist in my own skin. My career in education left me feeling distant and isolated from the black community. I had tried doing community outreach with my universities and theaters, but I felt like an interloper, a black man performing white savior. An Uncle Tom, preaching the good word of bootstraps and black responsibility. I felt like I was there for my peace of mind and not for their progress. Mostly, I felt angry that there was a divide between them and me; and I felt guilty that I was not one of them.

Even when I was on Match.com, I rarely got black women in my results. While I never marked a racial category in my searches, numerous preferences I did select had a covert racial component. Distance from zip code—I'm in La Jolla, which is mostly UCSD students or wealthy people, and few in each category are black. I wanted someone who was a college grad or at least pursuing a degree—I figured since I was in a PhD program, I wanted someone who was seeking to educate themselves and increase their earning power. But this requirement also weeded out a lot of black women. I didn't want anyone with kids. I don't know if this affected the number of black women in my results or if I am reading media tropes of young black mothers onto this.

On a few rare occasions, a black woman would appear in my results. Often, I would message them and, often, I would not receive a response. This isn't necessarily a racial thing—I probably only got an answer to 2 percent of the messages I sent, but I never made a match with a black woman on Match.com. On the rare occasion when a black woman would respond to my initial message, they usually gave some variation of the same five-word response that echoes the isolation and liminal status I myself felt in relation to the black community—

"I don't date black guys."

FACET: 2

Age: 26
Location: San Diego, CA
Status: To All the Girls . . .

January 2011. I was in my first year at UC San Diego, and a friend from undergrad, J-Muss, had invited me to an SDSU alumni tailgate for the San County Credit Union Poinsettia Bowl at Qualcomm Stadium. San Diego had recently experienced a freak January torrential rainstorm that flooded the stadium and half of the parking lot. While the grounds crew had managed to pump the water out of the arena bowl so the game could take place, the only place they could put the water was the already-flooded parking lot. The day was a sunny, cool mid-seventies—so perfect you'd never know a storm had occurred so recently, except for the fact that the pregame tailgating crowds conducted their barbecues and parking lot football games in about a third of the expected space. This forced groups who under usual circumstances would be on opposite sides of the blacktop expanse to congregate and mingle with one another.

The grills were on full blast, the coolers were full, and the air resonated with soundwaves ranging from pregame commentary to reggae. With an hour of beers and hot dogs in me, I joined a game of catch with fellow SDSU alums. The condensed space meant that we were constantly throwing the ball in, out, and through other groups of tailgaters. Even at peak sobriety, accurate passing is not my strong suit. I was a lineman, not a quarterback. So, a six-pack in, my aim was teetering between comical and pathetic. I overthrew my buddy J-Muss on a pass, and before he could retrieve the ball, I heard a voice I didn't recognize shout at me, "Go long!"

The voice came from a beautiful black woman with luscious light brown skin, natural hair, and bright eyes that narrowed into sultry daggers when she smiled. She was close to six feet tall, her body fit and toned from a childhood as a figure skater and gymnast, I would learn. She was a graduate of Thomas Jefferson law school and attending the tailgate with her law school friends.

I took her instructions and turned away to go long, sprinting as best I could through the overcrowded parking lot. She pulled back and unleashed a pass better than any of my own. I dug in and leapt for the ball. As I stretched to make the one-handed grab, I quickly realized I had overjumped, and I had to choose between catching the ball and sticking the landing. I managed to do neither, and as the ball sailed over my outstretched hands, I stumbled uncontrollably, eventually finding myself on the ground.

I remained on the blacktop for a moment; nothing hurt but my pride. As I began to get up and brush myself off, the woman approached and offered me her hand.

"That was awful." She laughed.

"Yeah, it was," I agreed. "That throw was terrible."

We both chuckled at my lack of athleticism. Then, she offered an introduction, "I'm Angela."

"Hi. Matt," I responded.

"What brings you here?" she asked.

"I'm with the SDSU group," I said. "You?"

"Thomas Jefferson Law," she said, pointing across the lot.

"Can I get you a drink?"

"Sure," she said. "Corona?"

"Let me check." I walked over to the SDSU alumni cooler and returned with two Coronas.

"Cheers," I said, handing her one of the beers. We clinked the rims of the glass bottles with a smile, and she thanked me.

We searched for a place to sit and eventually made the open tailgate of a stranger's Ford pickup truck our camp.

"So, Matt, what do you do?" she asked.

"I'm a PhD student at UCSD," I said. "You're clearly in law. What is your specialty?"

She gave a look that I read as surprise, as though most people outside of the field of law never bother to question any deeper about her chosen occupation.

"Corporate litigation," she said.

"Does that mean you help corporations sue corporations, or that you help corporations sue people?" I asked.

"Neither, right now," she responded. "I just graduated, and the job market for attorneys sucks. None of my friends have jobs yet, at least not in the field. I'm lucky to be a paralegal."

"Better than still being a student," I said, mocking my own current situation.

She gave a small chuckle.

We continued our conversation, and the tenor shifted away from polite small talk into the depths of our lives. We spoke of our pasts as athletes, our educations, our families, our history, our blackness. We spoke of isolation and community and purpose. She was born in New York, the daughter of a naval officer and a professor. She still enjoyed going figure skating when she could. She had gone to a Catholic high school.

"I still have the skirt," she said sheepishly.

We conversed for over an hour, and gradually the language and

voices that we wore to satisfy the standards of an antiblack society—
the coded language of professionalism that many assume is universal
but is the product of hegemony—slipped away. The endings of our
words softened from "-ers" to "-as" and the "hmms" became the "tch"
of a tongue click. The laughs became louder, and the polite smiles
became playful bumps and thigh pats.

Suddenly, "Yo, Angela!" called a man. "Game's about to start!"

"I gotta go," she said, standing from the tailgate. She leaned in
and gave me a hug. "It was so nice to meet you, Matt."

"Nice to meet you as well," I said as we released one another.

She hesitated for just a moment. I sensed she wanted me to ask
for her number. For us to get to know one another more. I wanted
that as well. Instead, I froze. I sat silently on the back of the pickup
truck and waved good-bye. As she turned and walked into the stadium, I regretted my cowardice. But I didn't go after her.

I spent the entirety of the game thinking about her, thinking
about how I had blown it. Why didn't I ask her out? For most of my
life, I had been a coward when it came to girls. It wasn't the fear of
rejection—being in theater and academia have taught me that rejection is a fact of life. Whether it's auditioning for a role in a play or
submitting an article to a journal, the supply of actors and articles
far outstrips the demand for them. Being rejected means you are putting yourself out there. Rejections are a badge of something between
effort and honor. Or at least that's what we tell ourselves to cope with
the fact that rejection is much more common than acceptance. I
wasn't afraid of rejection.

Maybe I didn't believe I was worthy of love.

The possibilities were still swirling in my head as I sat in the pas-
senger seat while we tried to exit the parking lot. With thousands of
drivers in varying states of sobriety all trying to leave at once, traffic
had cemented itself into place.

After not moving for what felt like hours but was probably closer to five minutes, we were assaulted by a car horn. I looked at J-Muss, and he rolled his eyes. It must just be some drunk fan celebrating.

But the horn didn't relent.

"What the fuck, man," said J-Muss. "Where do they want me to go?"

"I got this," I said.

I rolled down my window, prepared to give the nagging honker my best black shit to try to scare some patience into them, but my eyes didn't see some annoying fan. Instead, I saw Angela's face sticking out the rear window of a car in the next lane. I couldn't believe it.

"Hey, buddy," she shouted, "how's it going?"

It was fate. It had to be. Someone blessed me with a chance to redeem myself for my earlier cowardice.

"Ya wanna go rolla skatin'?" I shouted across the engines and brake lights.

It would be the last time I ever asked out a black woman.

SLIVER

Maybe It's Me?

I rationalize away my shortcomings. I blame external factors. But the truth is, I, too, have antiblack thoughts.

I do not, however, engage in antiblack actions. I don't wear a white hood or celebrate Negro bodies swinging from trees. I don't say All Lives Matter or Blue Lives Matter. I don't call my brothers and sisters thug or ho. I don't even engage in the backhanded compliments that code the normative black person as uncivilized, descriptors such as well-spoken, well-dressed, or tidy.

I try not even to think them.

But try as I might, some of these urges still infest my thoughts. They pop into my mind—haunting apparitions that chill my spine and vanish into the ether between pure imagination and conscious thought.

Maybe not the more violent

manifestations and examples mentioned above—lynchings are not my dreams, but my nightmares. No, I am not that ghoulish and self-loathing. My antiblackness is more insidious, confined to instincts and reflexes that conscious thought must override.

I am not immune to the constant barrage of dehumanizing images and tropes of blackness. I find myself often struggling against the current of deplorable representations of blackness—swimming upstream against the welfare queens and shiftless niggers, hos and pimps, and thugs and druggies—that our news media and scripted dramas deploy for profit. On occasion, my faculties relent, and I get swept away in thoughts of "if I did it, why can't they?" and "maybe if they had more jobs and fewer kids . . ." Even though these brief thoughts are more a product of exhaustion than malice, I still feel guilty for letting them happen at all.

Just because I am not of the antiblack world does not mean I am not in the antiblack world. I recognize the tension between the two, and I have to actively work against the psychic impulses to hate myself and others like me for our blackness. I have to actively work against the subconscious antiblackness that structures both human civil society and my social death. I actively work in my pedagogy, my art, and my life to advance black life. At every break, it's never enough. The river is too strong.

On occasion, I can take one of my brothers or sisters by the hand and drag them against the overwhelming torrents of black inhumanity that bombard our senses and psyche. But these individual advances, these personal successes—the students I mentor to graduation and grad school, the ones I help find jobs, the ones I buy groceries for—do nothing to dam the flow. I can fight against the current, but how does one make a river flow in the opposite direction? That is the struggle of black life: we can fight against people and narratives and institutions, but how do we fight against the world

itself? How do we imagine outside
of all so revolutionary progress
does not just realign into repetitive
oppression?

How do I fight when even my
thoughts are formed and informed
by the very antiblack world I seek
to dismantle?

My psyche is also the product of
an antiblack world. I am particularly susceptible to negative images
of black women. I have my own
experience, my own life, to counter
narratives of black masculinity
and blackness as a whole, but
when my thoughts on blackness
intersect with the specifics of
womanhood, I struggle to find
stability. Like crossing the streams
in *Ghostbusters*, the intersection
of blackness and womanhood is
a plane of existence beyond my
capacity as a man to comprehend,
let alone articulate.

I hope with all my hope that
the preconscious antiblackness
that occasionally makes its way to
my conscious thoughts isn't the
reason I didn't seek out more black
women, that I didn't date more
black women, that I didn't marry

a black woman. If I am completely honest with myself, I don't know. This is not to say the factors of systemic racism do not matter. What I have written earlier certainly creates obstacles to partnerships with black women. However, I also must recognize that these obstacles, while monumental, are not insurmountable. Maybe it was a result of systemic racism. Perhaps it was a coincidence of geography, education, and economics.

Maybe it wasn't.

Maybe it was a deep-seated, subconscious revulsion to blackness that kept me from pursuing more black women.

Maybe it wasn't.

Maybe it was a recognition of the work it would take to look past the world's view of our black flesh to see each other as we truly are and not to see each other through the kaleidoscope of black tropes.

Maybe it wasn't.

These questions join the innumerable antiblack notions in the haunting parade of ghosts and zombies and phantasms that invade my mind.

FACET: 3

Age: 26
Location: San Diego, CA
Status: To All the Girls . . .

Angela and I did go ice skating.

About a week later, we met up at the Escondido Iceplex for our first date. I am a terrible ice skater. I can barely stand on the skates. She literally skated circles around me as I drifted aimlessly near the wall, praying I wouldn't do anything too embarrassing or painful.

"Wow," she said, "you really suck at this."

"Thanks," I replied.

I think she was a bit smitten by the fact I wasn't some controlling, macho guy and was, instead, willing to put myself in a potentially embarrassing situation to engage in something she enjoyed.

"Let me help," she said as she took my hand and guided me around the rink.

We kissed goodnight next to her car.

We continued seeing each other over the following weeks. We texted every day and spoke on the phone most nights. We went to a small Italian cucina for dinner together on Valentine's Day. We made out at the movies. All the signals were there as we spent the next couple of months never fully dating but "seeing each other" in that way that young professionals and progressive youths *see* each other, eschewing labels and commitment.

Until one evening in late April when I invited her over to my apartment. We had spent quite a bit of time discussing cooking shows and recipes we had seen prepared on TV, and I proposed that she find some recipes she'd like to try, and we could make them together. She liked that idea, so on this evening, I was preparing the *mise en place* for panzanella, pasta carbonara, and raspberry crème brûlée. She arrived wearing a yellow sundress with lacy shoulder straps and white canvas flats. Her makeup was sparse but well done—enough to accent her eyes without diminishing their beauty.

After dinner, we made the short cross from the small nook that held my dining table to the couch in the connected open area that constituted my living room.

"What do you wanna watch?" I asked.

"I don't know, something stupid," she said.

I turned on some insipid comedy film and leaned into the plush back of the couch. Angela leaned into the crook of my shoulder and curled her feet behind her, kicking off her flats in the process. We cuddled on the couch for a few minutes, sinking into one another, before I leaned in to kiss her. The sounds of the TV slowly faded into the background. I placed a hand on her hip and made my way underneath her sundress.

"Be my girlfriend," I said, hoping the request would speed our momentum.

Instead, it ground to a halt. She exhaled sharply as though blowing out all sexual energy.

"I'm sorry," she said. "I can't."

"Why not?" I asked.

She pulled herself out of my embrace and sat up, sitting straight forward.

"I'm sorry," she repeated. "I like you. I do. I have a lot of fun with you. You're smart. You're funny. But . . ." she trailed off.

"But?" I spurred her on.

"But I'm just not in a place where I can have a relationship," she said. "I mean, I just passed the bar, and I'm looking for a job. If I get an offer in LA or San Fran, I need to be able to move. I can't have someone I'm attached to here. I don't want to have to make the choice between a relationship and my career."

"I get it," I said.

And I did. Being in academia, I knew how dire a job market could be. I had friends who fell out of the profession because they couldn't find a job that didn't require them to move their kids or their spouse or their life. So I knew that if we did get together in four or five years, I would be in the same position, if we made it that far.

"I really get it," I said. "Can we still see each other?"

"I hope so," she said.

She leaned back in, and we cuddled until the movie was over. I walked her to her car and gave her a goodnight kiss.

ABSENCE
Status: Between the presence of woman
and the absence of blackness.

"De nigger woman is de mule uh de world so fur as Ah can see."
—Zora Neale Hurston, *Their Eyes Were Watching God*

Afropessimism as a critique of the human as a construct
requires a critique of the constituent elements of humanity in
relation to blackness.
This fragment uses the phrase "black woman" uncritically.
Digestibly.
Coherently.
What if we challenge this phrase?
What if instead of relying on a humanist assumptive logic,
we interrogate the oxymoronic,
impossible intersection of black absence with the presence of
human gender?
What if instead of using the master's tools
to distinguish between the variations of black sentient flesh
we create our own?
How do we then come to understand the unique violence
that "black women"
face as beings
and as a phrase?

I don't have the answers,
but these brilliant black women are asking the questions:
Hortense Spillers, Audre Lorde, Sylvia Wynter,
Patrice Douglass, Selamawit D. Terrefe,
Zakiyyah Iman Jackson, Tiffany Lethabo King,
Katherine McKittrick, Michelle Wright,
Saidiya Hartman, Claudia Rankine, Karen E. Fields,
Barbara J. Fields, La Donna Forsgren,
Octavia Butler, Toni Morrison, Toni Cade Bambara,
Alice Walker, Kara Walker,
Kim F. Hall, bell hooks, Zora Neale Hurston, Brittney Cooper
And too many more to name.

Read them. Know them. Love them.
As though our lives depend on it.

This is not me pandering.
This is me recognizing my own shortcomings.
As a scholar. Theorist. Author. Teacher.
"Man."
Attempting to grow.
Using my voice, my privilege,
although I have little
to amplify those of others.

FACET: 4

Age: 26
Location: San Diego, CA
Status: To All the Girls . . .

Less than two weeks after telling me she wasn't ready for a boyfriend, Angela's Facebook status changed to "in a relationship."

Her new boyfriend was white.

Maybe she was just being polite with her reasons for turning me down. Maybe she just wanted something fun with me. Maybe she wasn't interested long-term and wanted to let me down gently.

Maybe.

FRAGMENT 11

FACET: 1

Age: 31
Location: Washington State
Status: Terror Alert Yellow

"Terrorist" is such a vile, disgusting word. In our current world, it is among the most damaging racially coded signifiers in common English language parlance; second, perhaps, only to nigger. The FBI divides terrorism into two classes based on the terrorist's relation to America: international terrorism, which is "perpetrated by individuals and/or groups inspired by or associated with designated foreign terrorist organizations or nations (state-sponsored)";[1] and domestic terrorism, which is "perpetrated by individuals and/or groups inspired by or associated with primarily U.S.-based movements that espouse extremist ideologies of a political, religious, social, racial, or environmental nature."[2]

If we consider these definitions at face value, I struggle to identify what distinguishes domestic terrorism from mainstream American policy. When voter suppression, militarized police, and mass incarceration exist as the lawfully wedded spouse of the bias in our criminal justice and policing systems, how is being black in America not living in a constant state of terror? Are not these policies "extremist"? Are they not "racial"? In America, black life is a life governed under the auspices of race-based terror perpetrated by a government of, by, and for a people who once owned blacks as slaves and continue to build their communities based on our exclusion and destruction.

"HE'S A TERRORIST!"

As my eyes passed over the seventeen characters, empowered by caps lock and inflated by an exclamation point, my heart sank. How was I a terrorist? What had I done other than speak my truth? I had offered no violence other than my presence, no political agenda other than my skin. But here, in my new home of Washington state, that was more than enough for me to be the victim of this second most heinous of (racial) slurs.

SLIVER

Trump Country

Washington state, and the entire Pacific Northwest for that matter, is entirely different from San Diego, yet precisely the same. Much like my other Pacific coast home, Washington has a reputation of liberalism and progressiveness. Companies like Microsoft and Amazon make the Seattle metro area their home. The national discourse surrounding the state focuses on technological advances, income growth of the clean-cut, made-for-mass-media white programmers, and executives with high salaries and stock options, which replaced forty acres and a mule as the American Dream.

Occasionally, the narrative shifts to one of the many subplots that also construct the region's story. Only rarely do the less benign subplots, such as the high cost of housing driving long-term citizens

from their residences and causing a
homeless crisis, ever reach our ears.
More often, these stories of gentrification and out-of-control housing
prices come dressed in the hipster
new bohemian aesthetic of eclectic
clothing, overgrown beards, and
craft breweries—the tales the
tourism board and popular culture
emphasize to draw in the dollars
of those claiming to seek tolerance
and the peaceful coexistence of cultures. There may be some truth to
this narrative, as long as you never
attempt to see behind the mirror
glaze that allows white people to
look at themselves and one another
and see nothing but acceptance
and love.

However, this thin, reflective
veneer of liberal reconciliatory
fantasy conceals a thick foundation
of racial segregation and violence.
Oregon, for example, was founded
as an explicitly all-white state.
In 1844, fifteen years before the
territory became a state, the pro-
visional government led by Peter
Burnett passed a law that expelled
all blacks from the region. Those
who refused to go willingly would

be subject to "not less than twenty and no more than thirty-nine stripes."[3] That means whippings. The Oregon law allowed any white person to whip any black person. All the violence of slavery with none of the labor.

But I don't want to imply that Oregon and Washington weren't slave states. They were. But the violence of slavery offended the white, liberal conscience of the colonists in these areas, so they allowed only a three-year grace period for slavery before ending the practice: once the slaves built the foundation for the colonizer's civilization, they were violently expelled from the master's house. And I am sure the well-being of the black slaves factored little into the decision to "free" them. Most likely, it was probably just cheaper and made them feel safer than building prisons.

The urban landscapes of Portland and Seattle have divorced their present narratives from this violent, antiblack past. But these metro centers compose only 10 percent of the total land area of

Oregon and Washington. The other 90 percent is mainly rural, primarily white, and largely uninterested in challenging the narrative. I lived in Ellensburg, which was ninety miles from Seattle on the map, across Snoqualmie pass. In the winter, that ninety miles may as well have been nine thousand, as the unpredictable snowfall at that altitude would often render the pass uncrossable, isolating Ellensburg from the outside world.

While this isolation was often climate-induced, in reality, it was a guiding factor in creating Ellensburg's culture. Many of my students, mostly in their late teens and early twenties, had never been outside the Ellensburg city limits. They had spent their whole lives where any being who was not white was an anomaly. For many of them, I was the first black person they had encountered who was not serving them. For many, their only encounter with nonwhite humans was the annual summer hiring of Latinx migrant laborers by their parents, who paid the workers slave wages.

And it was this history, this culture, this insistence on denying their complicity and reveling in their false superiority that caused my words to become a terrorist act. In this 86 percent Trump-voting county in the center of the Pacific Northwest, my presence, my voice, and my truth were more than enough for a student to interpret my—no, not my, as it was nothing I possessed, but rather, to interpret *me* as an enemy of the state.

How was I to react to such a slanderous, false accusation? Couldn't this student see that my being here was not of my agency but rather the byproduct of late-stage capitalism's devaluing of the professoriate combined with liberal academia's hunger for black flesh as a means of distracting from its antiblackness? I was not a terrorist. I was not an enemy of the state, far from it. If anything, I was a tool of the state. I was the state's evidence of racial progress and equality, of diversity and inclusivity. I was not in any way, shape, or form a terrorist.

If anything, I was a sellout.

SHARD: 1
Status: Movin' on Up

I moved to Washington by myself. The academic job market is an absolute bloodbath. About 40 percent of new PhD grads in the field of theater and performance studies get jobs in academia in any given year, and if you don't get a job in your first three years out of school, you probably won't get one. Having a full-time job outside of academia keeps most candidates from producing the research output to remain competitive in the field. But also, after three years, you are old news—damaged goods—compared to the dozens of bright, shiny new grads.

I was one of the lucky 40 percent. I received an offer for a nine-month, non-tenure-track, full-time position at a small, rural state school in central Washington. The job came with an exploitative thirteen-course teaching load over three quarters—all for the whopping sum of $43,000.

The offer came in the last week of July.

Classes started the third week of August.

I had three weeks to decide whether I wanted to spend nine months living in a town I had never visited. Three weeks to pack my things, find a place, drive 1,200 miles, and design four courses to teach in the fall.

There was no decision to make. Not taking the job would have put me one hiring cycle closer to untouchable.

But Steph was still in nursing school.

But I had to take the job.

Since the job wasn't permanent, Steph stayed in San Diego to finish school. I took what I could fit in my car—mostly clothes and a few of the books I'd need for my classes and my research—and began the twenty-hour drive to Ellensburg, Washington. Alone.

SPLINTER

Shard: 2
Status: Communist Pervert

"What the fuck?"

I didn't expect to find this on my windshield.

Especially not on Martin Luther King Jr. Day.

I stood in the parking lot of the Ellensburg Fred Meyer grocery store. The flyer froze me in place. Three letters and three words that cauterize the souls of black folk were emblazoned at the top.

Loyal White Knights.

KKK.

When the next faculty senate meeting came, both the chief of police and the university president were in attendance. They thought it necessary to discuss this act of terrorism. They thought it necessary to protect the university's few minority students and fewer minority professors.

Or so I thought.

"We have investigated the incident of racist flyers appearing on cars in the city," said the chief, "and we don't think there is a viable threat."

"After working with the police, we believe the campus is safe," said the president, "and these flyers were the work of one individual and not an organized event."

I couldn't believe what I was hearing. They made the same leap that the mainstream media makes in discussing white terrorism— dismissal. A lone wolf. A troubled soul. These flyers aren't about our town or its residents; they are about one lost sheep.

But these two men—one in his black uniform embellished with medals and patches, the other in his fine, tailored suit—did not teach. They didn't have students approach them with tears. They didn't have to explain to students' faces how and why this happens. And they wouldn't have to justify their actions in person to the young people targeted by these racist attacks. They could hide behind emails and university letterhead containing vague statements condemning hate in all forms and pat each other on the back saying, "Job well done."

"We have drafted a statement concerning this incident," said the president, "that we would like the faculty senate to sign off on."

The police chief read the statement aloud. Their message, as expected, was full of boilerplate denunciations of all forms of hate, even though the group perpetuating the hate in this instance had a particular breed of violent racist underpinnings. They then assured the community that the KKK posed no threat.

A strange buzzing overtook my ears as this white police officer spoke to a group of predominantly white professors that the white person who wanted to kill black people wasn't a threat. I couldn't believe my eyes as the white faces of the faculty nodded in understanding and approval at the chief's dismissal of the danger.

No threat.

They may as well have called them "some very good people."

No threat? For whom?

"I feel fine." The words of Carolyn Bryant, whose false accusations led to Emmett Till's murder, echoed in my head. When asked how she felt about his murderers being acquitted of Till's death, Bryant responded, "I feel fine." They feel fine, so there is no threat. Of course, the KKK was not a threat to the majority of this town, whose black families could be counted on one hand. The flyers were a threat to black and brown and Jewish and Middle Eastern people in the city—those whose numbers rendered them voiceless in the face of the Trump-voting populace. As such, the "I feel fine" crowd dismissed the concern of these people offhandedly without ever asking them if they felt threatened. This public promise of no threat served to implicitly support these racist actions by announcing to the perpetrators that they were free to continue their plots unimpeded by police interference.

Less than a week later, two men in a passing pickup truck hurled racial epithets and a glass beer bottle at a young black woman who attended the college. I never heard a police res-ponse to that incident, but I am sure they said it wasn't a threat.

When the police chief finished, the faculty senate president chimed in. "Before we vote on the statement, we will open it up for comment."

I looked around the room for allies. I looked for one of my colleagues of any color to look beyond their myopic perspective and attempt to see the incident through the eyes of the oppressed.

But there was no ally.

"If there is no comment, I motion we vote on the statement," said the faculty senate president.

My hand shot up before there could be a second.

"The chair recognizes Dr. Chapman," said the senate president.

My mouth immediately dried. My throat closed, knowing that I was risking both my reputation and my job. I was terrified. Speaking up at this moment, speaking truth in the faces of so many powers— police, union, university—could be my downfall.

But I persisted, as I had so many times before.

The words left my mouth barely above a whisper, "No threat to you."

"Excuse me?" said the police chief.

"You keep saying that the KKK is no threat," I said, more loudly and clearly than before. "The KKK is no threat to you. They were never meant to be a threat to you. They are a threat to me."

Judging by the faces of my colleagues, no one could believe what I had just said. From the back of the room, I heard a slight chuckle. I turned my head no more than two degrees so that just out of the corner of my eye, I could see the source: Dr. Conners—one in a handful of black faculty at this institution. Her laugh made me recognize my mistake. It wasn't the laugh of humor—she was not responding as though I had told a joke. It was the laugh that so many black people know, the signifyin' laughter of an elder that screams "boy, you fucked up."

Neither the police chief nor the university president offered a response to my comment. The only reply other than Dr. Connors's lesson in black positionality in the university came from the faculty senate president. "Thank you for your comment," he said. "I move to vote."

"Second," came a voice from the opposite side of the room.

"All in favor?" said the chair.

I looked around and saw all of my colleagues with their hands in the air.

"The motion passes."

I was not even allowed an opportunity to vote nay.

This is the type of racism that American society refuses to discuss. Most citizens recognize the spectacular racism of police violence and lynchings. Many can have polite discussions about the systemic violence of mass incarceration. But the subtle, paternalistic infantilization from our institutions often goes unaddressed. Antiblackness always approaches blackness with a "father knows best" attitude that denies black agency, black suffering, and black fear. It disavows our world view, our concerns, and our truths.

Imagine being told every second of every day that what you experienced didn't happen. And even if it did happen, "it's not that bad" or "there's no reason to make a big deal out of it." How long would you last before you ceased to believe, either out of defeat, out of self-preservation, or out of sheer (in)sanity, that perhaps your life wasn't actually happening how you experienced it? How long before you recognized that the world doesn't value your experience unless it serves someone else's agenda? How long until you concluded that the world didn't acknowledge your ownership of your truth?

I had just told this collective group that, despite the safety afforded them by sharing a flesh color with the attackers, there was, in fact, a threat. I had just positioned the danger on an axis of skin color where the degree of threat escalated in direct correlation with the amount of melanin visible in the epidermis.

And the collective group responded that as long as they were safe, I wasn't under threat.

SLIVER

Know Your Place

"I define know-your-place aggression as the flexible, dynamic array of forces that answer the achievements of marginalized groups such that their success brings aggression as often as praise. Any progress by those who are not straight, white, and male is answered by a backlash of violence—both literal and symbolic, both physical and discursive—that essentially says, know your place! . . . Understanding the country's tendency toward know-your-place aggression is crucial for black literary theory because it will keep the field attuned to how profoundly focused on success black communities have always been. It is because they have so consistently achieved [success] that white-authored violence has constantly emerged to check their progress . . . I vow to continue to make a priority of 1) identifying know-your-place

aggression and 2) highlighting
how often white mediocrity is
treated as merit. Violence is done
whenever there is know-your-place
aggression, no matter how subtle,
and whenever whiteness is treated
as if it always signifies merit."
—Dr. Koritha Mitchell,
"Identifying White Mediocrity
and Know-Your-Place Aggression:
A Form of Self-Care"[4]

Know-your-place aggression is
real, and it is damaging. But when
it comes to blackness, know-your-
place aggression is not limited to
policing achievements. The world
also polices our thoughts, our
bodies, and our emotions. Banning
critical race theory is nothing more
than backlash against blacks for
having the audacity to say, "We
built this country, too." Riot gear,
tear gas, and tanks unleashed on
peaceful protestors for having the
temerity to say, "Hey, we deserve
to live." If black people asking
for a history and a life is stepping
outside of our place, then what
place does this antiblack world
have for us?

FACET: 2

Age: 32
Location: Washington State
Status: Terror Alert Level Orange

"I've never had to light black skin," he whispered, partly ashamed of this gap in his experience and partly ashamed of the potential reaction from his classmates.

The department's antiblackness was the less obvious kind. The department did not engage in the active, explicit hatred of black people. Rather, they did not consider them at all. I was the only black faculty or staff member within the department's walls. The only minority period. There were no courses in American minority theater in the curriculum; the department's only recognition that nonwhite people existed was the Asian drama course taught by a white man who spent a summer in Japan. In the century plus between the campus's opening in 1891 and my arrival in 2015, the theater department had produced a total of two plays by black playwrights. After digging through the archives that dated back to the early 1990s, I was able to find a handful—a literal handful—of five or six productions that were written by any minorities at all.

I began to ask around to other faculty about the lack of diversity in production. Most faculty responded with either platitudes or victim blaming. I heard "I never thought about it" more than once, which should tell you about the overall attitude of the department toward diversity. "We don't have the students for that" was the most common refrain, even though when I began, the department had at least five black students and four students of Latinx descent, numbers sufficient to perform thousands of plays by minorities. I had one faculty member tell me "you know how it is when you cast those people," a quote that to this day I wish I had on record. I had no idea how it was, truth be told, and I hope never to find out how he thought it was.

I later learned during a faculty meeting that the real reason was at best unethical and, at worst, a violation of federal law. The department put on so few plays by minorities because numerous faculty members considered the desires of their church congregations over the needs of their students and the university in selecting productions. Their congregations' old white conservative sensibilities were offended by anything more daring than Golden Age musicals and midcentury American realism. They wanted their theater free of any potential political interpretation, and the incorporation of minorities' voices and bodies was inherently political.

I took matters into my own hands. I approached and partnered with numerous organizations across campus—student organizations and university-sponsored programs focused on diversity, community organizing, and leadership—to produce a play with black students by a black playwright: Katori Hall's *The Mountaintop*. It would be the flagship event of the university's annual Martin Luther King Jr. week.

While I was grateful for the opportunity to show the department what black students could do, the timing of the production left much to be desired. MLK week always began at the end of the winter term's first week. This meant that, for the play to work, I would have to find students willing to surrender half of their winter break to return to campus and begin working ten-hour days building and rehearsing the show. Thankfully, I assembled a fantastic group of fifteen students who desired to trade their time and their labor for the opportunity to work on a diverse, modern production. In addition to racial minorities, the production team also included people of many different genders and sexualities and even a few non-theater majors. With everything set, we embarked on a whirlwind production of the play: we had four days to rehearse, three days to load in the lights and sets, two days for technical rehearsals to set cues and focus lights followed by three performances, and then strike. The whole shebang, from first rehearsal to final curtain, would be twelve days.

I could never have prepared for some of the obstacles I encountered. Our return to campus the day after Christmas came during a snowstorm that threatened our daily commutes to the building. On the third day of rehearsal, my lead actress came down with the flu. My assistant director stayed at the theater to run lines with our lead actor while the lead actress and I spent the day waiting at the clinic. Despite her illness, she refused to be the reason the show failed, as though she recognized that department was looking for any reason to say "we told you so" when it came to black theater. Instead, she demanded to rehearse the next day—our last day of rehearsal—so we arrived armed with soup, juice, and high dosages of cold and flu medicine.

I took each of these delays in stride. "Shit happens," I thought to myself, "let's just roll with the punches and do the best we can."

But the subsequent delay was a little harder to roll with and left me wanting to punch back.

On that last day, as I began to draft the schedule and annotate my script, my lighting designer, Matt, approached. I had handpicked Matt for this project, as his time in my classes had shown me that he was both responsible and hardworking and, most importantly, had proven he would be straightforward about what he could and could not do.

"Hey," he said, nervously folding his hands in front of his body, fidgeting a pattern with each finger. "I was wondering if I could have a little bit of time when we came back to do a light lab?"

I hesitated and cringed. We couldn't afford any more delays, not if we wanted to mount a show.

"Is it absolutely necessary?" I asked. "Part of the reason I asked you to do this is that you're a senior, and I knew I could trust you to do the job independently."

"Yeah," he said, "ummm, I mean, I can. I totally can, but, ummmm..."

"Ummmm, what?" I asked.

"I've never had to light black skin before."

"What?" I responded, part in sheer bewilderment, and part in anger that our faculty was going to allow him to enter into the professional world with this gap in his experience.

Just like the more tangible design disciplines of costumes and sets, lighting design uses texture, shade, and color to help tell a story. To produce color, designers rely on colored sheets of thin plastic called "gels." Often, to get the correct tone and depth of color requires a blending and layering of multiple gels, most commonly yellow, pink, and brown to imbue the life of blood into the flesh that would otherwise appear pale and ghoulish under the unfiltered purity of the intense stage bulbs. But this standard mixing of colors to produce life in the flesh only works on white skin. Shining those same lights on black skin makes it appear a dull, pale, lifeless green.

Watching my lighting designer rotate gels in and out to make my two black actors look alive, I couldn't help but view this moment as a metaphor for social death. Things we take for granted as truth, whether it be what groups and actions represent a threat or even what gels to combine to give life to flesh, tend to exclude and damage blackness. The unspoken truths of our world are not universal but racialized. As I watched these two actors blend into and out of the white sheet hung behind them so their true colors could be seen, I couldn't help but think how showing these two black bodies under the light of white truth rendered them dead and lifeless. That to see their life, to accept and interpret their experience, required reevaluating the truth through which the world views them—to see them as they are and not just how the world wants them to be.

Although we lost a day and a half of rehearsal, and my star got sick, and we almost had the show canceled on opening night because the invoice for performance rights never got to me, we managed to pull it off. We more than pulled it off; we packed the house every night. Despite the blizzard that had left the roads and walkways treacherous, people braved the elements to see our humble show.

One night after the production, we had a *talkback*—an opportunity for the audience to discuss the show with me, my assistant director, my two stars, and three black faculty members from across campus. One young, black gentleman whom I recognized from around the department but did not know rose to ask a question. Before he could form a coherent thought, emotion overcame him, and he instead just offered tears and thanks. For that brief moment, I was reminded why I got into the arts. I was reminded why I got into teaching.

After the talkback, the cast and production team surprised our backers with signed, framed photos of the entire production ensemble and a toast. It was a true celebration of blackness. Not blackness as it exists in its degraded, vile state in American society, but rather a celebration of the capacity for the rising tide of blackness, when given the chance, to raise all ships.

Thanks to the success of this production, which was done within their walls but without their blessing, my relationships with all but a few faculty members soured. I had blown a hole through their weak excuses, and through that opening washed a wave of resentment. Not only had I pulled it off, but I had rallied students to do work above and beyond the narrow lens they had applied to each student. I had pulled these students out of their pigeonholes and allowed them opportunities to shine. I gained a reputation among the student body as someone who had their best interests at heart, someone who would fight for them and fight for opportunities. A reputation as someone who got shit done.

That reputation would be the source of my coming troubles.

ABSENCE
Status: Letters from the World

"Dear Matt,

I debated if I should reach out to you in this manner.
I decided that it's best that I let you know my thoughts and how upset I am with my department.
I just want to let you know that even though you aren't getting an offer, I voted for you.
I think you would have been a great asset to our department, as this recent incident with Uncle Tom's Cabin shows.
However, some people on the committee thought you asked too many questions,
and when they didn't know the answers,
it made them feel ignorant.
I don't know if this is helpful to you at all,
but I really think someone should hire you,
and I want you to know honestly why you didn't get the job here.
But it was a pleasure meeting you, and I am disappointed that you will be working somewhere other than here.

Sincerely,

REDACTED"

Translation: "Quit asking questions and be grateful you aren't still a slave."

Translation: "Know your fucking place."

Academia:
Where an original contribution to knowledge is a qualification.
And asking questions while black is a disqualification.

FACET: 3

Age: 32
Location: Washington State
Status: Terror Alert Level Red

"It's getting harder and harder to defend you," she said, cutting through greetings as I sat at the round glass table in her second-story office.

Funny, I wasn't aware I had done anything that needed defending.

The Mountaintop had been well-received outside of my department, and I began receiving inquiries from others about how they could partner on my next show. I spent the next few months at work more engaged with the campus at large—I had meetings with professors in black studies, English, education, and anthropology to discuss creating more art that engaged with life on campus instead of life in church halls. I partnered with the campus museum on a staged reading series that focused on contemporary social and political issues such as immigration and sexual assault on campus. I led workshops in the English department and served on a search committee for them. In between all this, I continued teaching my classes and preparing for my next production, a version of Shakespeare's *A Midsummer Night's Dream*, which would be staged in an abandoned second-floor dancehall above the town's Western culture museum.

As things churned along for me, they also churned along for the department. Before my production of *Midsummer* would be put on, there was another production in our season: a retelling of the Chinese folk novel *Journey to the West*. Keeping with the department's rich, white tradition, the script chosen was an adaptation by a white playwright from Australia. It was to be directed by our department's resident scholar of Asian theater—the one mentioned earlier whose only education in Asian drama was a summer trip spent training in Japan, a tale he loved to recount by calling himself "the one grain of white rice in a bowl of brown rice."

He had no credentials in Asian theater, but that didn't bother me—he was free to direct whatever he wanted. If the playwright would grant him the rights, who am I to say he shouldn't direct this play? And if he wanted to cast all white students to fill the roles, despite the presence of a few Asian actors in our department, that was artistic freedom.

But producing this play in this department in this city did bother me. However, I did my best to stay out of it. By this point, the faculty who wanted me gone far outnumbered those who wanted me around. They would never admit that; doing so would smear the thin icing of liberalism that frosted the thick cake of *regressivism* and racism. So, I kept to myself, kept my head down, and tried to do my job.

Then students began to approach me. The director's handling of issues of representation concerned them. Because of my work with race in *The Mountaintop,* numerous actors from the production came to me to discuss the racial politics involved in performing Chinese characters and Chinese culture as white students. I tried to thread the needle between not condemning the students, the director, or the production while also letting them know that many aspects of the show were incredibly problematic. I ended each of these discussions with the advice that if they felt this way, they should discuss the issues with the director because he deserved to know his actors were struggling.

All was quiet for a couple of weeks. But then, one day, as I headed to class, a group of students accosted me outside of my classroom door in a panic.

"You have to help us," said Annie. Annie was young and angry, and rightfully so based on the misogyny that served as the bolts that held together the department's racist scaffolding. But Annie could be overzealous in her activism, often wielding it as a machete when a scalpel would be more effective.

"What happened?" I asked, responding to the panic on her face.

"Andrew told the director how we felt about the play," she said, "and he threatened us!"

I didn't know what to do. I didn't want to get involved, but I couldn't stand aside while this tenured professor became the police and shifted from educating to coercing. I did what I thought was the right thing.

"Well, have you talked to the department chair?" I asked.

"We don't trust him," she replied.

"Then let's go to the dean," I said.

I poked my head into the classroom and told the students that we still had class, but I would be a few minutes late. As I walked Annie and her fellow students across campus to the dean's office, she filled me in on the details of the encounter. When the students had tried to approach the director about the lack of diversity and what they perceived as yellowface, the director's response terrified them. According to the students, the director threatened to hurt their careers. He claimed he "knew people" and that their attitudes "wouldn't fly in the professional world." He said if any of his friends in the business called asking about them, he would have to tell the truth: they weren't team players, they were terrible collaborators—they shouldn't be hired. These threats were empty, as no one in this small rural town had any meaningful connections in the industry, but the students didn't know this. They just knew he was a professor, so they assumed he had an extensive professional network, one he used to coerce them into doing what they knew was wrong.

As we approached the dean's office, I instructed the students to wait in the hall except for Annie.

Annie and I walked through the door of the dean's office and, before the office assistant could greet us, the dean, Dr. Robinson, saw me from her office.

"Hi, Matt," she said, looking puzzled. "What's going on?"

Dr. Robinson was a tall redhead in her late forties. She had a kind voice and kinder eyes but was fiercely professional and immensely intelligent. I am confident her past was littered with the bones of men who saw her beauty and underestimated her.

"I don't know the details," I lied, "but this is Annie, and she said a faculty member threatened her."

Dr. Robinson's eyes narrowed. She was familiar with many of the issues plaguing my department. She took it upon herself to hold monthly meetings with the new faculty members to mentor them through the transition and tenure process. As such, we had met on multiple occasions, and each revealed some problematic process or outright lie within the walls of the theater building.

"Thank you for bringing her here," she said. "You shouldn't get involved in this. You can go."

I took her advice and left. I was not present at their meeting nor any of the following sessions. But I know the dean met with my chair, and the chair met with the director of the show. I know because, eventually, all the shit rolled its way down from the dean's office and landed on me.

The chair called me into his office, where he gave me a long lecture on collegiality and chain of command—a lecture whose words I can't recall because I can only remember the thick ooze of condescension and infantilization that came with them. I sat in his office for over half an hour, vaguely nodding, as this man reminded me of my place. He was so in love with the sound of his voice and so smug in his superiority that he never asked why I didn't bring the issue to him. I can only assume this is because he either already knew or didn't care. There was no response to such a query that would have satisfied him, no answer or apology that would have made my actions okay in his eyes. To him, that department was his domain, and I needed to know my place in it.

I left that office determined to get the fuck out of that school.

It turned out, unbeknown to me, they had also already been working on getting rid of me.

At the request of students—and against my better judgment—I attended a production of *Journey to the West*. They asked if I would sit with them in the balcony and discuss the aspects they found troublesome. Although I knew nothing good would come from this, I was an educator, and the department had shown that they were not willing to have productive conversations about race. The show was appallingly ironic; at one point, the group of actors who had spoken out against the show's problematic racial and cultural politics delivered lines that encouraged the audience to be respectful of all peoples and cultures. In the context of the backstage drama, I couldn't help but laugh. I laughed long and loud, the tenor echoing through the theater.

I arrived on campus the following Monday with an email flagged as urgent telling me to report to the dean's office at 10 a.m. She was summoning me like a child to the principal.

"It's getting harder and harder to defend you" were the words that opened this meeting. I was, up to that point, completely unaware that she was defending me to anyone. What had I done that needed defending? Was producing work by a black playwright some transgression that needed justification? Was bringing students to a place where their voices were heard some great sin? Was it a crime to attend a show and educate students on how it was potentially problematic? "What did I do?" I asked sincerely.

"Students said you heckled them at the show," she responded. "A student was crying because you heckled them."

Heckled? I laughed. I groaned. I clapped. I fully engaged with the play as an audience member. But heckle? I had done no such thing nor had any such intentions. I reacted as audience members are expected to; I laughed when something was funny, I groaned when something was inappropriate. But my truth was illuminated by the light of whiteness—through the gel that projected sickly onto my blackness. Regardless of my intentions, my actions had caused white tears, and thus they had to be policed and punished. White tears are a powerful thing—they helped get Emmett Till murdered; they helped Casey Anthony get time served; they helped Brett Kavanaugh get confirmed. This university was no different from the world outside when it came to blackness. The dean was not interested in my explanation; she had white tears on the other side. Those tears had to be recognized and satisfied. Like so many before me, I was being washed away. Drowned in a deluge from white eyes.

"I did not heckle anyone," I replied.

She didn't acknowledge my response. She instead spoke of rumors, slights, and misdeeds that she neither witnessed nor provided evidence of. Only that she had heard or someone had mentioned, only whispers that I had said or done something disrespectful, something not "collegial."

"Who is saying these things?" I asked.

"You know I can't reveal their identities," she scolded me.

The air left my lungs in a sigh of submission and defeat. Of course, she couldn't tell me. Even if she could, why would she? Just as the KKK is only a threat to blackness, so are these disembodied voices against whose truth my blackness has no recourse. To tell me would be to reveal the trick—to show how the scaffolding of the institution relies on the fugitivity and criminality of blackness. Just like the police had attempted to control and criminalize my life and my body. Just like how EJ, my thesis advisor, had tried to control and criminalize my words and my truth. Now, Dr. Robinson and her unnamed sources were policing and criminalizing my very emotions—my joy. The ears and minds of people who viewed my voice as terrorism perverted my joy. They read my laughter as their taunt. My pleasure is torment to them. I cannot be happy in this antiblack world because black happiness incites white rage. It triggers the masochistic impulse to dismember black flesh—*How can you be happy in this world that delights in your death?! We'll show you!*

So instead of creating a situation where we could have a discussion and I could defend myself, she moved straight to punishment. The carceral apparatus operating under the guise of education.

My body. My movements. My words. My truth. My emotions. My affect. What part of my being is left? What part of me can exist as my own? What part of this world will ever accept any of me or my kind? If every constituent element of my physical and emotional being is subject to the policing and control of an antiblack world, then what is the possibility of freedom? Of peace? Of life? Antiblackness is a vampiric force, subsisting on the flesh and blood of blackness, draining these forces from our being on a metaphysical level, denying us our humanity in the first ontological instance. There is no black life in an antiblack world. There is only black criminality. There is only black flesh. There is only violence and control.

And with these thoughts in my head, I began to question my choices—I suppose, perhaps, I could have handled things differently. Looking back on it, I could have been more "collegial" by following the "proper channels" that allowed my department to bury the voices of dissent as they had done so many times in the past. I could have shown up and shut up. I could have submitted, bent my knee at the altar of antiblackness, kissed the rings of my own oblivion, and become the minstrel they wanted me to be. I could have relented and begged this white woman to shine her light on me once again, so that I could be seen as a person and not just an ungrateful slave, as the one who refused to accept the crumbs they had deemed "enough."

I could have done many things differently. But not in a way that would have allowed me to "live" with myself—even in an altered state of social death. Had I submitted, the results would perhaps have been different but the process unimaginable. Doing things differently would have required me to inflict the violence they inflicted on me onto myself. And that is the paradox of black violence: either we exist as ourselves, and the antiblack world inflicts violence on us, or we submit, bend and mold our will and our flesh and our being to their desires and inflict their violence on our own being for them. There is no space in this world for blackness, unfiltered, unburdened, unviolated.

But in this case, it was not just my own being at stake. Doing things the way they had always been done would have resulted in the mistreatment of students—especially students of color. Even though I was on the verge of losing my job, I didn't regret anything I had done because I had done it for my students. I did it so my students could have experiences and opportunities that the university apparatus repeatedly denied them. I did it so my students could, for the first time, have someone claim them as students and not dismiss them as some necessary imposition. And my students recognized that I laid it all on the line for them. They showed their appreciation by awarding me the black student union's inaugural Muhammad Ali Award, which they created recognize the faculty member who "stood up for students of color when no one else would."

When. No. One. Else. Would.

Those five words sum up our university system better than any research study ever could.

FACET: 4

Age: 31
Location: Washington State
Status: Terror Alert Level black

Had this comment "He's a terrorist" come in one of my more theoretically engaged courses, perhaps in my seminar Afropessimism and the Stage or in Shakespeare, Race, and Performativity, I could have better understood the thinking behind it. In the context of a course, I could have chalked it up to nothing more than the student giving voice to the antiblack university's implicit and inherent positioning of black thought as politically radical and culturally dangerous. I could have related the claim of terrorism to the subject's challenging of white male hegemony. I could have positioned it within current conversations of banning critical race theory and making professors declare their political beliefs. I could have at least seen how being forced to take a course that deconstructs everything you know and experience could be interpreted as political violence.

But this was not a part of a text from a course. It was explicitly about me.

Still, in the end, I don't blame the poor, misguided soul who felt it appropriate to call me a terrorist behind their anonymous student evaluation of instruction. While I was aware that the antiblack university viewed black knowledge as violence, I learned then that even the presence of my black body in the university's alabaster tower was a coup—a violent insurrection against the construction of knowledge itself. I was disappointed, not in this new lesson I had learned, but that this student was so afraid of me, both who I was and what I represented, that they interpreted my presence as politically motivated violence. They didn't insult me with their words; the insult was in the fact that nothing I did was able to get this student to question their world.

My only real regret from my time in the literally and metaphorically cold Pacific Northwest is that I never got a chance to speak with the student, listen to their reasoning, and perhaps teach them something or learn something about myself.

FRAGMENT 12

FACET: 1

Age: 33
Location: Houston, Texas
Status: Après Moi le Deluge

My car is underwater.

SLIVER

The City of the Future

Houston is a strange city.

Houston is one of the oldest cities in Texas, founded in 1836. It is the city "where seventeen railroads meet the sea." As a result, Houston was a global hub of both the shipping and the oil industries throughout the nineteenth and twentieth centuries. As the calendar turned to the twentieth century, these industries produced over $120 million combined in revenue.

I love Houston's history. Houston is where Juneteenth originated. With the federal government recently declaring Juneteenth a national holiday, everyone knows the name, but what is it really? It's not as simple as "the day America freed the slaves." Juneteenth is the day on which some African Americans celebrate the abolition of slavery in the state of Texas.

In 1862, Abraham Lincoln
issued the Emancipation
Proclamation, which freed slaves
in the rebelling states during the
war. Emancipation was actually
Lincoln's plan B to his plan A of
deporting all black people. But life
is full of compromises. Although
Texas was technically a member of
the Confederacy, it was not used as
a battlefield because of its remote
location compared to the rest of
the US. This lack of bloodshed
within its borders meant that the
US did not consider it a rebelling
state. Therefore, the Emancipation
Proclamation did not apply. Slaves
in Texas would have to wait three
more years until June 19, 1865, for
their freedom. Although most of
the state's slaves were in rural areas,
the highest concentrations were
along the Gulf Coast in Houston
and Galveston. On June 19, 1865,
General Granger, backed by two
thousand soldiers, stood on the
balcony of Galveston's Ashton
Villa and declared "in accordance
with a proclamation from the
Executive of the United States, all
slaves are free."

Once black people were free, it
didn't take long for them to thrive.
Jack Yates moved to the Fourth
Ward in 1865, and he started the
first black church in Houston,
the Antioch Missionary Baptist
Church. Shortly after, he founded
Houston Academy, a school to
teach black children employable
skills such as carpentry and
running a business. He was a pre-
cursor to later black leaders such
as Booker T. Washington, Bayard
Rustin, and Martin Luther King Jr.

Today, Houston touts itself
as the "City of the Future" after
being declared so by Resonance
Consultancy's 2020 ranking
of America's best cities. Major
international corporations have
begun opening headquarters
in Houston, giving it the
fourth-highest concentration of
Fortune 500 companies in the
US, after New York, Chicago, and
cross-state rival Dallas. The city
has become a significant center
for the health care, technology,
aerospace, engineering, and finance
industries, rebuilding a modern
reputation that hearkens back to

its nineteenth-century importance in shipping and oil.

The "City of the Future" designation also signals the city's ethnic and racial diversity. According to a study conducted annually by personal finance website WalletHub.com, Houston was the most diverse metropolitan area in the country in both 2019 and 2021. Its population's racial demographics have shifted from white dominant to "majority-minority," one of the many linguistic gymnastics the world deploys to center whiteness. Rice University sociologist Michael Emerson estimates that in the year 2050, the entire United States will mirror Houston's current ethnic breakdown: 40 percent non-Hispanic white, 37 percent Latinx, 16 percent black, and 7 percent Asian, with the small remainder being of two or more races.[1]

With so much of the city's focus on the future, those seventeen railroads serve as a present reminder of Houston's past. Despite the influx of international businesses and technology firms, the city

is still marked with thousands
of miles of steel and wood that
sutures the present and the future
to the white American fantasy of
the past's "simpler times." Despite
the countless and immeasurable
technological advances of the
past century and a half, railroads
remain the primary means of
overland shipping in America.
They also serve as a monument to
oppression. Each length of track
is a time machine to America's
nineteenth-century manifesting
the westward destiny.

Those seventeen railroads also
keep the city in the past in terms of
social progress. Weaving thousands
of miles of steel string through the
land and the entirety of the city
produced the civil engineering
equivalent of redlining; the plan-
ners created innumerable borders
between good neighborhoods
and "the wrong side of the tracks."
Despite its diversity, Houston lacks
inclusivity. While the bodies, when
counted as a whole, create the appearance of cosmopolitanism, the
city is still primarily composed of
racially segregated neighborhoods.

The East End, where I lived, is still almost entirely Latinx. Move west to River Oaks, and the percentage of white occupants rises as sharply as the median income.

The Second, Third, Fourth, and Fifth Wards of Houston, however, are historically black, impoverished neighborhoods and are home to the starkest divides. The distance between the Third Ward and River Oaks cannot only be measured by distance; any calculation of how far apart they are must also include wealth, opportunity, income, crime, policing, and race as variables in the equation. The Second Ward has already succumbed to the progressive force of urban development, more colloquially known as gentrification. The Fourth Ward is hot on its tail. The swallows who flew from the city center sixty years ago in the great migration of white flight are now returning as vultures. The Third Ward resists, standing proudly as the last bastion of black community in Houston.

But even the Third Ward is slowly being encroached upon.

Not by investors and speculators, mind you. Instead, it's being overtaken by the state apparatus in the guise of enlightenment. Scott Street serves not only as a geographical border, but also as the line between entrenched blackness and unrelenting antiblackness. Scott Street is the boundary between the Third Ward and the University of Houston.

After I resigned from that unspeakable Pacific Northwestern hellhole, I secured a position at the University of Houston. The university follows the example set by the city and lauds itself as the most diverse Carnegie Tier One Research University in the country. Based on particularly cherry-picked bits of data, their claim can be supported.

Not all diversity, however, is created equal. Although the proportions of most racial and ethnic groups at the University of Houston have moved ever closer to matching those of the city at large, blackness still lags far behind. The student body is 33 percent Latinx, only about 10 percent lower than the city's population as a whole. The Asian population actually triples that of the city as a whole, elevating from 7 percent in the city to 22 percent on campus. While blacks, however, have been left behind. Although the city is 16 percent black, the campus body barely reaches the double digits with a percentage of 10.1 at last count. The overall diversity of the campus consistently places the University of Houston high on the list of most diverse colleges, however, not all racial groups are proportionately represented. When it comes to blackness, America's most diverse city fails to place a proportion of black students within its flagship university that matches the national average of 14 percent black students—let alone the city's high bar of 16 percent black residents.

Instead, black students often find themselves at Texas Southern University, an HBCU across Scott Street in the heart of the Third Ward. Texas Southern was founded in 1927 as Houston Colored Junior College, a byproduct of

the separate but equal ruling of
Plessy v. Ferguson and the racially
qualified simultaneous establishment of Houston Junior College,
which would go on to become the
University of Houston. Although
having substantially less funding
than the University of Houston,
Texas Southern University would
become the first university in
Houston to be incorporated into
the state university system.

I wish I could say this event was
the product of a black university
kicking down the doors with unde-
niable achievement. But, sadly, the
designation as a state institution
was the result of antiblackness. In
1946, Heman Marion Sweatt had
his application to the University
of Texas School of Law denied
because of his race. Instead of
enrolling in another program,
Mr. Sweatt threatened to sue.
The University of Texas refused
to concede, offering neither integration nor a settlement to Sweatt.
To keep a black man out of UT,
the entire state banded together
and incorporated what would later
become Texas Southern into the

state university system as the Texas
State University for Negroes. The
state then started a segregated law
school at the college. Separate but
equal.

Admission to TSU Law School
did not mollify Sweatt, and he
continued to pursue litigation
against the University of Texas.
But what chance did he have?
A future law student versus the
University of Texas School of Law
and the Texas State Government?
After close to four years of appeals,
the case reached the Supreme
Court. In 1950, they ruled that
while separate but equal was
okay, the facilities, faculty, and
education offered at Texas State
University for Negroes were not
equal to those provided at the
University of Texas at Austin. As
such, the Supreme Court forced
UT to integrate. Sweatt won
the lawsuit, but only because the
courts ruled that blacks could not
offer a legitimate legal education,
saying nothing of the inequality in
funding and other resources. Even
in victory, the court found a way to
insult blackness.

The racial inequality established in the divide between the University of Houston and Texas Southern University still manifests in the flesh that inhabits the campus and its hallways, more pronounced in some departments than others.

6/1/2020

"There is a certain shape to memoirs.
We have to see the character struggle
then overcome those struggles
and come out the other side.
If we don't see the other side, then there's no point in
reading it.
It's too depressing."

Afropessimism is about hope.
It is about hoping I find the other side.
Black is not the other side of white.
Nonwhite is the other side of white.
And white and nonwhite alike take solace in being not black.
Afropessimism is also about questions.
If both sides take solace in our not,
then what is the other side for us?
Afropessimism is about hope.
It is about hoping I get to someday write a book
from the other side.

FACET: 2

Age: 33
Location: Houston, TX
Status: Après Moi le Deluge

My car was underwater.

As I stood on the small, concrete balcony of my second-floor apartment, I couldn't help but think that the apocalypse had come. In the few hours between falling asleep to the sounds of *Longmire* and waking to the sound of Chester, our small basset hound mix, slamming his low body into the black wood of our bedframe demanding that we take him outside for his morning relief, the ground had disappeared. Bray's Bayou and the small unnamed bayou hiding behind the corrugated aluminum fence of our apartment complex had united during the night. Floodwaters had caused them to swell over their banks and meet in the middle, turning our apartment complex into an island.

I stood on our balcony with my mouth agape, my gaze fixated on the parking space where I had parked my Honda Civic. I could just make out the black void of the sunroof through the rippling of the newly formed sea.

I had fallen asleep to the sound of pouring rain and woken up with my car underwater.

Better the car than me, I supposed.

I thought back to the text message I had received Thursday night from one of my new coworkers, Adrian. "Hey, I don't want to alarm you," it said, "but we used to live in those apartments, and the parking lot floods. If you have somewhere else you can park your cars, you may want to move them."

I chuckle now at the tone of his text. It had been so mundane that Steph and I almost ignored it, but she had trouble sleeping with the warning ringing in the back of her head. So we had crawled out of bed, put clothes on over our pajamas, and driven our cars the few miles to the fifth floor of Texas Women's Hospital's parking structure.

"Will this be high enough?" Steph yelled to me through the open window of her Subaru Outback.

"Honey," I yelled back, "if the water gets this high, our cars will be the least of our worries."

Unfortunately for my Honda Civic, we had moved the cars in the middle of the night, and to avoid walking through some of the sketchier neighborhoods of Houston at midnight while half dressed, we had driven the poor car back to the apartment.

Twenty-four hours later, the Civic had a burial at sea.

We had arrived in Houston the last week of July in 2017. We moved into our apartment the first week of August. I started class at my new job three weeks later, and the following week my car was underwater. On the fifth day of the semester, the campus closed due to the storm. With good cause, mind you—the city was underwater. But how long would it last? I had spent that first week of classes learning my students' names and, now, everything was in limbo.

Our electricity cut out. Losing power is to be expected during a storm of that magnitude, but the consequences of losing it in Houston can quite literally be deadly. Without power, the air conditioning cannot maintain its fight against the one-hundred-degree days and thick, humid air. No AC, no internet, and no way out, as the floodwaters were anywhere from waist deep to well above the top of my head.

I stood on that balcony, watching the water and chuckling at the absurdity of the situation. Just then, my phone chimed.

"How are you guys making out?" It was Adrian, the savior of the more expensive of our cars.

"My car is underwater," I replied, attaching a picture of the newly formed Houston Sea.

"Do you have power? Can you get out? Do you need a place to stay? If you can get out, you are welcome to stay with us. We're pretty unaffected," he replied. Unaffected? Adrian's home was less than five miles from ours, and while we were underwater, his local watering hole never even had to alter its hours.

"We're trapped," I responded, "but thanks."

Then, a miracle. As quickly as the waters had risen, they receded. Had I not lived through it, had I not witnessed it with my own eyes, had the city not been overtaken with an eerie, pained silence and lingering odor of sewage and death, I would not have believed it happened.

Steph, who at that moment was much stronger emotionally than me, immediately thought of others. She put her own trauma aside and volunteered her medical skills and empathy at the George R. Brown Convention Center. She spent the next few weeks aiding those whose homelessness was either long-term or a new experience.

I sat at home and drank.

The university shut down for eleven days while the city fought to keep from drowning. We had not yet reached the damage assessment phase of disaster recovery, and the city was months away from beginning the rebuild. The city was still in crisis mode when the campus reopened with each and every one of us still too actively living the present traumatic moment to begin considering the post-traumatic effects of the most devastating climatological event ever to befall the city.

The FEMA disaster counselor who visited the school told us there are three basic steps to disaster recovery: emergency, restoration, and reconstruction. They define emergency by the duration of the natural disaster—how long the city was in the immediate crisis of rain, winds, and flooding and the time it takes FEMA to arrive. Houston was in crisis for nine days during Harvey. The next step, restoration, is how long it takes to restore essential functions and stabilize the population—provide food and housing to those directly affected and displaced by the disaster and return those people to work.

"To estimate how long your restoration will take, take the number of days in crisis," he said, "and multiply it by two. That's how many *weeks* you can expect restoration to take."

Eighteen weeks. Based on his math, it would take eighteen weeks, a third of a year, to restore basic necessities such as food and housing to all of Houston's residents.

The last phase, reconstruction, is how long it takes the city to return to its pre-disaster level of economic productivity. "Reconstruction takes years," he said. "Typically, the number of weeks you are in restoration is the number of years it will take for full reconstruction."

Eighteen years before the city would be back to normal.

Most of my students had barely been alive that long.

Nine days in crisis. Eighteen weeks of restoration. Eighteen years of reconstruction.

SHARD: 1

Status: 292,000 Years

August 20, 2019, marked the 400th anniversary of the San Juan Bautista landing at Point Comfort in the Jamestown colony. Among its cargo was "20 and odd" Negroes who, upon their sale, would later be called the first African slaves in America. This crudely inaccurate but widely accepted date exists some 146,000 days in the past at the time of the anniversary. One hundred forty-six thousand days of crisis, of emergency, for blacks in America. By our government's own standards, if we were to somehow end the crisis today—to end the for-profit prisons, the killing of black men and women by the police, the school-to-prison pipeline, and all of the other structural crises that define the daily experience of black people—we would have 292,000 weeks of restoration. Two hundred ninety-two thousand weeks—over 5,600 years—to restore blackness not to equality, but just to safety, to stability. Thus, 292,000 weeks of restoration becomes 292,000 years of rebuilding. The timespan to black equality, for black life, is beyond our comprehension: black humanity is as far into our future as the first homo sapiens are into our past.

While these events—the rain, the flood, and the post-traumatic-like symptoms—accompanied me to my job on that day in a literal sense, they served as an appropriate metaphor for every day I am coerced by capitalism into entering that place. I am the only minority faculty member in my department. Not the only black member. The. Only. Minority. Period. Even the most diverse Research One university in the country still leaves me entirely isolated in my blackness.

There is only the stark opposition between myself and everyone and everything else around me. The rain is antiblackness. The flood is in me. And every second of every day, the rain threatens to cause a swell that will eventually overtake me and sweep me off the edge.

There is no escape from the isolation. There is no escape from the sea between black expectations and black excellence, between just enough, not enough, and too much. The crisis continues, unabated, as it has for the last 400 years. I am trapped, forever, between who I am and what society makes me. I am in between the in-between—the thought that causes a reaction but escapes expression.

This is the life I have chosen.

No.

This is the life.

This is the life that blackness, all blackness, from the lowest criminal to the highest leader, has as the only option for us. The living death of recognition and being in absentia.

This is our life. This is our death. This is our dying. Always. Always already. Always dying and always fighting—to live, to breathe, to love.

This life is a constant reminder that we are not and can never be.

FACET: 3

Age: 33
Location: Houston, TX
Status: Après Moi le Deluge

We returned to classes twelve days after Harvey.

Many of the city's freeways were still underwater.

After being away from campus for close to two weeks with no new precipitation, the rain decided to join us as we made our way back to our classrooms and office hours. The same eerie pall that covered the city swept through the university. I had no idea how my students had been affected: Were they injured? Were their families? Did they still have transportation? Food? Homes? With the rain beating down all around us, I addressed my class.

"Welcome back," I began. "How many of you saw the rain today and had a mild panic attack?"

I raised my hand, and most of my students soon followed course.

I looked across the room at this sea of faces. Despite the university's reputation for diversity, mostly white faces looked back at me. Most university theater programs still struggle with diversity. This particular course only had a handful of black and brown students. But on this day, every face—be it white, black, or brown—shared the same expression. Behind eyes and mouths that remained locked in stoic professionalism, I saw fear. Death had crept into the room. At that moment, the same uncertainty and terror that hangs over every moment of black existence hung over the whole city. I had spent thirty years of my life aware of how close I was to the reaper: its hand touching every relationship, its eyes watching every action, and its breath falling on every word. I had come to know and accept this specter that walks alongside my blackness.

But for most of these students, this was the first time they were aware of the precariousness of life. This was the first time they were aware that their lives, too, even if temporarily, could be lived hand in hand with death. They had come into the same shadow that hung over my existence. The anxiety hovered in the air, and with each shuddered exhale from their shaken flesh, the room became more and more claustrophobic. We began to breathe in unison, but the breaths were not calm—the stale, moldy air of the flood went in and the terror and pain came out. We didn't want to be in this classroom. We wanted to be with our families. We wanted to be safe and comfortable.

We wanted to know that we wouldn't die.

With each breath, the pressure mounted, until the room seemed to bend at the seams, struggling to contain what each of us tried to conceal. With each breath, each and every one of us yearned to breathe free again, free of the lingering presence of death.

Bearing witness to these children's reckoning with death was heartbreaking.

"Nigger."

I was transported back to that word that made me first encounter my own death. I remembered my mother disemboweling my metaphysical being. I tried to imagine what it would be like to sit in a classroom pretending everything was okay when I knew in my mind and my heart that nothing would ever be the same. I looked into the eyes of these students—legally adults but, in many ways, still socially children—and saw a suffering they had no idea how to navigate because they had no idea what the destination was supposed to be. Death had crept into their awareness. Mortality no longer existed solely in the abstract; death became a tangible, palpable part of their experience. At that moment, my classroom became a mirror. In that moment of impending and concurring tragedy, each of my students looked at me from the same pit of internal despair from which I awake each morning. They were, however momentarily, exposed to and engulfed in the suffering that structures my own being.

What could I do? Or, as Christina Sharpe asks, "What does it look like, entail, and mean to attend to, care for, comfort, and defend, those already dead, those dying, and those living lives consigned to the possibility of always-imminent death, life lived in the presence of death; to live this imminence and immanence as and in the 'wake'?"[2] What could I, whose entire existence had been and continues to be haunted by the afterlives of trauma and genocide offer to these children who had unwilling been brought under this ghastly shadow of immeasurable suffering and death?

I don't know if what I did was right or wrong. What I did was what I could.

"Yeah, this isn't right," I said. "How can the school expect anyone to care about American drama when a lot of its faculty, staff, and students may not have homes? If there is anything I can do to help any of you, please let me know. Otherwise, class is dismissed. Go take care of yourselves, and we'll try again next week.

"Just know that this won't last forever. You will get through this. You will get through this," I added.

You. Not me. For them, this was temporary. This would end. For me . . .

Less than five minutes after that class began, I did the human thing and ended it. I couldn't in good conscience expect anyone in that room to give a fuck about American drama. What value does William Wells Brown have when your life has just been destroyed?

No one's mind was on *The Escape*; everyone was focused on how much rain had fallen and questioning if there would be more floods. Instead of offering education, I offered empathy and assistance. Let me know how I can help. I offered them humanity.

Into their newfound awareness of death, I offered a lifeline.

Acknowledgments

The number of hands necessary for a book like this to ever see the light of day is as countless as the stars in the sky. Thousands upon thousands of hands have all touched the clay that would eventually be sculpted into these stories. Attempting to give thanks to those hands who molded those memories into a book is a daunting task, but the joy of giving thanks to some outweighs the fear of forgetting someone.

First off, I would like to thank Derek Krissoff and my editor, Sarah Munroe, at WVU Press. Derek and Sarah saw the potential of these stories when they existed in a completely different format, and they believed in this book from the beginning. Sarah especially deserves praise and thanks for pushing me to write the book I needed to write, to push the form and language beyond the standard memoir, and be fearless both with form and content.

I would like to thank my copyeditor, Troy Wilderson, who helped to bridge the gap between what I write and what you read.

I would also like to thank Frank B. Wilderson III, who believed in a previous version of this book enough to tell me not to publish it, even though I had an offer. He saw something special in the stories I had to tell, and taught me how to better tell them. He believed not only in what the book was, but in what the book could be.

Thanks to Frank, early versions of the manuscript passed through countless knowledgeable and professional hands, each of whom offered encouragement and feedback: Eric Chinski, Faith Childs, Sarah Burnes, Tanya McKinnon, and others took time out of their lives to give advice to someone who could offer them nothing in return, and I am grateful for their wisdom.

I would also like to thank the friends who read and commented on early versions of the text: Rachel Kelly, Kim Brigner, Joshua Kelly, Rohit Puri, and Julie Burelle.

I would like to thank my anonymous reviewers who provided both resistance and guidance to my arguments and narratives.

I would also like to thank all the people whose work and engagement with me and my work over the years helped me build a vocabulary to tell these stories: Jaye Austin Williams, Patrice Douglass, Selamawit Terrefe, John Murillo III, Janet Smarr, and Miles Parks Grier.

Lastly, I would like to thank my wife, Steph, and my daughter, Roar, for allowing this extra member of our family to live with us for a few years. He's now grown and out of the house and into the world.

Notes

These notes are only from published sources that I cite directly or for whom engagement with the text will offer a deeper understanding of the work being done and the stories being told. Quotes from memory, unpublished sources, and discussion of events, studies, and history that are referenced though not cited are not included here.

AUTHOR'S NOTE

1. La Marr Jurelle Bruce, *How to Go Mad without Losing Your Mind: Madness and Black Radical Creativity* (Durham, NC: Duke University Press, 2021), 6. Emphasis in original.

FRAGMENT 1

1. Emma Green, "When Mormons Aspired to Be a 'White and Delightsome' People," *The Atlantic*, September 18, 2017, https://www.theatlantic.com/politics/archive/2017/09/mormons-race-max-perry-mueller/539994/.
2. Matthew Bowman, "Mormons Confront a History of Church Racism," *The Conversation*, May 29, 2018, https://theconversation.com/mormons-confront-a-history-of-church-racism-95328.
3. Lester E. Bush, "Mormonism's Negro Doctrine: An Historical Overview," *Dialogue: A Journal of Mormon Thought* 8, no. 1 (1973): 11–68.
4. Saidiya Hartman, *Scenes of Subjection: Terror, Slavery, and Self-Making in Nineteenth-Century America* (Oxford: Oxford University Press, 1997), 5.

FRAGMENT 2

1. "Facts about Bullying," Stop Bullying, https://www.stopbullying.gov/resources/facts#stats.

FRAGMENT 3

1. Frantz Fanon, *Black Skin, White Masks*, trans. Richard Philcox (New York: Grove Press, 2008), 45.

FRAGMENT 4

1. Frantz Fanon, *Black Skin, White Masks*, trans. Richard Philcox (New York: Grove Press, 2008), 90.

FRAGMENT 7

1. Frantz Fanon, *Black Skin, White Masks*, trans. Richard Philcox (New York: Grove Press, 2008), xviii.
2. Fanon, *Black Skin*, 84.
3. WEB DuBois, "The Talented Tenth" (1903), Teaching American History, https://teachingamericanhistory.org/library/document/the-talented-tenth/.
4. Casey Dougal, Pengjie Gao, William J. Mayew, and Christopher A. Parsons, "What's in a (School) Name? Racial Discrimination in Higher Education Bond Markets," *Journal of Financial Economics* (JFE), June 16, 2018, https://ssrn.com/abstract=2727763.
5. Dougal, Gao, Mayew, and Parsons, "What's in a (School) Name?"
6. "Black Historians Abound at High-Ranking Universities, but Almost Always They Teach Courses in Black History," *Journal of Blacks in Higher Education*, no. 25 (1999): 17–18, https://doi.org/10.2307/2999355.

FRAGMENT 8

1. Liz Dwyer, "Good Luck Getting a Therapist If You're Black or Working Class," Take Part, June 6, 2016, http://www.takepart.com/article/2016/06/06/good-luck-finding-therapist-black-working-class;

Monnica T. Williams, "Why African Americans Avoid Psychotherapy," *Psychology Today*, November 2, 2011, https://www.psychologytoday .com/us/blog/culturally-speaking/201111/why-african-americans -avoid-psychotherapy.
2. Christina Sharpe, *In the Wake: On Blackness and Being* (Durham, NC: Duke University Press, 2016), 9.

FRAGMENT 9

1. Among the many texts used in this seminar were Orlando Patterson, *Slavery and Social Death: A Comparative Study* (Cambridge, MA: Harvard University Press, 1985); David Marriott, *On Black Men* (New York: Columbia University Press, 2000); Jared Sexton, *Amalgamation Schemes: Antiblackness and the Critique of Multiculturalism* (Minneapolis: University of Minnesota Press, 2008); Saidiya Hartman, *Scenes of Subjection: Terror, Slavery, and Self-Making in Nineteenth-Century America* (Oxford: Oxford University Press, 1997); Frantz Fanon, *Black Skin, White Masks*, trans. Richard Philcox (New York: Grove Press, 2008); and, of course, Frank B. Wilderson III, *Red, White, and Black: Cinema and the Structure of US Antagonisms* (Durham, NC: Duke University Press, 2010).
2. Jared Sexton, *Amalgamation Schemes: Antiblackness and the Critique of Multiculturalism*, (Minneapolis: University of Minnesota Press, 2008), 83.
3. Wilderson, *Red, White, and Black*, 54.
4. Fred Moten and Stefano Harney, "The University and the Undercommons: Seven Theses," *Social Text* 22, no. 2 (2004): 101–2.
5. Wilderson, *Red, White, and Black,* 58–59.

FRAGMENT 10

1. Asher Price, "A Secret 1950s Strategy to Keep Out Black Students," *The Atlantic*, September 19, 2019, https://www.theatlantic.com/ideas /archive/2019/09/how-ut-used-standardized-testing-to-slow -integration/597814/.
2. Victoria Clayton, "The Problem with the GRE," *The Atlantic*, March 1,

2016, https://www.theatlantic.com/education/archive/2016/03/the
-problem-with-the-gre/471633/.

FRAGMENT 11

1. Federal Bureau of Investigations, US Department of Justice, "Terrorism 2002–2005," https://www.fbi.gov/stats-services/publications /terrorism-2002-2005.
2. Federal Bureau of Investigations, "Terrorism 2002–2005."
3. DeNeen L. Brown, "When Portland Banned Blacks: Oregon's Shameful History as an All-White State," *Washington Post*, June 7, 2017, https://www.washingtonpost.com/news/retropolis/wp/2017 /06/07/when-portland-banned-blacks-oregons-shameful-history-as -an-all-white-state/.
4. Koritha Mitchell, "Identifying White Mediocrity and Know-Your-Place Aggression: A Form of Self-Care," *African American Review* 51, no. 4 (Winter 2018): 253–62.

FRAGMENT 12

1. Elise Hu, "In Houston, America's Diverse Future Has Already Arrived," *NPR*, July 1, 2013, https://www.npr.org/sections/itsallpolitics/2013 /07/01/195909643/tx2020-houston-racial-ethnic-diversity-americas -future.
2. Christina Sharpe, *In the Wake: On Blackness and Being* (Durham, NC: Duke University Press, 2016), 38.

Further Reading

Bruce, La Marr Jurelle. *How to Go Mad without Losing Your Mind: Madness and Black Radical Creativity*. Duke University Press, 2020.

Douglass, Patrice D. "Assata Is Here: (Dis) Locating Gender in Black Studies." *Souls* 22, no. 1 (2020): 89–103.

———. "Black Feminist Theory for the Dead and Dying." *Theory and Event* 21, no. 1 (2018): 106–23.

Douglass, Patrice, and Frank B. Wilderson III. "The Violence of Presence: Metaphysics in a Blackened World." *Black Scholar* 43, no. 4 (2013): 117–23.

Hartman, Saidiya. *Lose Your Mother: A Journey along the Atlantic Slave Route*. Macmillan, 2008.

———. *Scenes of Subjection: Terror, Slavery, and Self-Making in Nineteenth-Century America*. Oxford University Press on Demand, 1997.

———. *Wayward Lives, Beautiful Experiments: Intimate Histories of Riotous Black Girls, Troublesome Women, and Queer Radicals*. Norton, 2019.

Hartman, Saidiya V., and Frank B. Wilderson III. "The Position of the Unthought." *Qui Parle* 13, no. 2 (2003): 183–201.

Jackson, Zakiyyah Iman. *Becoming Human*. New York University Press, 2020.

Judy, Ronald A. *Sentient Flesh: Thinking in Disorder, Poiēsis in Black*. Duke University Press, 2020.

McDougall, Taija. "Left Out: Notes on Absence, Nothingness and the Black Prisoner Theorist." *Anthurium: A Caribbean Studies Journal* 15, no. 2 (2019): article 8.

Murillo, John, III. *Impossible Stories: On the Space and Time of Black Destructive Creation*. Ohio State University Press, 2021.

Patterson, Orlando. *Slavery and Social Death: A Comparative Study, with a New Preface.* Harvard University Press, 2018.

Sexton, Jared. *Amalgamation Schemes: Antiblackness and the Critique of Multiracialism.* University of Minnesota Press, 2008.

———. "The Ruse of Engagement: Black Masculinity and the Cinema of Policing." *American Quarterly* 61, no. 1 (2009): 39–63.

———. "The Social Life of Social Death: On Afro-pessimism and Black Optimism." *InTensions,* no. 5 (2011).

Sharpe, Christina. *In the Wake: On Blackness and Being.* Duke University Press, 2016.

Spillers, Hortense J. *Black, White, and in Color: Essays on American Literature and Culture.* University of Chicago Press, 2003.

———. "Mama's Baby, Papa's Maybe: An American Grammar Book." *Diacritics* 17, no. 2 (1987): 65–81.

Terrefe, Selamawit D. "The Pornotrope of Decolonial Feminism." *Critical Philosophy of Race* 8, no. 1–2 (2020): 134–64.

Terrefe, Selamawit, and Christina Sharpe. "What Exceeds the Hold?: An Interview with Christina Sharpe." *Rhizomes* 29, no. 1 (2016).

Wilderson, Frank B., III. "Grammar and Ghosts: The Performative Limits of African Freedom." *Theatre Survey* 50, no. 1 (2009): 119–25.

———. *Incognegro: A Memoir of Exile and Apartheid.* Duke University Press, 2015.

Wilderson, Frank B., III, Saidiya Hartman, Steve Martinot, Jared Sexton, and Hortense J. Spillers. "Afro-Pessimism: An Introduction." Racked and Dispatched, 2017.